To Matt Greenfield, the ver

Thank you for your friend.
and always willing to be there.
will not be forgotten!

John Day

IMPACT INVESTING

The Practical Guide

Connecting Capital to Impact

C. John Duong

Contents

CHAPTER ONE: INTRODUCTION

"Dreams are just goals yet to be achieved."

The field of impact investing is rapidly growing in its acceptance and popularity. Millennials, in particular, seem to have a strong affinity for this field, given their desire to seek purposeful professions, not just something that pays the bills or makes a lot of money. People often come to me at conferences where I speak and ask how to get into impact investing. As much as I would like to give them a straight answer and advice on how to get into the space, I can only tell them how I got into the sector, which isn't necessarily the right path for them.

After nearly ten years as an investment banker on Wall Street and multiple stints in between jobs consulting and advising entrepreneurs and nonprofits, I finally found what I now know is my calling. But the journey was not intentional. It would sound too much like a cliché to say I have always wanted to be an impact investor. Heck, I didn't even know what impact investing was back then. I fell into it from simply applying to a job posting on the Sponsors for Educational Opportunity (SEO) job board for alumni of the nonprofit organization.

In 2010, the world was still recovering from the 2008 financial crisis. I was one of the many unemployed individuals falling prey to the numerous layoffs on Wall Street. It was not the first time in my career that I had been laid off due to a corporate restructuring, but certainly one of the most prolonged periods that I had been out of a regular professional job…nearly 18 months. I was burning through my savings while applying to various job opportunities and was down to about a month left of funds available in my checking account by year-end. Yet as luck would have it, I had received three job offers after months of interviewing for each that were opportunities that I would seriously consider. All of them were outside of the New York City metro region, a key factor in my decision-making.

I had never planned on staying in the NYC metro long term, and in hindsight, I am still surprised I was there almost fourteen years! One opportunity was with SMTC, one of the world's five largest semiconductor chip manufacturers headquartered in Shanghai. The second was working for Atlantic Lottery, a quasi-governmental organization based in Moncton in Canada, much like the lottery system in the US that supports education and other public causes. And the third opportunity was with the W.K. Kellogg Foundation, at that time one of the ten largest private foundations in the country with over $8 billion in assets, based in Battle Creek, Michigan. It was a difficult decision as each had its advantages and disadvantages. The opportunity in Shanghai was likely going to be the most lucrative as I was an "expat" (hence likely to enjoy a generous expatriate package), and I knew China was a booming opportunity. It would have been a short-term role to transition into something else to ride the booming Chinese economy leveraging my network of friends there. The Atlantic Lottery opportunity was based in the middle of nowhere Canada—Moncton was described as a "scenic" area far from the hustle and bustle of a major metropolitan hub. It was where some of the episodes of the reality TV series The Deadliest Catch were filmed—so this would likely be a lifelong career change, and I could kiss my social life goodbye. As much as I love nature, I had no plans to become a recluse at that stage of my life. Ultimately, I chose the opportunity with Kellogg Foundation, not necessarily because it was the dream job at the time—I didn't know anything about philanthropy or what exactly the role entailed—but merely because it was the least drastic and least limiting among all my options. The key benefit was that I would be a little closer to my family in the Midwest, a seven-hour drive versus having to fly to see my parents.

While I knew nothing about the foundation world back then, I always hoped I would do something useful with my life. Joining Kellogg's Mission-Driven Investments (MDI) Team to help build and manage a $100 million impact investing portfolio as one of the early members seemed intriguing, even though it too was located in a tiny town. I had a history of helping to build things and launch new initiatives at prior firms, so it was something I enjoyed. Hired by Tom Reis, a nineteen-year veteran of the foundation, I would be the "finance guy" while my counterpart Tony Berkley was an internal transfer who was the Deputy Director that led the education portfolio on the grant-making side. Together, the three of us would build one of the most exciting impact investing portfolios among foundations with the help of Imprint Capital, a leading impact investing advisor that Kellogg Foundation helped to create as its first client. My friends had warned me I was committing social and career suicide when I accepted the Kellogg opportunity. But early January 2011, in the dead of winter, I would pack my stuff into my little 2002 Acura RSX hatchback and drive across the country to Battle Creek. Excited and nervous about the new job, I was still oblivious to how that wintry drive would take me to the forefront of the emerging sector that many today are trying to get into and change my career trajectory.

My official first day of work was January 17, 2011…Martin Luther King Day. It was coincidental, of course, but to this day, my boss Tom would joke that he should have known I was a detailed oriented "sneaky banker" picking my first day at work as a vacation day. After nearly five years into the position, my friends were half right: my social life took a dive, but I would successfully transition into a new field that was gaining increased public attention and completed an executive MBA from Northwestern that the foundation primarily funded. In addition, I would gain expertise helping to pioneer some of the approaches to impact investing within Kellogg (creation of the Michigan Good Food Fund and the Entrepreneurs of Color Program-Related Investments Fund in Detroit) and at Lumina Foundation. In addition to the rare opportunity to help build the MDI Program, I gained an extensive network and made some incredible friends along the way that would open up new opportunities and empower me for the next phase; for that, I am eternally grateful to the Kellogg Foundation.

By the time I left Kellogg, the MDI portfolio had comprised nearly fifty investments across various programmatic areas in support of the foundation's mission. These investments span both mission-related investments (MRIs) as well as program-related investments (PRIs)—don't worry if you don't know the difference; we will discuss that more in detail later. From early-stage direct investments to international funds, the MDI Program became an example that other foundations were looking to learn from as they explored making their own entry into impact investing.

Taking the lessons learned from my experience at Kellogg, I joined Lumina Foundation to lead the impact investing strategy in the fall of 2015. Like Kellogg, Lumina's initial entry into impact investing was through fund investments in 2010, but much more narrowly focused on higher education given the foundation's sole mission, referred to as Goal 2025 back then: to increase the proportion of Americans that have a high-quality postsecondary credential. Although smaller than the MDI program at Kellogg, the $50 million for direct investments and $30 million committed to fund investments, all dedicated exclusively to a singular focus area, allowed Lumina to build a brand as a leading higher education impact investor in the foundation world.

Over the years, I've been asked numerous times to do calls with newer impact investors looking to enter the space. Some are college students asking for advice, while others are seasoned professionals looking for a career change to get into impact investing. Some individuals have already made the transition into impact investing, having convinced their institutions to move forward but don't know what to do or how to do it. Today, more and more are jumping into the space but lack the technical expertise to execute successfully. There is no one size fits all solution. You may have heard the saying: you know one foundation, you know one foundation. This book is meant to help you think through the various strategies and tools to accelerate your learning curve, avoid mistakes others have made (including many of mine!), and, most importantly, contribute to the impact that makes the world a better place. Below are some links to resources that may help you in your journey:

- http://missioninvestors.org (Mission Investors Exchange)
- http://thegiin.org (The Global Impact Investing Network)
- https://sdgs.un.org/goals (United Nations Sustainable Development Goals)
- https://impactmanagementproject.com (The Impact Management Project)
- https://www.impactprinciples.org (Operating Principles for Impact Management)
- https://iris.thegiin.org (IRIS+)
- https://www.pitchbook.com (Pitchbook)
- https://www.crunchbase.com (Crunchbase)

CHAPTER TWO: HISTORICAL CONTEXT

"For four-fifths of our history, our planet was populated by pond scum." J.W. Schopf

Purist nonprofit professionals and some of my philanthropic colleagues may view profit-driven capitalists as "pond scum" and perhaps, in some cases, justifiable in that classification. Without pond scum though, the world wouldn't be what it is today. One of my early observations about the impact investing sector was that most of the early practitioners came from nonprofit backgrounds. Given that conceptually the intent of impact investing was meant to drive impact more than financial returns, it would seem logical that some early practitioners transitioned from their grant-making roles into impact investors. That is not surprising and helps put things into context for why deals are structured the way they are, which we will delve deeper into later in this book.

Ford Foundation and MacArthur Foundation have a long history in impact investing; in fact, Ford Foundation pioneered program-related investing (PRI) as an investment structure over fifty years ago, with its first investment in 1968. However, today's PRI is not your grandfather's PRI as its application and structure have evolved to adapt to the needs of modern time. We will delve into more details about PRI structures in later chapters.

In 2011, my friend Antony Bugg-Levine, CEO of Nonprofit Finance Fund and formerly at the Rockefeller Foundation, and his co-author Jed Emerson, published the book Impact Investing: Transforming How We Make Money While Making a Difference that would come to be a reference guide for those interested in understanding the field. For those interested in an in-depth background, I would highly suggest reading it. This chapter is not meant to be a replacement but a complement to provide updated information given the sector's rapid evolution, particularly within the last five years.

The turning point for impact investing was arguably the financial crisis of 2008. Not only was the global financial world in distress, but the trickle-down impact would permeate into the nonprofit world. The worse condition the world is in, the greater the need for the social sector. But due to the dire situation of the financial markets and philanthropic organizations seeing their asset bases reduced by 30 to 50 percent, the ability to support the heightened need for social services organizations was greatly diminished. Foundations struggled to keep their spending level at the same pre-crisis level, which would eat even more into their post-crisis, significantly-reduced endowment size. If they spent at the same required rate (for private foundations, that is the 5 percent of their endowment size in order to maintain their charitable status), simple math would imply that the given level of foundations' giving would be reduced by 30 to 50 percent, proportionate to the drop in their endowment sizes, putting even greater strain on the social sector that needed more significant funding, not less—it was the perfect storm!

This contradictory heightened demand for social sector support in the face of diminished resources available served as a wake-up call for both parties. For foundations, particularly smaller ones, maintaining the same level of support to their grantees would risk their own long-term viability as it would drain their corpus. That meant prioritizing and making tough decisions on which initiatives to continue supporting and which ones to sunset. Impact investing could be a hybrid strategy that would not drain the corpus the way traditional grant-making does while still supporting impactful initiatives.

For nonprofits, the intensified competition for even more limited resources forced some to rethink their funding options and strategic planning. Some social services organizations had gotten comfortable relying on key funders for years, rarely worrying about funding as those foundations with which they had strong relationships continue to write checks year after year. However, the 2008 financial crisis was a wake-up call to change the business-as-usual mentality and adapt to the new environment. As many nonprofits with concentrated funders that support their work came to realize, if that funder decides to change direction on their strategy or is forced to cut back on their grant making, it could prove detrimental. Sometimes, these organizations would no longer exist if they failed to find a new funder to support their work.

Ironically, to this day, some nonprofit organizations still have not learned this lesson and still rely heavily on key funders.

The more sophisticated nonprofits with earned revenue streams began dipping their toes into the impact investing space that reduced their reliance on critical funders. In fact, by doing so, they could tap into additional funding sources beyond their traditional reliance on grant making, allowing them to expand their services and scale. Thus, by leveraging impact investing tools, some of these organizations could not only replace some of their grant funding but also access incremental funding sources to support their work. Of course, it should be noted that impact investing is not suited for all organizations, so the points made previously do not and should not apply to every organization (we will discuss this more in the chapter on what the tools are).

CHAPTER THREE: SECTOR OVERVIEW

"The size of your audience doesn't matter.
What's important is that your audience
is listening." Randy Pausch

The latest statistics from the 2020 Global Impact Investing Network (GIIN) Survey show the growth of impact investing continues to gain traction. Of the 294 respondents in the annual survey, total managed impact assets grew to over $404 billion by year-end 2019 from $114 billion in 2017. This considerable increase provides evidence of the rapid acceleration of the sector as more capital is being shifted towards impact investing. While the GIIN Survey aggregated responses from only 294 organizations, it estimated the overall impact investing assets under management is closer to $715 billion, managed by over 1,720 organizations at the end of 2019. It should be noted that while the allocation of capital towards the sector does not necessarily mean the deployment of capital has been just as rapid, but still suggests an increasing optimism for the sector. Figure 1 provides an overview of various asset classes within the sector and their change over the past six years among the respondents:

Figure 1 Impact Investing Asset Allocation 5-Year Change (GIIN, 2020)

Instrument (in $ millions)	2013	2019	CAGR
Public Equity	$326	$19,968	99%
Real Assets	$1,591	$9,762	35%
Private Debt	$12,338	$27,600	14%
Private Equity	$7,222	$13,831	11%
Deposits & Cash Equivalents	$983	$1,148	3%
Public Debt	$4,012	$4,476	2%
Equity-like Debt	$2,673	$1,294	-11%
Other	$1,647	$1,884	2%
Total	$30,792	$79,963	17%

Total impact investing allocations have increased by 17% compounded annual growth rate (CAGR) between 2013 and 2019. Private debt has been traditionally the most significant source for impact investing and continues to be the largest allocation reaching $27.6 billion; this was historically followed by private equity, which reached nearly $14 billion in 2019. However, the fastest-growing impact investing allocation was public equity, which had only been $326 million in 2013. Still, it overtook private equity as the second-largest allocation for impact investors, reaching nearly $20 billion by 2019. That is likely due to the growth of environmental, social, and governance (ESG) factors being taken into account for investors and the increasing availability of ESG funds. It should be noted that this data only accounts for respondents of the GIIN survey; these figures under-estimate the actual size of the sector but are likely representative of the broader trends. The 2020 COVID pandemic has only accelerated the demand and focus on socially-conscious investing strategies.

One example of the growth of ESG being an increasingly attractive entry point into impact investing is a look at Generation Investment Management, an asset manager co-founded by David Blood (former head of Goldman Sachs Asset Management) and former U.S. Vice President and Nobel Peace Prize Winner Al Gore. The track record of Generation's sustainability-focused investment strategy provides strong evidence that it can provide superior returns when ESG factors are considered for securities selection. Founded in 2004, its assets under management (AUM) grew to $19 billion in 2018 from approximately $1 billion when it started fourteen years ago, which is a compounded annual growth rate of over 25%. To be clear, some of the growth is likely from additional investors pouring money into the firm net of any withdrawals. Still, some of the increase can be attributed to investment performance.

In his April 28, 2018, Financial Times article "Al Gore: sustainability is history's biggest investment opportunity," Owen Walker noted that Generation's flagship equity fund returned 13.5 percent before fees since inception over its 14-year existence compared to 7.3 percent for the relevant benchmark. Does this necessarily prove the case that sustainability investing does not sacrifice returns? Obviously one strong example is insufficient but still gives optimism for that underlying thesis. While the sector is still relatively new, it will take more evidence from other market participants to convince skeptics on the potential of impact investing without compromising on returns. There will undoubtedly be plenty of examples where impact investors have to compromise on financial returns, whether intentionally part of their initial strategy given their mandate, or simply because they are poor investors who cannot outperform traditional investors having the burden of the extra bottom lines. People must take an unbiased view when evaluating these data points to objectively assess the sector by considering all information rather than selectively only pointing to data points that support their preconceived opinions.

Traditional for-profit asset managers represent the largest segment among investor types, accounting for approximately 51% of the 2020 GIIN survey respondents. Nonprofit fund managers and foundations comprise the other major impact investor types, as shown in Figure 2.

Figure 2: Impact Investor by Type (GIIN, 2020)

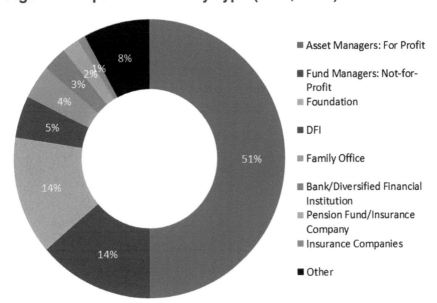

As growing acceptance of ESG investing continues, it would not be surprising to see the shift where family offices and pension funds become larger shares of the impact investing landscape. Two major trends drive this potential shift. Firstly, the continued transfer of wealth from the older generation to Gen X and millennials. Over 45 million American households are estimated to transfer their wealth to the next generation or charity over the next 25 years; Gen X will inherit $27 trillion from that transfer (Asher Cheses, 2018). Older generations stereotypically bifurcate the accumulation of wealth and philanthropy into mutually exclusive activities. You make your money through private enterprise endeavors and investing, then make an impact with charitable activities through giving money away as grants. Adherence to that philosophical approach is one of the core obstacles in the past to the acceptance of impact investing. However, Gen X and millennials are more open to values-based investing. As shown in Figure 3, according to Bank of America's 2018 U.S. Trust Insights on Wealth and Worth, it is estimated that nearly 80% of high-net-worth millennials screen their investment portfolios for ESG factors in 2018 compared to just over 30% in 2013.

Figure 3: ESG Investing Interest by Generation (Dieter Holger, 2019)

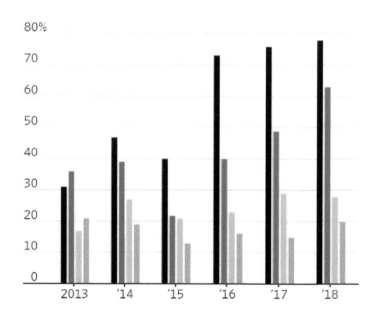

Growing Interest
Percentage of high-net-worth investors who have reviewed their portfolios for ESG impact

■ Millennials ■ Generation X
▨ Baby Boomers ▨ Silent Generation

Source: 2018 U.S. Trust Insights on Wealth and Worth; Bank of America

Assuming Gen X will dedicate 5 to 10 percent of the $27 trillion of inherited wealth to impact investing over the next 25 years, the implied potential opportunity is $1.3 to $2.7 trillion for the asset class.

US SIF Foundation's estimates of the impact investment market are even higher, although its screen for what qualifies as impact investing might be broader than others. According to its 2020 Report on Sustainable and Impact Investing Trends, there was already $16.6 trillion of US-domiciled assets in the US that practice "ESG incorporation," meaning that they apply various social, environmental, and governance criteria in their investment analysis and portfolio selection (US SIF Foundation, 2020). The survey and research of US SIF aggregated assets of 530 institutional investors, 384 money managers, and 1,204 community investment institutions.

The $16.6 trillion is split between $4.6 trillion managed on behalf of individual investors and $12.0 trillion managed on behalf of institutional investors. Figure 4 shows the dramatic acceleration of the trend from 1995 through 2020, particularly over the last eight years.

Figure 4: Sustainable Investing in the United States 1995-2020 (US SIF Foundation, 2020)

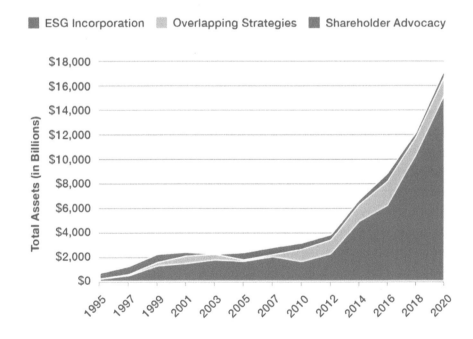

We can see from the graph that ESG incorporation accelerated particularly since 2016.

Figure 5: 2020 Money Manager Assets by Type Incorporating ESG Criteria (US SIF Foundation, 2020)

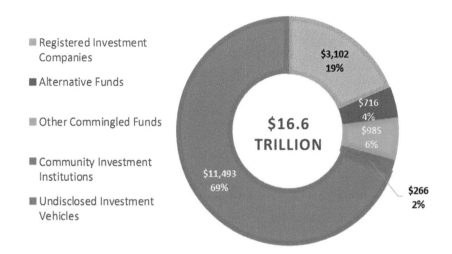

The combined effects of the COVID pandemic and the George Floyd murder protests provide the tailwind that is the second primary driver of the shift and acceleration of impact investing. These macro social and economic tsunamis spotlight the racial and social inequities faced by poor communities (predominantly communities of color) and the growing disparity between the wealthy and the poor. It was not that these issues didn't exist before; they were just less obvious to ordinary people and easily ignored when they didn't seem to have any impact on them in their daily lives directly. COVID and the protests washed away the barriers of complacency. They awakened sensitivities among those who might have easily separated themselves from the plight of the less fortunate when they get bombarded by constant news feeds of massive protests and a rapid increase in COVID infections domestically and globally. This time felt different, unlike previous calls for social and racial justice in recent history. Corporations are more aggressively putting out statements for supporting racial equity and increasing commitments to diversity, equity, and inclusion (DEI) initiatives as they see their consumers align their spending with their values. Just as consumers become more conscientious of where they spend their money, investors also become more thoughtful about ESG factors in their investing decisions.

Whether you believe the $16.6 trillion figure from US SIF or the more conservative figure of $715 billion from GIIN's estimate for the impact investing market's size, they agree that the trend is upward and accelerating for the sector. Some day we may even see prominent asset managers consider impact investing as an asset class, even though a lot of asset managers are still not sure how to think about impact investing. Allocating between debt versus equity, public versus private markets are classic decisions of institutional asset managers when constructing their portfolio allocation strategies, but will they add yet another dimension to their allocation decision matrix: traditional versus impact investing? Or "impact investing" may become synonymous with just "investing" and merely absorbed into every aspect of investment decision making that it is no longer considered a separate style of investing. I cannot say which would be the better outcome, but my guess is that there will be practitioners of both approaches, much like there are investors today who heavily favor fundamental analysis while others heavily favor technical analysis for their investment decisions. As long as impact investing is at least a factor in the investment decision-making process, our world would be much better as we connect capital to impact.

CHAPTER FOUR: TYPES OF INVESTMENTS

"Every complex structure starts with simple building blocks."

Before getting into investing itself, it's best to understand the different types of investments and structures. This chapter discusses a variety of ways that impact investments can be structured. Let's first start with some fundamentals. For some of you who are more financially sophisticated, you may want to skip this chapter as I'm covering it at an elementary level. However, getting the basics right before understanding the more advanced deal structuring concepts is essential. While I will keep the discussion at a higher level in this chapter, later chapters will dig more into how to explore the concept of capital stacking. These are the key topics I want to cover:

- Debt versus Equity
- Fund versus Direct Investments
- Mission-Related Investments and Program-Related Investments
- Social Impact Bonds
- Income Share Agreements
- Bank Deposits and Loan Guarantees

This chapter's purpose is not to turn you into a financial guru. Still, hopefully, for those of you who are not financially savvy, you will get enough of an understanding of these concepts not to be intimidated when you hear them. Sometimes they sound very confusing and technical, but when you understand conceptually what each instrument is, you'll realize none of this stuff is as complicated as some may have you believe.

DEBT VERSUS EQUITY INVESTMENTS

The type of instrument used to make an investment has significant ramifications on governance and risk specific to the asset class. We'll start with debt since that is one of the earliest and most common types of impact investment made. Debt is essentially loans. When you give someone a loan (you are the lender), you expect them to pay it back at some point (term of the loan). In addition, they (the borrower) will pay you some fee for borrowing that money from you in the form of interest. So how does a loan work, and what are the terms you often hear for loan investments? There are a couple of terms worth clarifying:

- *Lender* – the person or institution providing the money, a more technical term is "creditor" since they are extending you "credit." Credit cards are essentially a bank giving you debt on demand up to your credit limit.

- *Borrower* – the person or institution looking for a loan; a more technical term is "debtor" since you are taking on "debt" from the lender. The borrower is indebted to the lender when he takes a loan.

- *Interest* – when you borrow money, there is a cost for that money typically. For example, your rich uncle (or a foundation) might give you a loan with no interest, but in a normal situation, someone will lend you money for a fee. The amount of the loan and the fee/interest they charge are based on how likely they think you will be able to repay the loan back. It is also based on how long the loan is for.

- *Term* – this refers to the length of the loan. Conceptually, the longer the term, the higher the interest rate. Why is that the case? Well, imagine if you were to lend someone $1,000 for 30 days versus three years. The reasons you would charge them a lower interest for a thirty-day loan versus a three-year loan are: 1) you will have $1,000 less available to you for a shorter period; 2) the likelihood that the borrower will repay you within thirty days is higher than over three years (a lot can happen in thirty days, but a lot more can happen over three years!), and 3) lower repricing risk.

    You're probably wondering what repricing risk is, so I'll give this example. Let's say you lent someone $1,000 for six months at 5% interest. The prevailing interest rate at the time you made the loan was 5% for similar loans. Now let's say that at the end of six months (the "Maturity" date is the technical term), the prevailing interest rate jumped to 10% for similar loans. By that point in time, the borrower would have repaid you the $1,000 loan plus the 5% interest, which totals $1,025. (Interest rates are quoted on an annual basis, so if that had been a full-year loan, you'd have gotten $50 of interest, but the loan was only for six months, so you're only getting $25 of interest earned.) You can now re-lend that $1025 at the new interest rate of 10%. What if you had lent the money for three years initially? Well, now you are stuck only earning 5% interest over the three years when others can lend at 10%. That is the concept of repricing risk. It can also go the other way where interest rates might fall to 3%, in which case you benefit from getting a higher interest rate for the two and a half years remaining on the loan. Speaking of repricing risk, one way to avoid or mitigate that is the concept of "floating" interest rates.

- *Fixed versus Floating Rate Interest* – A loan paying a fixed interest rate is simply whatever the set interest rate is over the loan's full term. Floating rate loans have what is called a "Spread" over some benchmark interest rate. All this means is that they add some incremental amount over the benchmark. The three common benchmarks for interest rates are the 10-year treasury notes, Prime rate, and London Interbank Offer Rate (LIBOR). An example of a floating rate loan is a one-year loan priced at LIBOR + 300, meaning that if LIBOR rates are 1.83%, then the one-year floating-rate loan is 4.83% interest. If LIBOR goes up to 2.83%, then the loan interest charge would go up to 5.83% because that rate "floats" with the benchmark rate. That is how repricing risk gets mitigated. The reason why fixed-rate mortgages are more expensive (higher interest) than floating rate mortgages comes back to that core issue of banks charging you a premium to take away your repricing risk. A lot of unsophisticated borrowers during the boom years preceding the 2008 financial crisis got sold low floating rate mortgages (adjustable-rate mortgages or ARMs) on their home loans but were caught off guard when those rates adjusted significantly upward after a couple of years, and they could no longer afford the monthly payments. The results were detrimental, as we saw in the 2008 financial crisis with numerous defaults on home mortgages and evictions. Going deeper into the financial crisis and its causes is beyond the scope of this chapter. The core point here is that repricing risk is the biggest concern for floating-rate interest structures for both the borrower and the lender.

- *Secured vs. Unsecured* – A loan is considered "secured" when there is an asset pledged to the lender if the borrower is not able to repay the loan ("default" on loan). For example, a home mortgage is essentially a loan secured by the home's value; if you default on the mortgage, the lender forecloses on the loan and becomes the homeowner. They have the right to sell the house to recover what was left on the mortgage. The technical term for an asset that secures the loan is the "collateral"; this can be anything tangible like a car or a home and intangible assets like intellectual property in the technology sector. Secured loans usually have much lower interest payments than unsecured ones because it is considered lower risk since you can sell the collateral if the borrower does not repay the loan, all other factors being equal.

- *Covenants* – This is the technical term for the terms that a borrower must abide by to comply with the loan agreement. Most covenants are financial by nature (having a set of specific financial ratios that do not fall below a certain level; for example, the total debt can't exceed 50% of the company's capitalization) but could also refer to specific things the company is forbidden to do. Covenants can be positive or negative in structure:

  ○ An example of a negative covenant: the borrower is forbidden from selling assets above $500K in value without pre-approval from the lender.

  ○ An example of a positive covenant: the borrower must maintain a minimum cash balance in its checking account of $1.5 million.

  Covenants serve two purposes. The first purpose is to notify and flag the lender that an event has occurred that could increase the borrower's risk profile. Secondly, it gives the lender the right to foreclose on the loan if the covenant is triggered (breached) and referred to as an "event of default."

- *Default* – This refers to when a specific term in the loan agreement has been breached. In every loan, there are typically some terms that a borrower must comply with. For example, sometimes, a specific financial ratio needs to be maintained according to the covenants set in the loan agreement. Other times, it might be reporting requirements on social metrics or mission drifted from the original business when the loan was issued. Default allows the lender to force an immediate repayment of the loan or seize the collateral securing the loan. In most scenarios, the borrower and the lender will try to do a workout so that a foreclosure (the seizure of the collateral) happens to see if there are less extreme ways to get the loan repaid.

Now that you know the key terms of debt investments, let's discuss what an equity investment is and why this may make more sense to the investee. Equity is essentially the shareholders of a company. When you invest in a company's equity, you become a shareholder owning a stake in the company. That means it entitles you to a share of the company's value, in simplest terms. There are many different types of equity structures, but I'll cover just a few key ones to keep things simple.

- *Common Equity* – Not to sound punny about it, but common equity is the most "common" type of equity. Every company has it that has shareholders. It is the form of equity with the least amount of seniority (I'll describe what seniority is shortly). When you own a share in a publicly listed company or if you started the company as an entrepreneur, the most likely type of equity you own is common shares in the company.

- *Preferred Equity* – These are shareholders with special (read "more favorable") rights that common equity owners do not have. When a company raises a financing round with a venture firm or any institutional investor, those new investors typically want some preferential right, so they are issued Preferred Equity rather than common shares. Sometimes these special rights include having a board seat with the company, getting paid a dividend, or being repaid at a premium if the company gets acquired within a specific timeframe. We'll discuss these special rights in the advanced structuring section, but just know that preferred equity has preferential treatment compared to common equity. As each new equity round is raised, an additional series of preferred stock is usually issued. Think of a multilayer cake; each new layer at the top gets more preferential treatment than the layer below, including other preferred shareholders in the prior rounds.

- *Convertible Notes* – These investment instruments are essentially debt, but their risk profile is closer to that of equity; for that reason, they are referred to as "quasi-equity" or equity-like instruments. With early-stage companies, these are structured as Convertible Preferred Notes that pay the investor an interest rate (accrues with the Notes value rather than being paid out the way traditional debt interest payments are) over the life of the note and convertible to the equity of the company. How these are structured is discussed later, but Convertible Preferred Notes are usually issued in bridge rounds for early-stage companies that need to raise capital due to cash flow issues or don't want to price the equity round because of valuation concerns. We will discuss why these situations arise and how to mitigate risks while providing necessary funding that isn't just putting more money into a sinking investment.

These are just three categories of equity structures, but the range of investment structures between debt and equity is extensive and well beyond the scope of this book.

So what are the main differences between being an equity investor versus a debt investor? We summarize some high-level factors and will go deeper into the more advanced topics in later chapters.

Seniority & Risk – when you are a debt investor, you get more seniority on being repaid when things go wrong with the company. For example, suppose the investee goes bankrupt, and the assets are sold off to repay the investors. In that case, debt investors will get repaid before any remaining value is paid to the equity investors. The following figure illustrates the waterfall of repayment when a firm goes bankrupt, and its assets are sold off.

Figure 6: Illustrative Example of Seniority

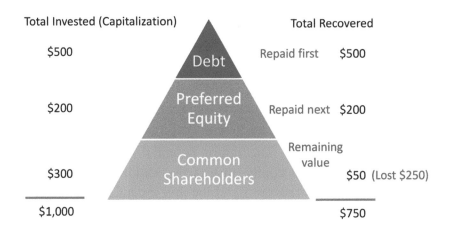

We assume the firm initially had a total of $1,000 invested into it by debt, preferred equity, and common equity investors. When the firm fails, its assets are only worth $750 when those assets are sold. As shown in the figure, the first investors to be repaid are debt investors because they are the most senior on the capital stack; they are fully repaid. Then comes the preferred equity investors; they are next in line in seniority (they get preferential treatment, as you may recall, over common shareholders). The amount remaining after the debt investors are repaid is $250 ($750 – the $500 repaid to debt investors), which is then used to repay the $200 owed to the preferred investors. What is left will then be used to repay the common stock investors: $50. As shown in this example, only common stock investors are taking a loss. Every common stock investor will only get back just under 17% of their investment ($50 divided $300). If the total amount recovered had been just $300 instead of $750. Every investor will have lost money, but at least the debt investors will recover some portion of their investment back. In contrast, the preferred equity and common equity investors lost everything. This example oversimplifies seniority but gives you a sense of how repayment works across the capital stack.

- *Governance* – This refers to the control of the company. Debt investors usually do not have a say in the company's governance. They have covenants to mitigate their investment risk and get seniority when things don't go well for the company, but they have no real control over the firm. Shareholders in the equity tranche of the capital stack have the right to control the direction of the firm; for the sake of simplicity, the largest shareholders who have the most votes will have the most control over the direction of the firm; this is typically represented by having a board seat. It should be noted that in real life, governance is not merely determined by ownership stake; some stock classes have super-majority voting rights even if they don't have a majority ownership stake in the firm.

• *Return Potential* – The return potential significantly differs between debt and equity, just as the seniority profile is. Not surprisingly, the risk profile of the investment structure directly correlates to its return potential: the higher the risk, the higher the return potential. In the example earlier, we showed that debt is a less risky investment relative to equity in the case of a company's failure, all else being equity. Not surprisingly, the return potential is also lower than equity. For a debt investor, the return potential is simply the interest rate paid for the loan. If the firm has an amazing year, the only upside for the debt investor is to be fully repaid with interest promised to them by the loan agreement over the life of the loan. For the equity investor, as shareholders of the company, the upside is only limited by the company's potential value. If the company is worth ten times what it was worth when the equity investor made the initial investment, then that investment has increased tenfold as its return compared to the debt investor getting just interest on the loan.

These key differences highlight factors for an investor choosing debt over equity. In some situations, there is not a choice. For example, investing in a nonprofit can only be in the form of a debt instrument. That is simply because nonprofits do not have shares, so consequently no shareholders. In the case of very early-stage companies, very rarely can they access debt because they don't typically have revenue or assets that give an investor confidence the loan would be able to be repaid by the startup. Thus, the only viable form of investment is equity. That is why most venture funds are equity investors, given how early in the development life cycle their investments are. They are at the highest risk but also the highest return. As a case in point, a renowned Silicon Valley venture firm, First Round Capital, invested $500K as an equity investor into the Seed round of Uber. That $500K investment was worth $2.5 billion when Uber went public through its IPO (initial public stock offering), an almost five thousand times return.

DIRECT VERSUS FUND INVESTMENTS

Now that you understand the difference between debt and equity, another question I often get asked is should I do direct investments or invest in funds. Let's start with what that question is asking before we discuss picking one over the other. When you invest directly into a company, you are essentially the lender (if you made a debt investment) or a company shareholder (if you are an equity investor). You are in "direct" contact with the entrepreneur, so you might be more actively engaged (if you would like to). As a direct investor, you will be the one structuring the investment, negotiating the terms of the investment, and ensuring you understand the risks entailed in the investment. You'll also be responsible for monitoring the investment.

On the other hand, a fund investment is essentially buying into a "pool" of investments. This pool of investments might already be known (in the case of a mutual fund, you are buying into the existing pool of companies in the fund's portfolio); but when it comes to private equity or venture capital funds, they are the tentative pool of investments that reflect the investment strategy of the fund manager. Investing in a fund essentially is investing in the fund's strategy and backing the fund manager to execute that investment strategy. For this reason, the fund manager's track record is vital when assessing the risk and return potential of the fund. In essence, you are outsourcing direct investing to a professional manager. Many reasons drive that approach, including:

- Domain or Industry Expertise – the fund manager might be much more experienced in a sector, asset class, geography, or stage of investment than someone in-house

- Diversification – Since the investment is in a "pool" of assets, there is immediate diversification created by the fund manager

- Time Efficiency – Since the fund manager is in direct contact with the portfolio of investees, you are one layer removed and do not have to monitor or actively engage with the entrepreneur.

- Staffing and Resource Access – If the department is leanly staffed, investing in a fund is much more effective since the fund manager will have a full team dedicated to the investment strategy, from diligence and deal execution to monitoring the portfolio. They will also have access to proprietary research resources such as Bloomberg terminals and Pitchbook that might be too expensive to subscribe to unless that cost can be spread across a larger set of investors.

- Co-investing Opportunities – Another advantage is the ability to leverage a fund manager with deep expertise in a specific sector for their access to deal flow that you can co-invest in. Because most likely they've been in the industry for a long time, the fund manager should have a solid network to tap for potential investment opportunities. In addition, investing in a fund can sometimes give you access to deal flow that you might not be aware of or have access to. The fund manager may allow or want others to co-invest in the companies that they invest in, especially if the co-investor brings other capabilities that the fund manager doesn't have.

While there appear to be advantages of having a professional manager by investing in a fund rather than directly, there is no right answer for which option is better. It all depends on the unique circumstances of the investor. Some family office investors prefer to be very hands-off and just know that their money is being used to invest in companies that do good. In contrast, others want to be much more actively engaged with the investee, so a direct investment is preferable. Strategic investors may want to be actively involved with the entrepreneur to see if other potential partnerships and value can be created beyond just the money invested.

MISSION-RELATED INVESTMENTS AND PROGRAM-RELATED INVESTMENTS

Newer impact investors often ask the difference between a mission-related investment (MRI) and a program-related investment (PRI). Unfortunately, even for experienced investors, sometimes the terms are misused, which leads to even more confusion. The easiest way to differentiate between them is to look at where they sit on the impact and financial return spectrum, as shown in the following figure.

Figure 7: Spectrum of Impact Investments Continuum[1]

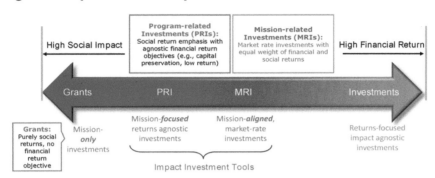

As shown in Figure 7, there are two opposite ends of the spectrum: the far left side represents investments solely with high social impact, while the far right side of the spectrum is focused exclusively on high financial return. In the context of a private foundation, generally speaking, grants are the tools to drive purely social impact, while the endowment assets managed by the investments team are solely focused on financial return. It should be noted that this continuum represents intent rather than the actual outcome with the specific type of tool utilized. That is an important point to remember, as I'll explain shortly.

Mission-related investments – MRI investments equally balance financial return objectives with social impact objectives; hence they sit squarely in the middle along the continuum, and the focus on mission is best deemed as "mission-aligned," unlike program-related investments. The bar for how strongly an MRI investment supports a foundation's mission is much lower than for PRIs. Private foundations typically make these with endowment assets because they have a strong financial return objective as part of their investment consideration. The financial return target is the "market rate" for similar types of traditional investments even though they have a second bottom line of social impact. What is often a bit confusing is that foundations sometimes refer to all of their work as "mission-related investments," which includes their grantmaking programmatic initiatives; this was the case even at Lumina Foundation, where I had built the impact investing strategy. Senior executives repeatedly kept using the term mission-related investments for all aspects of Lumina's work other than internal back-office operations because all the activities were in

---

[1]   Kind Capital LLC Overview Deck, 2021

support of the Foundation's mission. If the organization does not have an impact investing function or division, then perhaps it would not be as confusing. Every time I hear an executive use the term mission-related investments in the broader context rather than specifically to impact investing, a little of me dies and makes me want to pull my hair out. It's no wonder the W.K. Kellogg Foundation called their impact investing program "Mission-Driven Investments" and mitigated that confusion. Even more surprising is why not more foundations adopt that terminology to avoid the confusion of MRIs.

<u>Program-related investments</u> – Unlike MRIs, program-related investments are typically funded out of a foundation's grant budget. That is because private foundations can count these investments as part of their 5% payout requirement to maintain their nonprofit tax status; thus, instead of making a grant, using those funds to make a PRI investment counts as part of that year's payout requirement. Because of that benefit, the Internal Revenue Service (IRS) has very defined criteria of what can qualify as a program-related investment. A more detailed explanation is in Appendix A, but the primary three components are:

Criteria 1: The primary purpose is to accomplish one or more of the foundation's exempt purposes,

Criteria 2: Production of income or appreciation of property is not a significant purpose, and

Criteria 3: Influencing legislation or participating in political campaigns on behalf of candidates is not a purpose.

While these three criteria may appear simple, the ways foundations have interpreted what each component means have been very different among some foundations, particularly #1 and #2. We will discuss that in more detail shortly, but in the meanwhile, notice where PRIs sit on the spectrum of impact investments continuum in Figure 7: just between grants and MRIs. This signifies that program-related investments are mission-focused investment instruments rather than just being mission-aligned the way MRIs are. They are much more like grants than investments because their primary objective is to drive charitable purposes aligned with the foundation's mission. Being mission-aligned is not sufficient to satisfy Criteria 1; the investment's primary purpose must be focused on the foundation's charitable purpose. Note that focusing on charitable purpose in itself is not sufficient to qualify as a program-related investment; it must be the charitable purpose of the foundation. That is often something newer impact investors forget unless they have good lawyers experienced with PRI structuring, reminding them of the legal requirements under the definition of what qualifies as PRIs. Therefore, what qualifies as a PRI for one foundation may not qualify as a PRI for another foundation. For example, an investment into a school teaching technology skills to kids in slums of South Africa might qualify as a PRI for a private global foundation, but that investment would not qualify as a PRI for a small private foundation focused exclusively on healthcare access for vulnerable populations in New York City as its sole programmatic focus. Of course, a very creative lawyer might be able to draft a Legal Opinion that somehow can connect an investment into the South African school to be mission-focused enough to the small private foundation, but it would be quite a stretch.

The biggest confusion for program-related investments tends to be the interpretation of Criteria 2. Many traditional foundation impact investors have conservatively interpreted Criteria 2 as guidance from the IRS that PRIs must be targeting a below-market-rate investment return at the onset of the initial investment. That is not true, however, and not the intent of the Internal Revenue Service. In the early days of impact investing, most PRIs have been structured as debt instruments. While I don't have research data to support this, I believe a significant driver for that may have been due to the more conservative interpretation of Criteria 2. It is much easier to structure a debt investment to comply with demonstrating charitability as below-market-rate investments relative to other traditional debt instruments. This can be done by charging very low interest rates or even no interest on loans while taking similar or more significant risks than traditional debt lenders. In addition, foundations like to talk about how they "crowd in" or "catalyze" other market-rate investors into the investee through those investee-friendly terms, which helps them meet the charitability criteria. In the Side Letter section chapter, we will cover more ways to demonstrate charitability for PRI qualifications.

Program-related investments do not need to be below the market rate from a financial returns perspective. I've been on several conference panels with expert impact investors who insist that PRIs must be below market rate when it comes to financial returns, which confirms the misunderstanding among many practitioners. As of the writing of this book, the Internal Revenue Service's Criteria 2 merely reinforces the notion that PRIs' primary objective is not to generate financial return but to focus on the mission. As long as the primary goal of the PRI is to drive the charitable mission of the investor and is documented appropriately during the initial investment decision process, financial returns from that investment can be at market or even above market without breaching what qualifies as a PRI. Debt investments have a capped return and easily can be compared to what the "market" (traditional) investors are willing to lend against. Equity investments have uncapped returns and are much more nuanced when comparing returns. That is why documentation and record-keeping are crucial for program-related investments. If there is ever a question from the IRS, providing documentation showing that the initial investment decision was driven primarily by a charitable mission will be key. If the investment ends up doubling or even a one-hundred-fold return at the exit, it does not jeopardize its qualification as a program-related investment.

Legal Opinions – As an added level of ensuring an investment qualifies as a program-related investment, major foundations like The Bill & Melinda Gates Foundation, Lumina Foundation, and Kellogg Foundation have required Legal Opinions for all their PRI investments. An outside law firm (typically) engaged by the foundation issues a Legal Opinion to confirm that the investment meets the qualifications of a program-related investment. They will go into case laws and examples of how the investment specifically qualifies as a PRI specific to the foundation; in essence, a Legal Opinion is a confirmation from the law firm. They are not cheap ($3K to $10K on average, depending on the deal's complexity) and take time to put together, which extends the time of the deal process. Some foundations opt to do the Legal Opinions in-house for more straightforward deals to save costs (and time) and outsource more complicated deals to external law firms.

Whether you choose to invest in a Legal Opinion for your PRI investment will be driven by: 1) the cost you are willing to spend; 2) the timeframe available to get a deal done; 3) the size of the investment and 4) lastly, your concern that an investment may not qualify as a PRI and you need the extra insurance/confirmation from a lawyer. If you are a small private foundation making investments ranging from $25K to $100K per deal, spending $5K on a Legal Opinion for each investment just doesn't seem reasonable relative to the investment size. That doesn't even include the legal diligence fees. Sometimes investment opportunities have very short time frames. A legal opinion that takes three weeks to complete might be too long to extend a deal diligence process. The biggest concern executives (particularly general counsels) at major foundations use as the rationale for not doing PRIs is that if the IRS decides that the investment actually doesn't qualify as a PRI, the foundation may lose its charitable status. However, I have always found that explanation to be a feeble argument. To date, there has never been a private foundation that has lost its tax-exempt status simply because it had wrongly classified an investment as a program-related investment. Note that PRIs have been around for over fifty years since Ford Foundation initially created them in 1968. In most cases (unless the foundation intentionally tries to skirt the law repeatedly), should an investment be determined not to qualify as a PRI, the IRS will likely ask the investor to reclassify the investment and be responsible for any taxable outcomes as a result. As long as there is good documentation to show why the investment qualifies as a PRI using good faith interpretations of the IRS rules on PRIs, I would assume the risk to be reasonably low on not requiring a Legal Opinion.

OTHER INVESTMENT STRUCTURES

Now let's cover a few other investment structures you might hear about. Each has its own unique role to play in the impact investing space. I will only provide a simplified explanation of what they are so that you have some context when you hear the terms, but to go deeper into each of these would be beyond the scope of this book as there is plenty of public information on these structures readily available.

Bank Deposits and Loan Guarantees – These instruments are meant to provide a catalytic effect for the investees. Bank deposits are typically "certificates of deposits" or CDs that an impact investor provides to a community development bank or community development financial institution (CDFI), allowing them to have the capital to lend out. In some cases, the intent is to provide liquidity for philanthropic lenders who operate in underserved communities; in other cases, the capital also catalyzes other investors by giving the investee credibility. It can also be a way to reduce the cost of capital for the lenders so that the loans issued can be lower than what traditional investors charge, as shown in the following example of a $500 million CDFI.

Figure 8: Bank Deposits to Lower Interest Rate

CDFI Loan Fund	Traditional Investors Only		With Philanthropic Investors	
	Amount ($MM)	Interest Rate	Amount ($MM)	Interest Rate
Traditional Investors	$500	12%	$300	12%
PRI Investors	$0	1%	$200	1%
Total	$500		$500	
Weighted Interest Rate		**12%**		**8%**

In Figure 8, the example demonstrates the impact of a Bank Deposit on reducing the cost for end borrowers from the CDFI Fund by lowering the Fund's cost of capital. For example, the market interest rate for loans is 12%, but if impact investors provided $200M of the $500M loan fund at a 1% interest rate to the Fund, the impact investors have effectively reduced the cost of loans for end borrowers from 12% to 8%, assuming all else being equal.

Loan Guarantees provide a credit enhancement for traditional investors to be willing to lend to the investee that would otherwise not be attractive. For example, a traditional investor might feel that lending in a specific community or to a particular demographic (entrepreneurs of color as an example) may be too risky, so an impact investor such as a private foundation may guarantee the loan losses up to a certain percent, in essence, credit enhancing the structure of the loan. The Loan Guarantee can be just a portion of a loan portfolio (say 30%) or the full amount of a specific loan, as shown in the following example:

Figure 9: Loan Guarantee Example

$500 Million CDFI Loan Fund with $100 Million Loss

	Amount ($MM)	Implied Loss	Remaining ($MM)	With 30% First Loss Loan Guarantee		
				Amount ($MM)	Implied Loss	Remaining ($MM)
Traditional Investors	$300	($60)	$240	$300		$300
PRI Investors	$200	($40)	$160	$200		$200
Loan Guarantee Reserve	$0	$0		$150	($100)	$50
Total	$500	($100)	$400			

Similar to the previous example, we assume a $500M CDFI Loan Fund that lends to high-risk, underserved markets. All else being equal, if we assume that the Fund loses $100 million from its loans, we see in the example that the $100 million loss implies $60 million of loss for the traditional investors and $40 million of loss allocated to the PRI investors based on their pro-rata shares of loans outstanding, reducing total available loan capital to $400 million remaining in a normal situation. However, if the Fund had a Loan Guarantee of 30%, essentially a reserve of $150 million to cover losses, then even with a loss of $100 million in the Fund, both the traditional and PRI investors have not suffered any losses. The Loan Guarantee still has $50 million remaining for additional loss protection. The finance world refers to this as credit enhancing the loan fund.

In the Figure 9 example, the Loan Guarantee is structured to take the first $150 million of losses from its portfolio of loans; however, an impact investor may also structure the credit enhancement based on individual loans instead of the entire portfolio. Guarantee of the whole portfolio is a much stronger credit-enhancing mechanism than just on an individual loan basis because the traditional and PRI investors will not lose a penny until losses on the portfolio exceed the $150 million loan Guarantee reserve. If the Loan Guarantee had been structured to provide 30% loan loss protection on a loan-by-loan basis, those investors would take a pro-rata loss on anything exceeding 30% of each loan loss. In such a scenario, if we assumed a borrower defaults on a $100,000 loan and only $40,000 of the loan was recovered ($60,000 loss), the Loan Guarantee would cover the first $30,000 of loss, and the remaining $30,000 loss would be split pro-rata between the traditional investors and the PRI investors. Administratively the latter approach becomes more cumbersome to track every single loan and its performance but may better align incentives and underwriting risk tolerance.

Social Impact Bonds – Despite the term, social impact bonds (SIBs) are not "bonds" in the traditional definition. In the simplest explanation, they are specialized structures for aligning government payments with outcomes. Originated in the United Kingdom in 2010, the first SIB was launched to focus on reducing recidivism for incarcerated individuals, created by Social Finance UK as an innovative financing tool. It crossed the pond to the US-led by Tracy Palandjian, CEO and

Co-founder of Social Finance US. If not a bond, what exactly is a SIB? It's a complicated question, literally because it's a complicated structure and process. SIBs aim to connect government funding to the outcomes they are supposed to drive. That sounds logical enough: if the government agency is paying a service provider $25 million to provide a service that should achieve a specific outcome, it would make sense that the government agency would want to know what it is getting. Using incarceration as the impact area, imagine if the $25 million contract paid for tech skills training for incarcerated individuals so that when they are released, they are more able to find jobs and support themselves rather than repeat crimes and return to prison—research has shown that a major cause of recidivism is the lack of ability to find meaningful employment for formerly incarcerated individuals. The innovation of SIBs is to initially shift the service contract funding to private investors and then be reimbursed by the government agency based on the service provider's performance. To put it into an example, if the service provider achieves a baseline outcome (say, reducing recidivism by 10%), the private investors will get their $25 million reimbursed by the government agency with a 5% yield (this is the only "bond"-like aspect of SIBs); but if the actual recidivism achieved is 20% reduction instead, then the private investors would get a higher yield for their investment, say 6% instead of 5% for baseline outcomes.

On the other hand, if the service provider's outcome does not improve recidivism rates at all, then in theory, the government agency will not reimburse the private investors anything. That sounds like an excellent deal for the government agency, having to pay only if the outcomes are achieved, right? That is a core reason SIBs are referred to as "pay-for-success" instruments. The following diagram summarizes the various stakeholders involved in a SIB.

Figure 10: Stakeholders Involved In A Typical Social Impact Bond (SIB)

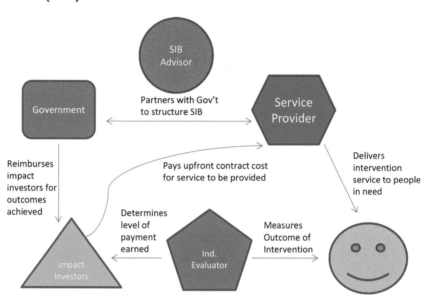

From the diagram, it's clear that SIBs involve many different stakeholders. The complexity involved requires an intermediary such as Social Finance to partner with the government agency to help structure the SIB by bringing in the various stakeholders. The cost to put together a SIB was not nominal, owing to its complexity and the need to customize legal contracts across each stakeholder. In fact, many early SIBs created were funded by philanthropic capital to pay intermediaries to structure them and provide the credit enhancement to entice the impact investors into the projects.

As of the writing of this book, there are over 160 social impact bonds globally across 28 countries, more than 25 of which are in the United States.[2] During the early years, there was significant excitement (and arguably hype); I remember just about every major impact investing conference had a dedicated session on SIBs as if they were the silver bullet philanthropy had been waiting for. SIBs were initially marketed as an innovative financing structure to save government costs when they first came out. However, as more and more SIBs were structured and lessons learned over time from their performance, it became clear that perhaps the more realistic objective was to shift the timing of

---

2   https://socialfinance.org/social-impact-bonds/

government funding rather than save government funding and better tie government funding to the performance of intervention services.

Today, I rarely hear anyone talk about SIBs, and relevant projects are more applicably referred to as pay-for-success projects nowadays. Having been a deal structuring junkie, I was always skeptical (albeit hopeful) that SIBs would succeed due to their complexity and the legal costs to create them that made SIBs highly difficult to scale without philanthropic support. Unless contracts were standardized across stakeholders and standard deal structures and terms to simplify SIBs, it would never scale; there are just so many variables in each project. I am doubtful they can be standardized. Today's pay-for-success projects do not have the level of complexity as SIBs had been, in essence carrying forward the outcome-based funding model of SIBs without their many customized, complicated multi-stakeholder contracts. As foundations' boards of directors seek greater accountability for their grants, outcome-based funding models provide an attractive alignment for funders to demonstrate what I like to call the impact return on their investment (iROI): the impact created per dollar invested.

Income Share Agreements (ISA) – Income share agreements have grown increasingly popular over the last few years as many educational institutions seeking to improve access and affordability tried to emulate Purdue University's Back a Boiler ISA Fund which provided an innovative alternative to traditional student tuition financing. While Purdue Foundation may have been the one to which most people attribute ISAs, the earliest example of an income share agreement being utilized should actually be attributed to Yale University through its Tuition Postponement Option from 1971 through 1978.[3] Regardless of which institution was first to implement an ISA, and despite their popularity (especially among coding boot camps), I have mixed perspectives on ISAs. On the positive side, in theory, ISAs offer greater accessibility for students who cannot access traditional forms of tuition financing through this innovative repayment structure. On the other hand, if structured poorly (always read the fine print!), an income share agreement can be usurious for students who enter them with their education programs.

---

[3]   https://www.savingforcollege.com/article/history-of-income-share-agreements

Before I explain why I am not as enthusiastic about ISAs, let me start by explaining what they are and how they work. Imagine if you are a low-income student or a previously incarcerated minority student. It's very likely your credit score is low (if you have a credit score at all), or your parents cannot guarantee your student loans. As a result, your options for a student loan are to pay a very high-interest rate if you can find a lender, or you can't even get a student loan. Income share agreements essentially allow you to attend the educational program or institution without paying the tuition upfront. Instead, the cost of tuition (and all related educational costs) are repaid when you graduate and have a job by taking a percentage of the salary (the "income" piece of ISA) you earn. You enter into a contract with the ISA issuer to pay some percentage of your salary over a specific period or a fixed amount over the accrued tuition. The ISA issuer can be the education program provider or a completely third party partnered with the educational institution.

Fundamentally these ISA "contracts" are no different from loans. I remember being pitched an ISA fund that sought to be the third-party issuer for educational institutions and turned it down within the first 30 minutes of the call when the fund founders claimed ISAs are not loans but merely contracts. To me, they either didn't understand the fundamental structure of what a debt instrument is—a "contract" between two parties where the borrower agrees to repay the lender with specific terms for that obligation—or they thought I was too stupid to recognize what they were spinning with their sales pitch. Calling it a contract rather than a loan makes it sound much more appealing, like how mortgage brokers pitched adjustable-rate mortgages (ARM) that artificially reduced monthly payments in the early years but jumped after the adjustment period. These affordability misrepresentations led to the foreclosures of many low-income families who didn't understand how ARMs worked. That is not to say ARMs are bad; they just need to be transparent in terms of their structure and how they work and could be entirely appropriate or even optimal depending on the individual. The same goes for ISAs.

The popularity of ISAs has primarily been in the realm of coding boot camps. General Assembly, one of the most well-known coding boot camps (since acquired by Adecco), started using ISAs to make its programs accessible under its Catalyst brand. During the early days of coding boot camps, most of the students pursuing them were already college-educated professionals who wanted to change careers to the tech field given its rapid growth and better pay, not to mention the coolness factor of Silicon Valley. The media would highlight stories of lawyers going to boot camps and successfully landing a software development job at a tech firm. Those of us in philanthropy were disappointed by coding boot camps because they offered alternative career pathways without a college degree in a shorter amount of time (usually two years or less) but were not affordable for underserved minorities. Because these programs were not accredited like universities are, the students could not qualify for Title IV funding (federal student loans) despite the high price of $30,000 to as much as $100,000 in some cases for the complete programs, not including any room and board. That is why ISAs became so popular among boot camps as a way to broaden their affordability: students didn't have to pay tuition to attend. The boot camp bubble promised high-paying job opportunities with their training programs, and they were so confident in your success that they were willing not to charge tuition if you couldn't afford it and offered you an ISA instead. Well, that was the pitch.

While the concept of ISAs enabling access to low-income students by making education more affordable and attainable sounds enticing, much depends on the structure of the income share agreement. The key drivers of an income share agreement that needs to be kept in mind include:

1. **Amount of the loan taken out** – this is for the tuition and, in some cases, stipend while attending the program since low-income students cannot just dedicate full time to studying

2. **Percentage of income deducted** – this represents the share of the student's income monthly that goes back to repay the loan

3. **Period over which loan is repaid** – the shorter the period, the more quickly the loan has to be repaid, which implies a higher percentage of the salary taken out monthly for the repayment

4. **The income threshold** – this represents the minimum salary in which the ISA would kick in or be forgiven. For some firms, it might be as low as a $30K salary job; for others, a $50K salary job. The lower the threshold, the less favorable it is for students/borrowers.

5. **The capped return** – some ISAs have a capped return so that once the cap is reached, the student no longer needs to keep repaying even if the period for the ISA has not expired. When ISAs were first introduced by coding boot camps, many did not have a capped return.

Although we only listed the top five factors in the structure of an ISA, many other minute details are often not considered when entered into until they are triggered. An example is what happens if a student never completes the boot camp program (they get a great job offer or simply fail the program)? Or if they get laid off during the period while they are still paying their ISA off? Covering every minute detail of ISA structures is beyond the scope of this book, but taking the top five factors listed into account will provide an excellent understanding of whether the income share agreement structures are student-friendly, lender friendly, or somewhere in between. It's one thing to compare one ISA to another, but an investor looking at an investment opportunity offering ISAs to their students should also compare the structure of the ISA with a typical student loan as they are essentially very similar tools.

Let me provide some rules of thumb to assess the structures of income share agreements. These should be taken in the context of assuming all other factors are equal.

- Amount of loan taken out: the lower the loan amount, the faster the loan can be repaid. A boot camp program charging $100K will take much longer to repay than a $30K program. Sometimes the amount of the ISA loan has an interest charge while the student is still in the boot camp program while others do not; obviously, no interest would be preferable.

- Percentage of income – the lower, the better because a higher percentage of a student's income taken to repay the ISA leaves less available for the student's living expenses. Usually, this is correlated with the ISA payback period; the longer the payback period, the lower the percentage deducted from the salary. In addition, the percentage of income allows the ISA to calculate an imputed interest rate on the loan. I've seen the range of 13% to as high as 16% for implied interest rates on the loans; there have been cases where the implied interest is even higher. Comparing the implied interest rates to traditional student loans, which typically are under 10% interest, makes ISAs much less attractive if you have access to conventional student loans.

- Payback period – this factor is harder to assess because a more extended payback period may imply lower monthly payments since it is a lower share of the student's income and leaves the student on the hook for a much longer period for repayment.

- Income threshold – by far one of the critical factors for income share agreements, having a lower threshold implies that the boot camp provider may not be as confident in the success of its graduates. However, we need to remember that depending on the boot camp and what training it specializes in, there is no absolute good or wrong threshold. For example, let's say the boot camp specializes in data science and coding. Well, graduates with those skills are typically in professions that pay $80 to $100K or more. The boot camp program that costs $75K setting the ISA threshold at $35K salary would be unreasonable, but something closer to $60K would be more appropriate. On the other hand, if the boot camp program costs $20K focusing on graphic designers or IT support where the graduates make between $60K to $80K instead, then setting an ISA threshold at $40K seems very reasonable.

- Capped return – all ISA should have a capped return in their structure because the imputed return for the ISA to the issuer could be considered usurious. It is usually capped at some multiple of the loan amount (say 2x); the lower the capped return, the more student-friendly the loan is. To give an extreme example, let's assume a boot camp program was $50K to learn data science for the entire program, and the ISA has a 10-year payback period and 10% of salary repayment. Upon graduation, the student somehow lands a dream job paying her $150,000 salary. Over the ten years of the ISA loan, she would be repaying $150,000 ($15K a year over ten years) for a loan that is only $50K which is three times the amount of the loan! Imagine if the share of income was 15% instead—the amount repaid totals $450,000 or 4.5x the loan amount. You can now understand why a cap is critical.

I had mentioned that each of these factors assumes all other factors being equal. However, the reality is that these factors must be taken simultaneously while not all other factors are equal. For example, one factor may be more beneficial to a student while another may be more favorable to the ISA issuer. Figure 11 summarizes these ISA structure considerations.

Figure 11: ISA Key Structure Considerations

Student friendly	ISA Structure Considerations	Issuer/Lender friendly
Low ISA Amount	← →	High ISA Amount
Long Payback Period	← →	Short Payback Period
Low % of Salary Taken	← →	High % of Salary Taken
High Salary Threshold	← →	Low Salary Threshold
Capped Return	← →	Uncapped Return

The next time you hear someone rave about an income share agreement, ask them the structure, and you can determine for yourself whether it is as good for students as they may claim.

While at Lumina Foundation, my colleague Elizabeth Garlow and I tried to structure an innovative financing mechanism to support one of our entrepreneurs. The Edtech company Edovo provided educational programs through customized tablets to serve the incarcerated population at various prison systems, including Cook County in the Chicago area. A key challenge for incarcerated individuals is that they cannot afford to pay for some of the training programs offered to them and cannot take loans. So naturally, the ISA structure seemed to make sense given their lack of funding alternatives. We thought that bringing major tech employers to the table to fund the ISA for these individuals where the tech programs train skills to fill many job openings at these employers would be mutually beneficial. The incarcerated individuals now have a funding mechanism and a guaranteed job if they graduate once they are released from prison; the employers can fill their vacancies and also have a built-in pipeline of potential hires. In addition, philanthropy would provide some credit enhancement guarantee so that if the individual does not complete the program, the loan (ISA) guarantee would be paid for by the philanthropic capital (grants). We called the structure a SIBISA—combining the pay-for-success (SIB) with an income share agreement (ISA). Unfortunately, due to other priorities and timing, we never got to launch SIBISA officially. Still, conceptually, it combined the fundamental structures to serve a population without access or affordability. Perhaps someone else will take the concept to market as I still believe the need and applicability have increased rather than decreased.

CHAPTER FIVE: IMPACT INVESTING PROGRAM SETUP

"Don't do it because it's cool, do it because it's right."

Interest in impact investing has continued to grow, even accelerating with the devastating impact of the COVID pandemic. Therefore, it is not surprising that more and more institutions are starting to dabble in impact investing. This chapter provides some fundamental factors to consider when setting up an impact investing program. My prior experience helping to grow and build the mission-driven investments program at the W.K. Kellogg Foundation and creating the Lumina Impact Ventures strategy has taught me many lessons. Hopefully, sharing these lessons with you will help you avoid the challenges I had faced while accelerating your own programs in a sustainable and scalable way. These are the key areas I want to cover in this chapter:

- Leadership
- Resources
- Setting the strategy
- Logistics and operations
- Talent and staffing
- The case against doing impact investing

Every organization will have more specific factors for its unique situations to keep in mind. Still, these core strategic issues will provide tactical guidance for implementing an impact investing initiative. Note that the context discussed will be from the perspective of a private foundation, but many of the issues are also relevant to other forms of institutions.

Leadership

Launching any initiative begins with leadership support. We'll look at three categories when considering leadership support for establishing an investing strategy: board, executive team, and staff. Each group will have its own motives and objectives. However, for an impact investing initiative to be successful, there must be advocates among all three groups.

Board of Directors – Get Your Board on Board

The board provides the governance and oversight for the long-term strategy of the organization, approving and disapproving strategies and budgets. It is rare for all members of the Board to be fully aligned when launching an impact investing initiative. Inevitably there will be one or more advocates in support of impact investing, but also the same number of skeptics if not more. Let's start with skeptics and the arguments used against impact investing:

- Traditional finance executives – Some board members come from a very traditional finance background (usually holding CFO, CIO, or Treasurer roles). They tend to feel that investments and impact are fundamentally mutually exclusive goals. Traditional financial theory suggests that for investors to drive a financial return (which is the core objective and responsibility of traditional investors), adding another parameter and objective handicaps the investor, making it even harder to drive the primary aim of a high financial return. Their job is to make money, while the grantmaking team's job is to have an impact; these distinct roles have been the operating model historically, and it's uncomfortable to blend the objective. Furthermore, their perspective is that all impact investing is likely to be low-return or money-losing initiatives that make it harder for them to reach a target return for their overall portfolio. That could impact their compensation if total financial return targets are considered in their performance evaluation.

- Nonprofit executives – Some board members come from major nonprofit institutions, typically CEOs or VP of Programs at other foundations. Just like the finance professionals, their experience has always been using grant funding to drive a singular role of impact. When grant capital gets allocated for impact investing, their perception is that the money could have been used for grant funding instead. And if money was allocated out of endowment capital, it may take away from potential returns from traditional investments that could grow the grantmaking funds.

Board buy-in and support are so critical to a successful impact investing initiative. There needs to be at least a majority in support of the initiative, or the odds of the program failing will be quite high, driven by unrealistic benchmarks for success and a lack of patience for the initiative to be given a fair chance of success. If you cannot get a majority of the organization's board to support the initiative, it would be better to wait until you can.

Getting the board on board takes extensive communication and politicking. I've watched it at organizations I've worked at and heard the stories of other organizations' efforts in their impact investing journey. Here are several things to keep in mind and suggestions on how to get your board on board:

- Your board will likely err on the conservative – Due to their fiduciary responsibility, most boards will tend to be more risk-averse in their decision-making. Keeping that in mind, you need to attack the risk aversion by a) getting the board comfortable with risk; b) showing that the initiative may not be as risky as they assume and how you would mitigate the risk, and c) that the upside for the risk is worth taking.

- Brand building and innovation – As a new initiative, framing it around innovation and a unique capacity to accelerate mission achievement will help alleviate some concerns about risk. In addition, having a new capacity at the organization will allow the board members to brag about their organization as being innovative and cool among their peers. As strange as that may sound, this is more common than you would imagine.

- Compare PRIs to grants – Suppose the funds for impact investing will be coming out of the grantmaking budget (program-related investment dollars). In that case, it's good to remind board members that you are seeking to drive the same impact as pure simple grantmaking, but you have the potential to recover the capital and also have potential upside. It would be best if you were not comparing PRIs to traditional investments, which is typically how finance professionals are trying to frame the comparison; that is the classic apples and oranges comparison.

PRIs should always be compared to grants, while MRIs can be compared to traditional investments. Unfortunately, many in the investment world and financial roles continue to compare PRIs to traditional investments as a basis for why they should not be making impact investments; this naïve simplification shows a lack of understanding of what PRIs are. It is imperative to remind board members that grants are not only 0% return but actually negative 100% return, meaning it is a 100% loss! Even if your PRI investment only recovers 25% of the capital invested, you're still way ahead of what the grant would have been. Remember, PRIs' primary purpose is to drive charitable impact, which is exactly the same purpose as grants. However, at least there is potential for upside and recovering some of the capital if the investment fails.

- Recycling of capital – For smaller private foundations where preserving the corpus is a core objective, PRIs would be much more preferable to traditional grants given the potential to recycle the capital that would have been lost and the potential to make a financial return on that grant capital. As noted in the last point in comparing grants with PRIs, PRIs allow you to double-dip by driving a mission AND potentially having a financial return.

- Learning return – Leveraging impact investing tools allows foundations to partner with entrepreneurs and social ventures in a way that is unavailable to traditional grantmaking. Through investments, the foundation may learn from the innovations of its investees that could help drive its mission even more effectively and efficiently.

- Leverage – As an impact investor, the capital from foundation investors can be catalytic and crowd in other investors, both impact investors and traditional investors, depending on the structure of the investments. Thus, instead of fully funding an investee, the foundation can put less of its capital into the mission-aligned opportunity and save its resources for other opportunities.

- Overcommunicate – Board members typically meet only once a quarter and a few additional meetings in between for the various committees they serve. As such, they are not in the organization's day-to-day activities, so they must be reminded…often! Always remind them of key points and objectives when presenting to them why the impact investing initiative is strategically sound. They may need to hear it ten times or more before it actually sinks in; it's not because they are not intelligent but rather that they need to be reminded at every meeting since it's not something they focus on every day. Have a slide or two that always serves as the grounding or framework for discussion that you can bring up at every meeting until you get your buy-in.

Executive Team – Support or Sabotage

It should not be surprising that without executive team support, the probability of success is practically nil. Every organization is different in terms of its readiness and appetite for risk and the assets within the organization. I have served on the board of two major non-governmental organizations (NGOs), and the culture of each NGO was quite different. Both had been around approximately the same amount of time—over six decades—although one was about a quarter the size of the other. Interestingly the smaller NGO was much more risk-tolerant despite having fewer resources available for risk-taking, while the larger one was more bureaucratic and risk-averse. There is no value judgment here on which was better in their operating approach, but having worked with executives of both organizations, it was clear that the approach to get buy-in would need to be different based on each organization's circumstances.

From my experience, the most likely naysayers within a foundation against an impact investing program tend to come from the investments side of the house and the legal team. The titles will likely be Chief Financial Officer, Chief Investment Officer, Treasurer, General Counsel, Chief Legal Officer, or Head of Compliance. The investments team are opposed mainly because of their fundamental role in solely focusing on financial returns; adding another bar to focus on adds more complexity to their roles, an added burden. The idea of being able to drive social impact while driving a financial return challenges their fundamental training in traditional finance. On the legal side, the main concern will be around the issue of compliance and risk. Doing something totally new, utilizing a new tool the organization is unfamiliar with, puts the organization at risk. By nature of their roles to protect the foundation—they are paid to be Debbie Downers—the legal department will always err on the conservative side of every situation. This position is better understood when considering that when the foundation gets excellent press, it's usually the program side that gets the credit. But when things go wrong, the legal department will bear some of the brunt, if not all, for not preventing the risk. If you have no upside but are held accountable for most of the downside when things go wrong, you'd be very risk-averse too! I had a lot of empathy and respect for my colleagues in those divisions, even if they did make my job a lot more difficult when I was still in the foundation world.

You would think that the finance department should be very supportive of impact investing initiatives since it aligns their roles more with the foundation's programmatic side. Furthermore, it also allows them to be "innovative," which is not a term that finance departments of foundations often get described as. I remember a situation where the Chief Investment Officer of a major foundation was outwardly touting the fantastic work of the impact investing team of the foundation that reported to him but internally was trying to sabotage and shut down the division. The reason for this was that the impact investing team initially reported to the Head of Programs (grantmaking) rather than to him before an organizational restructuring, so the credit was still going to the retired director who launched the initiative. The CIO was fundamentally opposed to the concept of impact investing in general, although the foundation had established itself as one of the leaders in the field.

Getting and having the CEO's support is critical to moving an initiative forward. The CEO is often the gatekeeper to the organization's board. While the CIO may also have some direct access to the board, the CEO is the de facto conduit with the board. For this reason, if the CEO is not an advocate for the initiative, which will likely require board approval, the initiative has a high probability of experiencing a failure to launch. Fortunately, CEOs tend to like initiatives that could build the organization's reputation, especially if it is seen as innovative. It makes for better water cooler talk among their peers.

Another executive is the Vice President of Programs, who leads grantmaking, and the likelihood they would be supportive is 50/50 depending on the individual. Similar to the CEO's viewpoint, impact investing could be seen as something innovative, leading to good branding for the foundation's grantmaking work. On the other hand, it is also deemed to be riskier. For a VP of Programs who is afraid of change, the opposition will likely be framed as "why change something if it isn't broken. Foundations have been doing grantmaking far longer than impact investing, so if we want to have an impact, that is what grants are for."

Navigating all the opposition to impact investing among the executives will take some serious jiujitsu. If you're lucky, there may be only a few skeptics among the executives, while most of them already support an impact investing initiative. One of my former clients was very fortunate to have an executive team and a board already on board which made her job so much easier. A core driver of that was likely a function of some board members who have already had prior experience with impact investing at their respective organizations so that they could serve as advocates within the board itself. Unfortunately, most organizations will not be so lucky, so here are a few ways that could help to gain executive support:

- Make the initiative about the organization's mission – you must show how an impact investing initiative will further the organization's mission

- Have individual conversations with each executive – having personal conversations with each executive will allow you to understand their concerns and show them that you genuinely care about their perspective. You cannot fight an enemy you do not know; to be clear, the executive is not the enemy; their perception and opposition to impact investing is the enemy. Of course, you might come to find out that the executive is fully supportive; that is a benefit of these one-to-one conversations!

- Do pre-meetings before the formal group meeting – Before the formal meeting to discuss the impact investing initiative, set up pre-meetings for two objectives. The first is to get the people who are champions and aligned with the initiative to be prepped and advocate for you during the formal meeting. The second is to tease out the potential objections to your key points so that you are not taken by surprise and better able to address them during the formal meeting. This is one of the most important tips that have served me well; while surprises do come up sometimes, these pre-meetings certainly mitigate them and allow you to promote your case confidently.

- Be armed with responses for potential objections – Related to the last two tips, if you know the key concerns of various executives, you can research and provide examples to counter objections that you anticipate. Again, no one expects you to have all the answers. But if you can provide data and rationale responses for anticipated objections during the meeting, at the very minimum, you will appear knowledgeable and give confidence in your ability to execute the proposed strategy successfully.

- Be humble – While it is essential to be confident when advocating for your impact investing initiative, be transparent about where you will need support to make the initiative successful. Honesty about knowing what you don't know will also disarm naysayers and saboteurs who may intentionally try to ask you a "gotcha" question in a group setting to make you look incompetent. I've had plenty of those situations in meetings with executives and board meetings where I openly let them know what we needed as areas of competencies that were not innate within the organization or me. When someone strongly opposed to what I was advocating asked me a gotcha question, I simply responded, "that is a great point. I honestly don't have the answer to that, nor do I want to make an assumption in responding, which is why I had discussed the need to supplement the team's capabilities with additional staff or outsourced consultant to position our initiative for success." Instead of looking stupid, it shows others that I am not going to try and pretend I know something I do not and will rely on folks who are more specialized and knowledgeable about the topic as a way to get the correct answer.

- Give credit to others – This sounds so simple and maybe natural for some people who do not like the spotlight, but actually quite difficult for many people. With many Type A personalities who are very competitive, typical of most leaders and executives, getting recognized for accomplishments is just one mechanism for defining personal and professional success. Giving credit to others and acknowledging their support in group meetings goes a long way; it will make them feel like they are part of the journey for the impact investing initiative. Now instead of "your" impact investing initiative, it becomes "our" impact investing initiative. When I spoke at conferences, I would highlight and acknowledge my CEO and the foundation board's support for the success of the program we had built; at board meetings, I would specifically highlight the CEO and key executives' contributions. These little acknowledgments significantly reduced friction when I launched the impact investing strategy at one of my former foundations.

- Don't oversell, be honest – It's natural to try and focus on the positive when pitching an initiative you want to implement. However, that can backfire because no one likes to be "sold" something. It's better to guide them to where you want them to be, and let them get there on their own. If someone pushes or pulls you into doing something, you'll be more suspicious and resistant than if you had decided without being blatantly pressured. While you are supposed to try and convince your executives and the board that the organization should launch an impact investing initiative, you can do it with a more balanced, rational framing with clear strategic reasons and benefits for doing while also being transparent about the risks. As an example, during my first 60 days at Lumina Foundation, when I made my very first presentation to the board on the five-year strategy and execution phases for launching Lumina Impact Ventures, the very first thing I made clear to them was that we will lose money on some investments. They need to be comfortable with that. For me, it was critical that they saw I would always be transparent, sharing both the positive and negative aspects rather than just focusing on the positive side.

- Dial a friend – When launching an impact investing initiative, leverage external resources to help, even if you are the first and only internal staff member. If this means hiring a consultant who brings deep experience to help you plead your case, the money is well-spent because it may add credibility for you and the initiative. In addition, sometimes hearing it from an outsider, even if you say exactly the same thing, will be more effective in getting the point through with some executives and board members. They may be less likely to filter their perception when they are hearing it from an outsider.

Resources

While leadership is critical to launching an impact investing initiative, just as important is understanding the resources or assets of your organization. They come in many flavors and are not always something quantifiable. Let's start with financial resources. We can look at the operating budget and endowment size at the very basic level. An organization with a multi-billion-dollar endowment size will have much greater resources to put at risk without jeopardizing the organization's viability compared to one that has under $50 million in its endowment. That doesn't mean that smaller organizations should not pursue impact investing as a tool. Each organization needs to consider why pursuing impact investing serves its purpose. There are nonprofits with no endowments at all that may benefit from an impact investing strategy. Why? Because it helps to diversify the funding sources! As a case in point, the smaller NGO I referenced previously brought me onto their Board because of my impact investing experience as it began to explore leveraging impact investing as a tool. Evaluate financial resources on the following key factors:

- Size of the endowment and operating budget – this should help to determine the size of the impact investing initiative if one were to be pursued

- Sources of revenue for the operating budget
  - Does the organization rely solely on its endowment for its operating budget?
  - Are there earned revenues (not including financial returns from an endowment)? And how much of the operating budget does that support?
  - Are grant funding and donations the sole source of revenue to support the organization's operations and programmatic work?

- Does the organization have any debt outstanding? If so, how much? – The more debt outstanding, the more risk-averse the organization should be. Furthermore, some lenders may require approval before an impact investing program can be pursued. This is especially true if they see the initiative as a materially different organizational strategy or adds significant risk to the organization. Therefore, it would be prudent to check with your lender or carefully review the loan agreement to ensure your organization doesn't trigger any debt covenants if it launches an impact investing strategy.

Most foundations launch their impact investing program with less than 5 percent of their endowment, although some are more aggressive with an allocation of up to 10 percent. Over time, some foundations have committed to being 100 percent mission-driven across all their assets, as exemplified by Heron Foundation. The $100 million mission-driven investments initiative that the W.K. Kellogg Foundation allocated to launch its impact investing "experiment" in 2008 was "immaterial" relative to its over $8 billion endowment size, an approximately 1.25 percent carveout.

Human capital is another asset that needs to be evaluated. Do you have the right staff to execute the strategy? A large organization may have many staff members who bring a variety of skills internally that can be aggregated for all the essential roles to play in launching a successful impact investing program. For smaller organizations, everyone will have to wear multiple hats, possessing many of the skills necessary to play various roles. I should caveat that even for some larger organizations, the impact investing programs tend only to have small teams. To give some examples and context, in 2012, Ford Foundation, MacArthur Foundation, Kellogg Foundation, and Kresge Foundation each had two to four people on their entire impact investing teams. Each of the foundations had endowments ranging from $3 billion to over $12 billion in total assets; their impact investing program commitments ranged from $100 million to $450 million. Thus the correlation between staff size and asset size is not linear. In fact, staff size is much more correlated to the investment strategy and approach.

The next factor to keep in mind is time. Even with the available assets and internal staff, is the use of staff time and resources worth dedicating to the effort? If so, how much of their time should be dedicated to an impact investing strategy versus their existing roles and responsibilities? More discussion of this will be covered shortly in the in-house versus outsourced model section.

Setting the Investment Strategy

At the center of an impact investing program is the investment strategy. Some organizations know what they want, while others are just starting their journey. You may be asking yourself, should you have an impact investment strategy before adding resources to execute that strategy? Or should you pull together the necessary resources before creating an impact investment strategy? We face the chicken and the egg scenario here. There isn't a correct answer because both will be iterative. If you start with the investment strategy, that will help determine the necessary resources to execute the strategy; on the other hand, if you start with an assessment of resources available, those resources may help to determine your investment strategy.

Not surprisingly, your available resources will drive much of your investment strategy. So let's begin with some fundamental drivers of the investment strategy:

- Impact vs. return mandate: Are you investing purely for mission impact? Or will financial return be an important factor? If the financial return is important for your organization, where along the spectrum of returns (market rate vs. below-market rate) will be considered satisfactory?

- Risk tolerance: What is your organization's tolerance for risk? That is probably the most significant factor to keep in mind.

- Active vs. passive strategy: How actively engaged will your organization be with the investees? Do you plan to sit on the board?

- Direct vs. fund investments: Will the organization look only at fund investments, or will it also make direct investments?

- Organization structure: How is your organization legally structured? Private foundations have different regulatory compliance requirements than other types of entities, such as a family office, as an example. On the other hand, Chan Zuckerberg and the Omidyar Network are structured as LLCs, giving them the flexibility to deploy whichever capital type best suits the purpose without the limiting PRI qualification requirements of private foundations.

- Geographic focus: Will the investable market be limited to a specific geography? Whether your organization is a small locally-focused entity or a major global entity, the geographic focus drives the available investable opportunity and complexity.

While these are not comprehensive drivers for determining your investment strategy, they provide sufficient guidelines that will ultimately drive the creation of your investment policy statement, which we will discuss shortly.

Logistics and Operations

We've been discussing the "why" and the "what" for most of this book on creating an impact investing program. Once your organization has decided to move forward on an impact investing program implementation, the next step is the "how." That is the execution part that can both be daunting for newbies and frustrating for organizations already with an impact investing program in progress but can also be exciting and satisfying if done right. No program will be exactly the same, and each organization must think through its own unique situation, resources, and intent for its impact investment program. In this section, I want to give you the essential components for the operational side of an impact investing strategy. Specifically, let's cover four areas:

1. Setting the organizational reporting structure
2. Forming the investment committee
3. Establishing the investment process steps
4. Creating the Investment Policy Statement

These components are listed in a suggested order, but not necessarily the case for every organization.

Organizational Reporting Structure

Much of the reporting structure will depend on the size of the organization and its culture. Small organizations, in theory, can be more nimble, while larger organizations may have bureaucratic processes in place. Setting up the appropriate organizational reporting structure is critically important for the success of any impact investing program as it will affect decision-making processes, accountability, and resource allocation. You may not have control over setting up the reporting structure. Still, if you should be in the position to make the recommendation or have that authority, there are two levels of consideration to keep in mind.

The first level of consideration is the board. Does the organization's board of trustees need or want to be engaged in an impact investing strategy? If so, the follow-on question is how much? There are many good reasons for having the board involved, but also some drawbacks. First, determine what type of board culture your organization has. Some organizations have very actively engaged board members, while others are much more hands-off. I believe that a good board should provide the necessary guidance to senior executives of the organization, knowing that as fiduciaries of the organization, they are liable but leave the decision-making and operational execution to the organization's executives. While it can be helpful for board members to actively engage where they have the expertise, there is a fine line between being helpful and micro-managing. For smaller resource-constrained organizations, it's more common to have actively engaged board members who bring additional expertise and capacity to support the organization. However, it isn't entirely unusual for board members of large organizations to be overly engaged in the organization's activities where they have a strong passion. That could be programmatic in nature, but areas with high visibility, particularly, seem to attract such active engagement. It would behoove organization executives to fully understand their board's culture and preference for engagement. Finding the balance between helpful active engagement rather than suffocating micromanagement could accelerate the impact investing strategy. Those board members who are actively engaged can help champion specific initiatives to move the strategy forward, both among their board peers and steer other executives in the organization along who may not be as supportive. The involvement could be very informal, where you can reach out for guidance when necessary, or more formally, such as a separate board committee created specifically to focus on steering the impact investing strategy. Lumina Foundation did the latter—it was that very board committee that worked with senior executives to pursue an impact investing program and ultimately hired me. About a year after I joined to build its strategy, the committee formally dissolved with its founding purpose achieved.

The second level of consideration is the executive staff. The organization's CEO needs to structure the reporting structure carefully if the program is to be successful, especially if there are significant differences in opinion for or against the impact investing initiative.

Figure 12 shows different options for a reporting structure. Two fundamental questions to answer: 1) does the impact investing function report to the Finance & Operations division (represented by the CFO/ COO box), or should it report to the Programmatic/Grantmaking division (represented by the Head of Programs). Note that sometimes there may also be a Chief Strategy Officer executive within the Head of Programs areas.

Figure 12: Reporting Structure Considerations

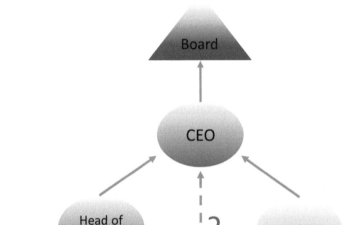

It would be naïve to tell you that there is precisely one right reporting structure. Frankly, there isn't, due to the differences among organization culture, resources, and risk tolerance, among other factors. Therefore, all I can do is provide you with decision drivers and some examples of the benefits and concerns with each option.

Option 1: Reporting to Finance Function (CFO) – This seems to be the most logical since impact investing is an "investing" function, after all. The Finance division would need to support the deal operations when investments are made and tracked. A significant benefit of reporting to the CFO is the financial and operational credibility of that oversight. It will also help integrate the finance and operations function from being purely "back office" to support grantmaking to something more integrated with the strategic aspect, which could be an exciting and motivating factor for those staff who rarely get such exposure.

The biggest challenge of this reporting structure is the potential emphasis or prioritization on financial return and less on the mission. This is driven primarily by what those staff members are trained to do, it's ingrained in their minds and core to their work, so it's natural for them to focus more on financial return and mitigating risk. Thus, if your organization decides to create such a reporting structure, it's imperative to ensure the mission is not lost in the deal discussions.

Another potential area of challenge is how supportive the CFO is of an impact investing strategy. When the CFO is not supportive of the impact investing strategy, it could lead to the complete failure of the program, even if the CEO and Board are supportive. Having control over the budget and operations, the CFO could easily create considerable obstacles to hinder the program. From simply trying to mitigate risk to real intentional sabotage to sink the program, the CFO could easily require unnecessary steps, make deal approval nearly impossible, or even reduce resource allocation. The internal politics of major foundations are not to be underestimated; the elbows are sharper in philanthropy than what I had ever witnessed on Wall Street. The worse part of it is that the motivations are often emotionally driven rather than logical, even if explanations for why a decision was made are often couched with supporting data.

Option 2: Reporting to the Program Function (Head of Programs) – Some organizations launch an impact investing initiative prioritizing impact as the driver and, as such, have a reporting structure that best aligns with that objective. The strength of this reporting structure lies in the emphasis on the "impact" part of "impact investing," which may mitigate risks for compliance of program-related investments where charitability is the primary driver for the investment. Secondly, a reporting structure under the Program Function's governance often makes integrating with other grantees and programmatic initiatives easier to achieve. The ability for investees to collaborate with grantees is one benefit that some entrepreneurs very much appreciate; that was certainly the case in the higher education sector. For example, Lumina Impact Ventures' investee, Credly, had been trying to find an opportunity to partner with the America Council on Education (ACE), a grantee of Lumina Foundation. The two organizations eventually collaborated on a small initiative that Lumina Foundation supported with a small grant ($10K Challenge Prize) and eventually formalized a partnership after that initial collaboration. It would be presumptuous to claim the investment by Lumina Impact Ventures drove that collaboration. Still, the entrepreneur has noted publicly that the strategic value of Lumina Impact Ventures as an investor was a core factor that drove their interest in LIV as an investor.

The biggest downside of having a reporting structure with oversight by the Program Function is the potential lack of discipline in the investment process, whether real or perceived. Because of the programmatic prioritization, the discipline needed to structure an investment appropriately might not be as stringently adhered to. As a result, there may be more willingness to be more lenient on the investment terms, which could expose the organization to greater risk while not optimizing the potential for a financial return commensurate with the risk level taken. Whether real or just a perceived risk, if the lead for the impact investing program possesses solid financial acumen, such a scenario would be alleviated. Ensuring there is strong involvement from the Finance Function at the very beginning will also help ensure better deal processes and investment structures.

Notice that in Figure 12, there is a dotted line showing the impact investing function having an indirect reporting line to the CEO. That is not a replacement of the other two governance options but rather a complement to them. Some organizations may want to have this indirect line to the CEO structure to A) give the impact investing function more visibility internally as well as externally, validating its importance to the organization; B) mitigate any internal politics when there are significant differences in opinions between the Finance Function and the Program Function, and C) engage the CEO who might want to have more active involvement on the initiative. Having the CEO aware involved will be very beneficial when they need to be an advocate for the impact investing strategy with the board.

Building the Investment Committee

Once the governance structure has been agreed to, the next step is constructing the Investment Committee. How do you expect decisions to be made? Does the Investment Committee have the authority to approve investments? Or is it merely "approving" a recommendation that would ultimately still need to be approved by the CFO or Head of Programs? In other words, is the role of the Investment Committee more of a vetting process rather than a decision-making body? You might ask what's the point of having an Investment Committee that merely approves a recommendation rather than having the ultimate authority to approve an investment. The nuance points to the internal politics, which some organizations will need to navigate.

Let me provide an example demonstrating this nuance, a deal I directly sourced and worked on. We had completed due diligence on a well-established mezzanine fund manager called Brightwood Capital, founded and led by two successful senior African American executives with deep experience on Wall Street: Damien Dwinn and Sengal Selassie. They have known each other for a long time. It was their third fund targeting $500 to $625M doing mezzanine loans, which they've had a long track record of successfully executing. After negotiating the terms, we were able to get approval from the Investment Committee for a commitment as a limited partner in the fund. It was one of the most straightforward deals to approve compared to others we had looked at that were much riskier. However, when I updated the CFO about the approval decision that needed his signature for the investment commitment, he didn't like the investment and created ("found") reasons to reject it. Instead of saying outright he would not approve the investment, he started by saying there was a particular risk that needed to be addressed, and we would have to get that addressed with Brightwood. After we addressed that risk, he then came up with another risk and then another risk. There was no rational explanation for why the CFO opposed the investment, so he had to create an explanation by pointing out risks that weren't truly risks to justify his opposition to the investment. I ended up apologizing to the Brightwood team in the end despite telling them the Investment Committee had approved the investment, but our CFO was vetoing the decision, even though he had no authority to do so based on our governance structure. To this day, when I come across Damien and Sengal at investment conferences, I feel embarrassed about what had happened. The moral of the example is that even if the Investment Committee has the legal authority to approve an investment, the actual authority may rest elsewhere. The classic saying that you shouldn't count the chickens till they hatch is very applicable; for investments, the deal isn't closed until the money is in the bank account of the investee.

With that example in mind, here are some considerations for building your Investment Committee. First is the size. How many members do you want or need on it? Is there a minimum size that makes sense? There's no rule of thumb, but I suggest no less than three members. In my opinion, five would be more ideal, but some may have even more members on their Investment Committees. The number of members in an Investment Committee will be driven by balancing the need for expertise, the logistical challenge of trying to get the full Investment Committee available for meetings (not to be underestimated when you have members from all over, including international ones), and the intended role of the Investment Committee.

I noted that five would be the ideal number of members because it balances diversity of expertise and logistics of coordination. Assuming a five-member Investment Committee (IC), selecting its members will depend on the IC's role and the types of investments the impact investing program will make. At a minimum, there should be at least one member who:

- Has deep program/impact experience
- Has deep finance and investment experience
- Is a senior internal executive
- An independent who is not affiliated with the organization to offer an "outside" perspective
- Has experience in the types of investments to be contemplated (asset class, geography, stage, etc.)
- A naysayer who will not be afraid of raising critical questions and challenges

Note that some members will bring not only one component but multiple components of these qualifications. That would be a significant benefit and allow for a smaller number of Investment Committee members necessary, although it compromises the number of opinions during the discussion and vetting process. It is imperative to structure the IC to ensure that a particular voice does not dominate the conversation or overwhelmingly influence the discussions. That can happen due to personalities, culture, and the individual's title, among other factors. One way to alleviate that potential scenario is to appoint someone as the Chair to run the meetings and maintain the balance in the discussions; the role can be a rotating one for a set term. In addition to appointing a good IC Chair, it is also critically important to ensure there is at least one voice who will be the naysayer willing to raise the tough questions during a deal vetting discussion. Some people may find those individuals to be annoying deal blockers who are always negatively biased. Still, they serve an essential role in ensuring the IC is not an echo chamber of like-minded opinions that rubber stamps a deal. Getting a deal approved easily might seem like a good thing, but a good Investment Committee should always raise challenging questions that might not have been thoroughly considered so that the deals are well-vetted. If (or when) a deal does not work out, then the reasons why the investment failed should not be a surprise but a strategic risk taken. And the factors that were risks were discussed and accepted rather than a surprise. Having the right members for the IC will make investment decisions smarter and give the investment process credibility to outside stakeholders.

While typically an organization may only have one Investment Committee, larger organizations may have multiple ones. As an example, there may be separate investment committees for the types of investments: the investment committee for mission-related investments may be totally separate from the one for program-related investments. And then, there is the investment committee for the overall endowment. As you can imagine, having multiple investment committees allows for specialization when selecting members but also may be a logistical nightmare to manage. One foundation I'm aware of had all three such investment committees due to its size; whether that was functionally more effective is questionable. Typically, one would see an investment committee for the overall endowment and a separate investment committee for just the impact investing function.

Creating The Investment Process Steps

Starting out, trying to create a roadmap for every investment could feel very daunting. For that reason, some may feel less inclined to be very detailed in mapping out the process. However, it would be in every organization's best interest to be as detailed as possible when creating the process steps. These can be broken down into core components:

I.   When to pull someone in on the deal?

That has to be thought through very carefully because there are political implications as well as governance implications. For example, are there certain executives who need to be given a heads-up early enough in the process? Make sure to provide some minimum guidelines on which individuals need to be engaged and when to ensure the deal process is as smooth as possible.

II. Which functional areas need to be informed and engaged?

It's critical to loop the right department in at the right time. For example, does the IT department need to set up something for the deal? What about the Program Team, where a program officer is highly relevant for a deal whose impact area is connected to help with due diligence? Does the Finance Team know the deal is coming and must manage cash flow so there is sufficient liquidity to fund the investment? What about the Legal Department when the legal documents need to be signed?

III. What are the internal and external processes necessary to get a deal done?

Is your organization using an external consultant to perform due diligence? What about external legal counsel for the review of agreements and other legal diligence? Understanding when they need to be looped in will ensure the most efficient and effective process.

Documenting the process with sufficient granularity will reduce key person risk. If the person leading the impact investing strategy resigns or gets hit by a bus, someone else can step in with enough of a roadmap to continue the program without too much interruption. There were two key documents when I created the deal process for my own program. One is a diagram showing the high-level flow of the deal execution process, starting from sourcing all the way through monitoring. This is helpful to visually gauge where a deal is along the investment process and the anticipated time frame for each phase. Figure 13 provides a sample of the investment process steps that my colleague Elizabeth Garlow and I had created. The actual amount of time for each stage is just an estimate. Some deals take longer, while others may be much more expedited; however, the diagram should give you a sense of what you should create for your program. There may be fewer or even more steps that need to be incorporated depending on the institutional infrastructure of your organization.

Figure 13: Sample Investment Process Steps

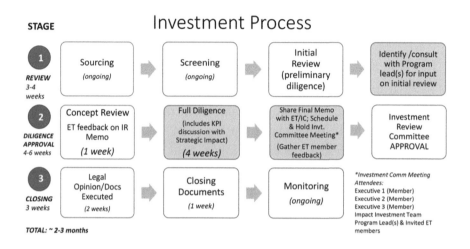

While the process steps diagram provides a useful workflow overview of the deal execution process, the more critical document to create is the granular step-by-step process itself. Start by listing every single step you can expect to go through, as detailed as possible. For example, let's start with deal sourcing at the top of the funnel. Then, just within that specific step or task, there are various components and layers to build into the list:

- What is the source?
  - Inbound – was it unsolicited, or was it referred?
    - Referrals
    - Other investors
    - Co-investors
    - Intake form submission
    - Other entrepreneurs
    - Internal staff
  - Proactive outbound
    - Who did the outreach?
    - How was the deal discovered?

- Response
  - Who is responsible for taking the first review?
  - Who needs to be on the intro call if one is set up?

How granular you want your process steps to be will depend on your organization, but at the minimum, the process steps need to incorporate a RACI as the column headings. The term RACI simply seeks to assign accountability and who to loop in for each step: Responsible, Accountable, Consulted, and Informed. Thus, the Excel process steps should have one column listing the steps, a second column with the estimated time frame to do each step, and four columns representing the RACI. I was an Excel junky, an old habit of being a former banker, but there may be much better tools to create your process steps nowadays. Keep in mind that the steps to make a program-related investment for some organizations are different from the steps to execute a mission-related investment, so you will need two separate processes. Furthermore, the steps for a fund investment may differ from those for a direct investment within your organization, which may also need its own process step document.

Whether it's the workflow diagram or the process steps, there will inevitably be iterations as the program launches. The more deals you do, the more you will refine the processes. Phases and expected timing for each step may take longer or less as you gain experience and staffing changes. Engaging all the different colleagues involved with each step to co-create the process will save a lot of time to know what is realistic compared to what is aspirational on timing for those specific steps. Once you have your investment process steps well documented, a valuable exercise to explore is to consider those one-off opportunities that might need to be expedited and which steps can be circumvented or accelerated. That should not be the norm but the exception; if you repeatedly bypass the process steps, then perhaps the process steps themselves may need to be tweaked to be the norm rather than the exception. Repeated circumvention of the process steps may also raise concerns about the process itself as well.

Creating the Investment Policy Statement

At the core of the impact investing program (any investment program, for that matter) is the Investment Policy Statement (IPS). Think of the IPS as the guiding principles for running the program.

For some organizations, it may be very detailed such as getting deep into Investment Committee membership selection or how consultants can or cannot be utilized for the program. For others, it should be as short as a page. Where your organization falls along that spectrum will depend on its culture & internal political dynamics, staffing, and size. There are advantages to each, as summarized below.

- Shorter IPS – A shorter IPS may make sense to start with for newer programs. This allows a general set of guiding principles for starting up the impact investing initiative and adding more details as processes get established. Having fewer details allows the impact investing leader to operate with greater flexibility. For some, this would be ideal, but others may find the ambiguity frustrating.

- Longer detailed IPS – A more detailed Investment Policy Statement provides more than just guiding principles for the impact investing strategy. To put things into context, if you think of shorter IPS as the guardrails or fences along a winding highway, then a more detailed IPS would add the speed limits, lane dividers, signage for falling rocks or deer passing, and flashing warnings, among other mechanisms to navigate through. These additional factors are beneficial to someone who might be a newer driver unfamiliar with the terrain to ensure safe passage. On the other hand, if someone is already a very skillful driver and familiar with the specific area, those additional details may not be necessary even if they may be helpful. A very detailed IPS provides the parameters for the impact investing team to navigate as they execute the investment strategy. These parameters give senior leadership and the organization's board confidence that the impact investing strategy being implemented is adhering to something they approved. I had created one IPS for a foundation over ten pages long, not including the various exhibits and appendices that supplemented the IPS.

Internal politics may sometimes dictate whether your organization starts with a short IPS or a longer detailed one. To clarify, imagine if the impact investing team reports to the Head of Programs as its governance structure and the CFO lacked confidence in the impact investing team's financial expertise. The CFO and Finance Team could require more detailed parameters in the IPS around financial diligence and types of investments that can be made, as well as requiring external financial expertise support on due diligence. What might be viewed as micromanagement may actually be good for reference for the impact investing team in institutionalizing the investment process. If a deal doesn't close due to adhering to a process that had been dictated, the process can be tweaked, but it would give the CFO and Finance Team additional confidence in the process.

Sometimes an organization may integrate impact investing into its core Investment Policy Statement for its entire portfolio. That might be something as short as just a paragraph referencing such a strategy as part of its overall investment strategy. Such an approach may suffice to start out a program to document the creation of an impact investing strategy, but insufficient longer term. A separate impact investment policy statement (IIPS) specific to the program provides the more particular guardrails and execution approach. Note that in the prior discussion about an IPS, I'm actually talking about an IIPS. While the IIPS may emulate a more generic Investment Policy Statement for a traditional endowment, it could also be materially different and narrower. To demonstrate the point, as with most traditional asset allocation and portfolio construction for a traditional portfolio, the concept of diversification is a fundamental objective; in an impact investing strategy, that may not be the case and is perfectly acceptable given the purposes of the program are different.

Regardless of how long or short your IIPS is, there are several specific components that a good IIPS should include. I'll briefly summarize them here:

- **Purpose** – This lays out the purpose of the Impact Investing Policy Statement as the guiding document for investment execution.

- **Objective** – This section lays out the overall impact investing goal. It provides the background for the creation of the impact investing program. It documents the intent of the investment priorities and helps to answer the fundamental question driving investments: mission first, financial returns first, or a balanced objective between impact and financial return. Documenting this in the IIPS may be one source of evidence that can be referenced by legal counsel when demonstrating charitability for PRI investments. This section may also be where the balance between risk and returns is addressed, as that directly connects to the prioritization of mission vs. financial return objectives.

- **Governance** – This section lays out the reporting structure and oversight for the impact investing program. It discusses the creation of the investment committee(s), its role, and decision-making authority or lack thereof. A more detailed IIPS may also discuss how members for the investment committee are selected, their term length, and even remuneration for external members—one major foundation paid external independent IC members for their travel and a $10,000 stipend annually.

- **Source of Capital Allocation** – This section lays out the program's size and sources of funding. Will the investment capital come from the endowment or grant dollars? Is the allocation annual or a one-time carve-out? Investment pacing will ultimately be impacted significantly by how the program is funded. Furthermore, what happens to investment returns? Does that go back into the endowment or to the grant pool for redistribution (note that returns from PRI investments need to get redistributed)? Or will the returns simply get recycled for future investments?

- **Investments** – This section lays out the types of investments for the impact investing strategy. It should discuss whether the program will invest in funds, direct investments, or both. Will the program invest in debt or equity, or both? What geography will the program target? How much will the average investment amount be in each opportunity? Will there be a capped amount per investment? These parameters steer the investment team to focus on the types of investments they should be looking for. However, the section should also lay out disallowed investments. While this may sound obvious, documenting that the program will not invest in certain types of investments will provide helpful guidance for the team to ensure resources and effort are spent on the right opportunities. For a detailed IIPS, a set of investment criteria is useful for reference in the appendix. It would also be helpful to discuss when investments might still be considered if they do not quite fit the investment criteria set contemplated initially. These one-off types of opportunities do happen, and you want the ability to consider them rather than completely turn them away if there are strategic reasons for why they should be considered.

- **Due Diligence** – This section may not be necessary but is sometimes included when there is concern about the technical/investment skills of the investment team. If included, this section lays out the due diligence process and discusses the sourcing of deals, screening, and structuring. Will due diligence be done by internal staff or external staff, or both? This section may include specific covenants expected for debt investments, for example. It could also include whether a board seat is required for an investment. Referencing the Investment Process documents discussed previously (which may be included as attachments in the appendix) will also be helpful.

- **Portfolio Construction** – Related to the Investments section, this part lays out the overall approach to portfolio construction. Tying back to the Objective section, the Portfolio Construction section should align with how the Objective will be achieved. Lay out the pacing of investments, concentration, and diversification approach for the portfolio and the target returns expectation for the entire portfolio. If there is one most critical section, this would be one to spend the most time on, followed by the Investments section because they are literally the sections that dictate much of the day-to-day activities of the investment team.

- **Resources** – This section lays out the resources available to the impact investing team. While not typically a topic most IPS will include, I have found documenting this useful, especially in highly political environments when various departments fight for the allocation of resources. How will the operating budget for the impact investing team get allocated? Does it come out of the overall carve-out for the program? Is it an annual expense that is no different from other program staff where annual budgeting is required? What about external resources, and how are those expenditures funded?

- **Valuation Policy** – This could be a section in the IIPS or an appendix item. How will investments be valued? Standard practices for valuing assets should be referenced and applied when marking to market the value of individual investments. This section should provide sufficient guidance that gives any third party a sense of how conservative or aggressive the investments team values the portfolio investments. It should also clarify who does the portfolio valuation and how frequently valuations are done. For example, will valuation be done through a third party, or will it be done entirely in-house?

- **Reporting and Monitoring** – This section discusses the reporting requirements for both the investees of the portfolio but also the reporting for the impact investment team to the relevant governing bodies, whether it's to the investment committee, the organization's executives, or even the organization's board. Are there specific metrics that need to be reported on? How are impact metrics determined, and are specific ones required for all investees? Who is responsible for monitoring the portfolio? While that sounds like a simple question, it is a bit more complicated. Monitoring a small portfolio is feasible if an organization has only a small number of staff (say two individuals) on its impact investing team. But it becomes nearly impossible to do effectively when you have over ten investments. Should the Finance Team be responsible for monitoring? Should the monitoring be outsourced to an external consultant? Each option will have ramifications on how engaged or disengaged the investment team needs to be, with implications on managing risk and accountability.

The components listed are just the core ones that every impact investment policy statement should include; how detailed each section is discussed will be up to your organization's unique circumstances. Just realize that the IIPS is not static and should be updated when appropriate to reflect the organization and the impact investing strategy as both evolve.

Staffing The Impact Investing Team: In-House vs. Outsourced Model

One topic that organizations sometimes struggle with is the staffing of their impact investing function. Some organizations have a completely in-house model, while others outsource that function altogether. What will work best for your organization will be driven by its resource constraints, impact investing strategy, risk tolerance, and objective for the program. Let's discuss the benefits and disadvantages of these approaches.

- **In-House Staffing –** In an ideal world with unlimited resources, an entirely in-house approach would be highly advantageous. First, no one will understand your organization's mission and objectives better than the internal team. Consultants will do their best, but no matter how much they try, being within an organization gives context to internal dynamics and strategic initiatives in real-time rather than through hearsay. An in-house team will be better equipped to navigate such dynamics much better than any external resources. Secondly, related to that same factor, internal staff will better facilitate the ability to integrate across other areas within the organization. Perhaps your impact investing program does not have that objective. Still, for major foundations looking to add impact investing as an additional tool to drive their mission rather than as a separate function that is entirely isolated, internal staff can achieve that integration much more efficiently and effectively than relying on outsourced consultants to drive that objective.

  Another benefit of an in-house approach is the fully dedicated team. Each staff dedicated to the impact investing team is 100% focused on that role and function; there's no question of them serving other clients. Good consultants might be able to have individuals wholly dedicated solely to your organization (assuming the contract with that consulting firm sufficiently compensates them for doing so, but it's extremely rare to see that. I've worked with numerous consultants in my career, and none of them have ever given me the sense that there were specific individuals wholly dedicated to the organization I was with. That's not to say they were not responsive when I needed them (at least most of them), but it is certainly not the same as having someone who is my internal colleague that shares the same accountability and objective. If a deal fails or the impact investing program fails, the internal colleague will be just as responsible, but consultants can just focus on other clients. An internal team only has one client: the governing body that oversees the impact investing function, so there is 100% alignment of interest.

Direct connection with investees may also be an important factor for some organizations. If the investment strategy seeks to partner with the investees through an active engagement approach, an internal staff member would be better suited. Part of the reason is related to the fact that internal staff is much more aware of other departments' objectives where there may be some opportunities to integrate and collaborate. Working with an internal team member rather than through a consultant/ intermediary will be preferable from the entrepreneur's perspective. Of course, there are exceptions, but most investees want a direct connection to their investor rather than through an intermediary who they feel may filter feedback/information from the investor or may even be gatekeepers.

There are many disadvantages to an entirely in-house approach, however. First, the need to build the infrastructure for pipeline development, execution, portfolio management, and monitoring can be extremely expensive. Not only is the cost a factor, but the time to build the infrastructure will take much longer than leveraging external resources. In order to have all the expertise needed, a large team is required to stand ready to be utilized but may be sitting idle; furthermore, maintaining the best of breed capabilities is very difficult. One of the most significant disadvantages is what I refer to as the echo-chamber risk—the lack of external perspectives that can be extremely helpful in driving innovation and diversity of thought. Lastly, the flight risk of talent is not to be underestimated.

- **Fully outsourced approach** – Since the world isn't ideal and resources are not unlimited, some organizations opt for a fully outsourced approach to building and managing their impact investing program. The cost could range from $100K or less for a limited engagement to over $1 million for a fully managed impact portfolio. It may seem like spending over $1 million for an outsourced team rather than using that resource to build an in-house team is illogical and wasteful until you understand the benefits of having an outsourced function. Keep in mind that sometimes outsourcing can start light and grow as needs evolve with the organization and the impact investing strategy. For example, if your organization needs someone to help with due diligence, that could be project-based and relatively cost-effective on a per deal basis. The caveat is that highly skilled consultants are less likely to accept such projects without the potential to grow the relationship into more of a partnership on a retainer basis.

One significant advantage of having an outsourced model is its flexibility. As alluded to previously, you can grow the contract much more rapidly than trying to build an internal team. If you don't like the consultant, the organization can simply terminate the contract and find someone else. Of course, the ideal scenario is to have a consultant be a partner for the long term, but sometimes, the consulting firm's capabilities are not sufficient to meet the needs of the organization as the impact investing strategy evolves. For example, perhaps your organization may focus on making fund investments only when it starts out but expands to make direct investments as part of its evolution; if the outsourced consulting firm only has experience with fund investing, you will either need to supplement by hiring another consulting firm with direct investing experience or completely replace the existing firm with one that has both types of expertise. Some consulting firms are competent at helping to set up the strategy for an impact investing program but have no real deal experience, so when the organization begins to make investments, a newer firm must be brought in. Hiring staff with the requisite skills could take significantly longer because you want to ensure they are the right fit for the program and the organization. One client I worked with took over two years to find someone to lead their impact investing program. Another foundation took over eighteen months before finding someone to lead their impact investing strategy. In my own experience, one of the roles I had taken took the headhunter, who ultimately recruited me, over two years to fill. It's a much bigger decision to hire someone for an in-house role than to hire and fire a consulting firm. In the context of the "great resignation" and general labor supply shortage, combined with a small pool of experienced senior executives who have long track records in impact investing, finding the right candidate will be even more challenging in today's market.

Another advantage of an outsourced model is access to requisite skills. I like to simply call it "plug and chug." If you need someone with debt experience or venture experience, there are plenty of consultants who can bring the specific competency required. The key difference here is that it doesn't have to be within one individual but a mix of individuals within the outsourced consulting firm. That's the beauty of plug and chug; pull in a competency when needed rather than having someone always dedicated with that competency in-house that might not get utilized. As an analogy, manufacturing firms have just-in-time inventory management systems where suppliers' raw material orders align with production schedules. The plug and chug approach essentially emulates that from a staffing perspective—the outsourced consulting firm should be able to meet your organization's needs at the time needed rather than having internal staff sitting idle until the competency is required. Unless your organization has unlimited resources to hire every skill needed to execute the impact investing strategy or have a very narrow scope for the program (e.g., will only invest in education funds in the workforce space), the cost for doing so would be much higher than utilizing an experienced outsourcing firm that provides the skills as needed. The $1 million consulting contract seems much more reasonable if you have a $100 million impact portfolio with a diverse investment mandate and active engagement approach to working with investees, as it represents 1% of the portfolio.

Another advantage of an outsourced strategy is stability. That sounds counterintuitive to what I had just mentioned about the ability to efficiently hire and fire the firm. Think of it this way: finding the right candidate takes a lot more time than hiring a consultant, and even if your organization successfully hires the individual, what if that candidate leaves after a couple of years? The days of someone spending a decade at an organization are much less common now; having someone stay for five years with an organization would be considered a long time these days as the evolution of work and career become more transactional than an enduring partnership. With that in mind, unless the impact investing team is large enough with good succession planning, there is a significantly higher risk with a purely in-house team than with an outsourced model. The irony is that even with good succession planning, sometimes, when the leader of the division leaves, the subordinates may follow. With an outsourced firm, even if individuals within that firm servicing your organization leaves, there will typically be someone else there who can step in without too much interruption, even if there is a transition period. The likelihood of the outsourced firm being a long-term partner is much higher than the likelihood of finding an internal staff to stay with the organization beyond five years. Program continuity and maintenance of institutional knowledge cannot be underestimated when weighing the decision to outsource versus build an internal team for the impact investing program.

Beyond flexibility and stability, outsourcing the impact investing function has the added benefit of an expanded network and institutional quality execution that your organization would not need to build in-house. All the activities discussed previously about creating an Impact Investing Policy Statement, structuring the investment committee, and setting up the investment process can be done in partnership with the consultant. Working with the right outsourced consultant can provide the program with added internal and external credibility. Any concerns upfront with the consulting firm's capabilities can be mitigated by ensuring that crucial executives (and sometimes even the board) within your organization are actively engaged when selecting the consulting firm. Since the consulting firm will have multiple clients, they can bring lessons learned from all their clients that your organization may benefit from; this may be in the form of market insights on sector trends or deal trends as well as best practices to replicate. In theory, if the firm or consultant is well-established or has a long track record, the firm will also bring a much more extensive network that would be nearly impossible to replicate from solely internal staff. A broader and deeper network will prove invaluable for deal sourcing, due diligence, partnership/collaboration opportunities, and co-investments. Furthermore, deal risks can be mitigated once an investment has been made since the outsourced firm may be able to help the entrepreneur with other value-added needs such as finding other investors, advisory board members, or even recruiting talent to join their team as the investee grows.

Lastly, an outsourced consulting firm will also have access to resources more economically. For example, below are some sample subscription costs to various proprietary research and resources:

○ Pitchbook – nearly $15K annually

○ FactSet – $12K annually

○ Bloomberg – Over $27K annually

○ Capital IQ – $13K annually

○ Refinitiv Eikon – $22K annually

An outsourced consulting firm can subscribe to various proprietary databases and resources that it can utilize to serve multiple clients, making the expense more justifiable, but for an organization to try and get its own license to these various proprietary resources for internal use may not be as practical if they are not frequently used or needed.

• **Hybrid Model (Combining Both In-House and Outsourced Approach)** – We've discussed the advantages and alluded to some of the disadvantages of a purely in-house or outsourced model. Fortunately, the choice need not be mutually exclusive, and a combination of the approaches allows for the best of both worlds, as shown in Figure 14.

Figure 14: Hybrid Model Optimizes Best of Both

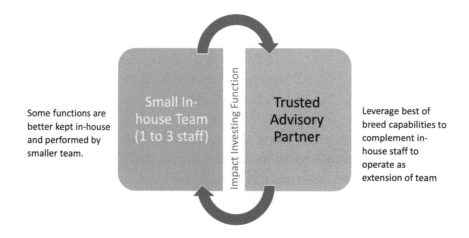

Hiring a small team or even just one key individual to lead the impact investing function while partnering with an experienced consulting firm that can handle many of the outsourced functions will be more cost-effective and accelerate the impact investing strategy implementation. This approach also mitigates risks that are inherent in launching any program. Even the major foundations committing over $1 billion to their impact investing strategy leverage consulting firms for advisory services.

Suppose your organization decides to pursue a hybrid model. In that case, the prioritization of what functions should be outsourced vs. kept in-house will depend on the existing infrastructure and talent, operating budget, size of asset base allocation for impact investing, and which skills may be harder to hire for. For example, portfolio monitoring is extremely tedious (if done right), so it would be much more pragmatic to pay an outsourced firm to perform that function, given their existing infrastructure. On the other hand, due diligence of deals may be a collaborative process rather than completely outsourced since the internal staff needs to be deep enough into the deals to understand and steer the process, assuming your organization wants to be more actively engaged. As a rule of thumb, if your organization plans to have just a handful of investments in total, a consulting firm may only be necessary on a project-by-project basis. The challenge with such an arrangement is that you may not get the best consultant when you need them because the good ones will be more dedicated to clients who have them on a retainer. The chapter on "Choosing an Outsourced Partner/ Consultant" will provide more details on how to go about finding and screening the right consultant.

The Case Against Doing Impact Investing

Impact investing has been proliferating, and many firms are actively exploring how to launch an impact investing program of their own. However, that may not be the right action for all organizations. Firms need to take a serious look at why they want to launch an impact investing initiative and ensure they are doing it for the right reasons. Otherwise, it could be a costly endeavor in both time and resources that could be better spent elsewhere. As a practitioner in the space for many years, I'm a big advocate of impact investing as a tool that better connects the capital to impact (the very driver of why I founded Kind

Capital). Still, sometimes the tool isn't suitable for everyone. You don't need a Ferrari to go grocery shopping (although that would be pretty cool!), just as you wouldn't drive a Formula 1 racecar to go camping. Remember our earlier discussion on social impact bonds that were all the rage during their early days but puttered out as more and more people realized the same purpose of the tool could be achieved much more efficiently and effectively with other mechanisms. Philanthropy sometimes behaves like a solution in search of a problem rather than like entrepreneurs creating solutions to a problem. Here are a few rules of thumb for why you should not launch an impact investing program:

- It is trendy – yes, impact investing is "in" these days and will probably continue to be so for a while, but that alone is insufficient justification. Of course, we all want to be recognized for being innovative, but perhaps there are other ways for the organization to showcase how it is innovative.

- Other ways to achieve the objective – if there are other ways to accomplish the same aim of having an impact investing program, then it must be carefully compared to why the impact investing program is the better option.

- Uncertainty with resources dedicated to launching the initiative – if the organization is unwilling to commit the necessary resources required to ensure a successful program, then why launch something with a high likelihood of failure? That is where hiring a consultant to do some preliminary analyses will be helpful in assessing your organization's readiness from both a mindset and resource standpoint.

- Uncomfortable with risk – launching any initiative inherently has risks, so leadership and the organization must be comfortable with the risks of launching an impact investing program. Some risks can be mitigated, but not all risks can be eliminated. (As a side note, I wanted to put that on a t-shirt and wear it to investment committee meetings when I was trying to get very complicated deals approved.)

- Significant oppositions exist – this may not be as common today as when I was just entering the impact investing space. However, plenty of diehard traditionalists exist who still do not believe in impact investing as a tool. If your organization has such individuals in executive-level positions or on your board, be sure that you are prepared to get them to change their perspective, or they will make launching the impact investing program much more challenging than it would typically be. It is much easier to go with the flow than swim upstream. It may not be impossible; it just requires much more brain damage and effort that may not be worthwhile until the tide shifts more favorably once more internal support exists.

Hopefully, your organization does pursue an impact investing program, and for the right reasons. With all the book chapters to this point, you should now have the fundamentals for launching your impact investing strategy. The rest of the book will cover more tactical aspects for your impact investing program.

CHAPTER SIX: THE ART OF THE DEAL

"The devil is in the details."

In this chapter, we will go through the types of investments in more detail and considerations to keep in mind for each. We've already discussed the various types of investments in earlier chapters, so this section will focus more on specific structures. By the end of this chapter, you may not become an expert, but you should be able to know the fundamentals for investing directly versus into a fund as a limited partner and comfortably rationalize them to your investment committee, leadership team, and board. Many of the concepts discussed focus on private investment funds (venture capital, private equity, etc.) rather than funds that invest in public markets like hedge funds or mutual funds, but they can be applied to both.

Fund Investments

Fund investments come in three general categories:

- Nonprofit funds – These funds invest for impact as their primary objective. They can be legally formed as a CDFI or even accelerators but are legally incorporated nonprofit entities
- Impact funds – These funds genuinely care about impact and have some formal alignment to a mission but are not structured as a nonprofit
- Traditional funds – Any fund that does not fit into the first two categories. Essentially they are funds focused on generating financial returns as their primary (sole) objective.

The first category is easy since they are legally established as a nonprofit entity. However, sometimes differentiating between an impact fund and a traditional fund gets less obvious when some fund managers market themselves as impact funds when in fact, they are not. Impact washing seems to be happening more today than in the past as impact investing has gained traction as a tool, and more capital is allocated towards the sector.

Key Reasons for Investing in Funds

As you may recall, investing in a fund is essentially investing in a pool of investments. Let's review the key reasons why your organization may want to invest in funds that we previously discussed:

- Domain or industry expertise – The fund manager might have much more expertise in a sector, asset class, geography, or investment stage than someone in-house.

- Diversification and lower risk – Since the investment is in a "pool" of assets, there is immediate diversification created by the fund manager. In theory, investing in a fund should be a lower risk since you are investing in a basket of opportunities rather than placing your bet on one company.

- Time efficiency – Since the fund manager is the one in direct contact with the portfolio of investees, you are one layer removed and do not have to do the monitoring or active engagement with the entrepreneur.

- Staffing and resource access – If your impact investing department is leanly staffed, investing in a fund is much more efficient and effective since the fund manager will have an entire team dedicated to the investment strategy, from diligence and deal execution to the monitoring of the portfolio. They will also have access to proprietary research resources such as Bloomberg terminals and Pitchbook that might be too expensive to subscribe to unless that cost can be spread across a larger set of investors.

- Co-investing opportunities – Another advantage is the ability to leverage a fund manager with deep expertise in a specific sector for their access to deal flow that you can co-invest in. Most fund managers will only consider co-investment opportunities with more prominent investors.

- Learning opportunity – There is something to be said for learning from an experienced investor by investing in and with a fund manager. If your relationship with the GP is strong, you may be able to request opportunities to shadow deals where you may be a co-investor.

Typically newer investors entering the impact investing space will start by investing in funds rather than a direct investment for the reasons noted above. It's a "hop" rather than a "jump" into impact investing, which can make the step to direct investments less daunting.

Disadvantages of Investing in Funds

While there are benefits to investing in funds, there are also plenty of disadvantages to doing so as well. Keeping these negative factors in mind may encourage a leap rather than a hop into impact investing with a direct investment instead:

- Fees – The biggest downside of investing in funds is the fees that must be paid to the fund managers. In addition to giving up typically 20% of the upside to the fund manager, the annual management fee can be a material drag on your total return. We'll discuss more details on the different fees owed to a fund manager shortly. The critical point is that you must weigh the benefit of having a costly professional money manager against making the investments on your own. A good fund manager should be able to more than justify their fees from the value they add, money that is well spent. Unfortunately, there is no guarantee that the fund manager will be able to deliver, so you may be stuck paying fees to an underperformer for ten or more years.

- Intermediary buffer from an entrepreneur – Just as being one layer removed from the entrepreneur could be a benefit by allowing you to be less engaged; this could also be a disadvantage for investors who want to be more actively engaged.

- Low or no control – Unless you are a major investor in the fund, it's likely to be challenging to have much influence on the fund manager. Should the fund manager steer astray from the investment strategy you originally invested in, your ability to pull them back is pretty limited without the support of other investors. That is why it is critical to make sure the diligence on the fund manager is thorough, and you have confidence and trust in their ability and commitment to executing what they say they will do. For example, I've seen impact investors invest in a fund where the fund manager pitched the mission part of their strategy early on during their fundraising process, but once the dollars were committed, it became readily evident the GP could care less about impact.

- Long commitment – A fund investment will, at the minimum, be a ten-year or more relationship. While secondary sales of fund commitments exist, it is nearly impossible to get out of the investment, and typically, when you can get out of the investment, you do so at a discount.

- Integration challenges – If your organization's decision to make impact investing is driven by the potential to integrate the program areas with investees, trying to do so through a fund manager is much more complicated than when you are directly interacting with the entrepreneur. Unfortunately, most fund managers do not prioritize that, although a few more mission-aligned (e.g., Rethink Education) do a decent job connecting their portfolio companies with their philanthropic strategic investors.

- Lower potential total return – As a pooled investment vehicle, the potential return on the fund is less likely to exceed the possible return of individual investments, especially when considering the fees paid to the fund manager. The trade-off for lower potential upside with lower risk in a pooled vehicle is to be expected.

The core downside factors for investing in funds may not be as material for some investors, but keeping them in mind may steer others towards making direct investments or some combination of funds and direct investments. Your organization may have unique circumstances beyond the factors discussed. A trusted consultant can help you with surfacing them to guide you in deciding what types of investments are most appropriate.

Some Key Terminologies for Fund Investments

Just like any area requiring specialized skills, fund investments have specific terminologies that can sound intimidating for the non-finance professionals going into impact investing and starting to invest in funds. Therefore, I'll cover a few key fund terminologies (some of which we previously discussed) very basically before we go into more details and get more technical on structuring considerations for investing in funds.

- **Committed Capital** – The amount of money an investor commits to the fund. The fund size is essentially the total of all the committed capital from all investors into the fund.

- **Drawn or Invested Capital** – Just as the term implies, it is the portion of the committed capital that has been drawn down to make the investment (and in some cases, to pay for the management fee)

- **General Partner (GP)** – The GP or general partner is the fund manager who will execute the fund's investment strategy.

- **Limited Partner (LP)** – These are the investors in the fund. They are "limited" because the maximum loss or exposure they have to the fund is the amount they committed/invested into it. When you invest in a fund, you are a limited partner of the fund.

- **Limited Partnership Agreement (LPA)** – The legal document governing the fund's partnership. This is where all the terms of the investments are spelled out in legal documentation.

- **Subscription Agreement** – When you become an investor, you must fill out the subscription agreement for the fund. It's the application to be an investor in the fund. Note that certain qualifications are required, such as being an "accredited investor" or "qualified institutional investor," to be an investor in a fund.

- **Gross Internal Rate of Return (IRR)** – The standard financial metric measuring the fund's performance that is time-sensitive. The technical definition for IRR is the discount rate applied to cash flows that make the Net Present Value (NPV) equal to zero in a discounted cash flow analysis…it is the annual return that makes the NPV equal to zero. We can spend a lot more time going into the technical aspects of IRR, but suffice it to say, the higher the IRR for a fund, the better the performance. You typically want to target at least a 20% IRR for a fund. Note that the earlier the return is generated, the higher the IRR will be: if you made $1 million on a $5 million investment within a year, the IRR is 20%; but if that $1 million was made over five years, then the IRR drops to less than 4%. The key point here is that the sooner an exit from an investment happens, the higher the IRR will be, even if the amount of money made is exactly the same.

- **Net IRR** – This simply means management fees/costs have been accounted for when calculating the IRR. It is the cleaner number for comparing one fund's performance with that of another, which we will discuss later in the structuring considerations.

- **Multiple On Invested Capital (MOIC)** – This is another standard financial metric often used for performance measurement. Unlike IRR, the MOIC is not sensitive to time and gives a much easier basis for comparisons. For example, if you invested $5 million and got $10 million back from that investment, your MOIC is $10/$5 = 2X. It's a simple measure of what you invested and the return you got from that investment. Whether MOIC or IRR is a better measure of fund performance depends on who you ask.

- **Management Fee** – The annual fee that a GP charges the investors for managing the fund. More details on this will be covered in the structuring section.

- **Carried Interest** – Think of this as the incentive fee, the pay for the performance portion of the GP's compensation. The better the performance of the fund, the higher the GP gets paid as opposed to the fixed management fee regardless of how well or poorly the fund manager performs.

- **Claw Back** – Sometimes, investors have a right to ask the fund manager to return what they might have been paid on the carried interest if specific performance benchmarks have not been met.

- **Right of First Refusal (ROFR)** – The term literally means what it implies: the investor has the right to do something before someone else, such as make an investment or co-investment before someone else does who might not be an existing investor.

- **Most Favored Nation (MFN)** – When an investor is given the same right as another investor who has negotiated additional favorable terms with the fund manager.

- **Side Letter** – When there are terms of an investment that are unique to a specific investor that the GP is willing to commit to, the investor will document those particular terms that are agreed to by the GP, which will be legally binding through a Side Letter. Some terms captured in the Side Letter include

Right of First Refusal, Most Favored Nation, Impact Metrics Reporting, Exit Rights, etc.

- **Preferred Return** – The minimum return that the fund manager must achieve before they get carried interest compensation.

- **Limited Partner Advisory Committee (LPAC)** – These committees provide oversight and governance for the funds and usually consist of representatives from the largest investors in the fund.

- **Legal Opinion** – This is the document from the legal advisors to the client certifying their belief that the investment qualifies as a PRI given the specific items that demonstrate charitability.

- Common Fund Financial Ratios definitions

    - **Investment Multiple or Total Value to Paid-in Capital (TVPI)** =

    $$\frac{\textit{(Cumulative Distributions + Residual Value)}}{\textit{Total Paid In Capital}}$$

    Think of this measure as similar to the MOIC but at the aggregate fund level, whereas MOIC measures the deal level return for each portfolio company.

    - **Realization Multiple or Distributions to Paid-in Capital (DPI)** =

    $$\frac{\textit{Cumulative Distributions}}{\textit{Total Paid In Capital}}$$

    This measures what actual money investors have gotten back from their investment. Notice the only difference is the Residual Value is not in the numerator, which represents the undistributed returns of the portfolio.

    - **Residual Value to Paid-in Capital (RVPI)** =

    $$\frac{\textit{Residual Value}}{\textit{Total Paid In Capital}}$$

    This measures the unrealized value of the portfolio remaining that has not yet been distributed to the investors.

    - **Paid in Capital (PIC) Multiple** =

    $$\frac{\textit{Paid in Capital}}{\textit{Total Committed Capital}}$$

This measures how much of the committed capital has been drawn down and gives a good sense of the pacing of the fund's investment during the investment period.

The are many other technical terms we can discuss beyond the scope of this book, but the ones I've provided should get you enough background for fund investing. The more esoteric terms will be something that can be dug deeper into by your consultants or legal advisors. Now let's get into the more specific considerations for fund investments.

Key Structuring Considerations

What should you look for when investing in a fund investment and fund manager? At the end of the day, when you invest in a fund, you're essentially investing in the thesis of the fund's investment strategy and ultimately investing in the fund manager to execute that thesis. Therefore, due diligence on the fund manager should be the most critical part of the process, even more so than the fund's investment thesis and operational aspects. So many factors need to be considered, and going through every one of them is beyond the scope of this book. But here is my checklist of crucial factors to vet when analyzing a fund:

- **Experience and track record** – Does the fund manager (the General Partner) have the relevant experience to execute the fund's investment thesis? If the fund is a first-time fund, do the founders have prior experience demonstrating their ability to continue doing what they claim with the new platform? Unfortunately, some investors automatically write off first-time fund managers. Still, frankly, while there might be more significant risks for a first-time fund manager (both real and perceived), the opportunity to establish a relationship early with a potential top performer can be incredibly beneficial for future allocation and negotiating the terms you want in the investment. Ideally, the fund manager can provide their track record at their existing fund or prior roles. Sometimes due to confidentiality and other non-disclosure concerns, a fund manager may not be able to share that information from their previous position. However, they should not hesitate to share that information for the existing firm if it is not a first-time fund.

- **Background check and references** – Just as you should do a reference check for picking your consultants, you must do the same for the key principals at the fund. Investing in a fund is a minimum of ten years of commitment typically, so make sure you want to partner with the right individuals. A simple Google search is a quick start, but if your organization expects to be a significant enough investor in the fund, requiring a formal background check (the General Partner would need to sign off on that) is not unusual. Most law firms can do that internally or have partner firms they work with since it's a common request from clients and well worth the additional cost.

- **Gross versus net return** – Fund managers will often focus on the gross returns rather than the net returns when reporting their track record of performance. Always ask for the net return information because it is the cleanest way to compare the fund's performance with other funds; otherwise, you will be comparing apples and oranges because the basis for the comparison is wrong. To clarify, let's say two funds both report a gross internal rate of returns (IRR) of 30% for the same period; however, based on the fee structure differences, one fund's net IRR drops to 22%, whereas the other fund's net IRR is 25%. The net IRR is what you as the investor should care most about because you pay fees to the fund manager. Your actual return on the fund investment is the net IRR. Unless the fund manager works for free, the net IRR will always be lower than the gross IRR. It would be a red flag if the fund manager is reluctant or unwilling to provide their fund performance on both a gross and net IRR basis if the information is available to them, with the caveat that such information from their predecessor roles might be subject to non-disclosure agreements.

- **Fee structure** – There are standard fee structures for funds, so make certain deviations from the norm are acceptable. For example, most funds typically have a two and twenty (2/20) fee structure. All this means is that the fund will charge a 2% management fee on the committed capital (which is 2% of the total size of the fund, not just the drawn amount of the capital) and a 20% incentive fee, which is sometimes referred to as "carried interest" since it aligns the interest of the fund manager with the investors when the investments are successful. Let's break the fee down a little bit further here to clarify.

○ Management fee – The management fee is paid to the fund manager regardless of how the fund performs and is meant to cover the overhead costs of operations for the fund. Typically this management fee starts at 2% during the investment period (typically 4-6 years, with most being five years) and steps down after that investment period ends, say to 1.5%. The stepped-down 1.5% will typically be calculated on the invested capital, not on the total fund commitment; your lawyers should be able to review the subscription agreement for details on the calculation. Something to keep in mind is that sometimes the fund manager may receive fees for work with their portfolio company (e.g., they get a monitoring fee or transaction fee for helping to structure a deal, etc.). You want to ensure those fees are used to offset the management fee for the fund. That helps to fully align the fund manager's interest with the fund's investors and avoids any conflicts of interest.

The management fee may be higher or lower than the standard 2%. The rule of thumb is that funds over $100M in size will typically charge a 2% management fee, but funds below $50M may charge up to 2.5%. The reason for that, in theory, is that a higher percentage for a smaller fund is necessary to support the fund's operations. However, for smaller funds, especially impact funds, the management fee is philanthropically supported rather than taken as a percentage of the assets under management. For example, the first-time fund manager might be a minority demographic that the investor wants to support that can only raise $10M; operating a fund with $250K (2.5% management fee x $10M) annual budget would be very challenging, especially in major markets like NYC or San Francisco where the cost of operations is much higher than other markets.

○ Carried Interest – The 20% standard fee helps incentivize the fund manager to perform since it is contingent on the fund's performance; if the fund does not achieve its return objectives, the fund manager will not get paid this fee in theory. Deviations from the standard 20% carried interest may occur for several reasons:

- First-time funds might need to lower their fees to attract investors. They use their first fund as the opportunity to prove to investors their ability and establish a track record, so they may be more willing to compromise on lower fee structures.

- Tiered fee structure – Some funds might be willing to structure the carried interest based on specific performance benchmarks. So, for example, if the fund reaches a target return of 20%, then the fee may be 20%, but if the fund's performance exceeds 30%, then the carried interest for the amount beyond the target return may be higher, say 25% rather than 20%.

- The fund is highly successful and popular, so it is oversubscribed, meaning that there is significant demand from investors. That gives the fund manager more leverage to negotiate more favorable terms, including a higher carried interest.

Ensuring the fee structure makes sense and is justifiable will be essential to getting the investment recommendation through your investment committee. In addition, a highly experienced finance member on the investment committee will want to understand why fee structures deviate from the standard; being ready to clarify will go a long way to getting their confidence in your team's technical and financial expertise.

○ Preferred return or "hurdle" rate – This is also fairly standard to include in the structure to further align the fund manager's interest with the investors. Essentially, this is the minimum return the fund manager must achieve for the fund before getting any carried interest. The preferred return or hurdle rate is typically 6 to 8%. If the fund does not reach a return of the hurdle rate, the fund manager is compensated purely from the management fee, which is not much of an incentive if the assets under management (AUM or fund size) is not very large. Figure 15 gives a basic example to show the impact of a hurdle rate on the General Partner's compensation from carried interest with and without a hurdle rate of 8%, assuming a total fund size of $100M, 20% standard target return, and 25% carried interest for returns exceeding the target 20%.

Figure 15: Sample Carried Interest With and Without Hurdle Rate

Total Fund Size: $100M	Carried Interest	Preferred Return	Total Carried Interest	Investors Receive	GP Receives	Comment
Actual Fund Returns						
5%	20%	0%	$5.0M	$4.0M	$1.0M	No hurdle rate, GP will get their full carried interest
	20%	8%	$5.0M	$5.0M	$0.0M	GP did not achieve hurdle rate of 8%
20%	20%	0%	$20.0M	$16.0M	$4.0M	No hurdle rate, GP will get their full carried interest
	20%	8%	$20.0M	$16.0M	$4.0M	GP achieves hurdle rate of 8%, gets full carried interest
30%	25%	0%	$25.0M	$19.8M	$5.3M	No hurdle rate, higher carried interest for portion exceeding target return
	25%	8%	$25.0M	$19.8M	$5.3M	

Note that the example does not incorporate the concept of an American waterfall or European waterfall fee structure to keep things simple and demonstrate the point of hurdle rates. We will clarify the difference in waterfall structures next.

- **European versus American waterfall fee structures** – Fee structures can get a bit more complicated when analyzing the waterfall calculation for carried interest. Many investors don't dig deep into this level of analysis which can come back to bite them when the fund performance does not hit the target return. Let's start by clarifying the difference between the two. A European waterfall structure means that the return calculation is based on the entire fund's performance, whereas the American waterfall structure is done on a deal-by-deal basis. On the surface, this may not seem like a big deal, but for the fund manager, the implications can be extremely important on whether they get compensated or not when there is a hurdle rate. The standard structure is the European waterfall structure and better aligns the fund manager's interest with the investors. When a fund utilizes an American waterfall structure, be sure to understand the implications of that and go into the investment fully aware so that you are not caught off guard when fee calculations may differ from what you had expected if the fund underperforms.

To understand why a fund manager would prefer the American waterfall structure, let's walk through an example in Figure 16. We'll assume a $100M fund with a typical 20% carried interest and 8% hurdle rate, and the fund makes ten investments of $10M each. To keep things simple, we assume that the first investment does amazingly well and generates a 50% return on investment while the other nine investments only return the amount invested (0% return).

Figure 16: European vs. American Waterfall Fee Structure

	Deal 1	Deal 2	Deal 3	Deal 4	Deal 5	Deal 6	Deal 7	Deal 8	Deal 9	Deal 10	Total Portfolio
Amount Invested	$10.0M	$10.0M	$10.0M	$10.0M	$10.0M	$10.0M	$10.0M	$10.0M	$10.0M	$10.0M	$100.0M
Capital Returned at Exit	$15.0	$10.0	$10.0	$10.0	$10.0	$10.0	$10.0	$10.0	$10.0	$10.0	$105.0
Return on Investment	$5.0	$0.0	$0.0	$0.0	$0.0	$0.0	$0.0	$0.0	$0.0	$0.0	$5.0
Return %	50%	0%	0%	0%	0%	0%	0%	0%	0%	0%	5%

Assumptions
Carried Interest	20%
Preferred Return	8%

European Waterfall
Return to Investors	$5.0	
Return to GP	$0.0	Portfolio return was 5%, which is below Preferred return of 8% so GP receives no carried interest

American Waterfall
Return to Investors	$4.0	
Return to GP	$1.0	First deal was 50% return which is above Preferred return so GP gets 20% carried interest on deal

Notice that the portfolio return is 5%, which is below the Preferred Return of 8%, so in the case of a European waterfall structure, the investors get the entire return while the GP earns nothing on the carried interest. However, in the case of the American waterfall fee structure, which calculates carried interest based on a deal-by-deal basis, since the first investment was such a success exceeding the 8% Preferred Return rate, the GP gets 20% carried interest on the return of the first investment equal to $1M. Our assumption in Figure 16 assumes the remaining nine investments broke even, but even if they all got wiped out, the GP would still get the $1M carried interest from the very first deal. That is the very reason why a fund manager would prefer an American waterfall fee structure if they can. Sometimes clawback provisions in the limited partner's agreement (LPA) require the GP to return some of that carried interest if the other deals don't perform, even if the fee structure is an American waterfall structure.

- **Impact reporting** – There has to be some accountability for alignment to mission, and the requirement for impact metrics reporting is fundamentally at the core of achieving that alignment. Some fund managers will bulk at being required to provide such metrics reporting, which can indicate how aligned they are with the mission. Understandably, impact metrics need to be appropriately determined (we have a chapter dedicated to performance evaluation and metrics later). Still, if your investment is authentically an impact investment, the unwillingness of the fund manager to provide impact reporting should be a deal-breaker. In fact, if the investment is structured as a PRI, it would be very challenging to demonstrate qualification as a PRI without requiring impact reporting.

- **Valuation approach** – Dig deep to understand how the fund manager values their portfolio. Note that we are talking about private investments, not publicly traded securities, where the value of the stock is readily quoted on a stock exchange. Some fund managers are much more aggressive than others in how they value their portfolio of investments to make the performance numbers look good. Here are a few recommendations on digging into the valuation approach of the general partner:

  - External vs. internal valuation – Does the fund manager use an external third party for valuation? Conceptually using an external party will be less biased when valuations are done of the portfolio, but that may not always be practical and expensive. For example, imagine a third-party consultant performing a valuation analysis of ten to fifteen companies annually. That can get very costly and add to the fund's operating costs, not to mention the annoyance to the portfolio companies if they have to spend their valuable time with the consultant. Some tools now are much more efficient such as Carta (www.carta.com), where their enormous proprietary database allows for third-party valuation without the typical processes of hiring a consultant and is much more cost-effective for the fund manager.

  - Frequency of valuation – Since fund managers provide quarterly updates to their limited partners, in theory, the valuation should be updated quarterly. But, again, depending on the valuation approach, this may not be practical. Accounting rules dictate best practices on how and when to mark to market an investment's value, and the fund manager should have a valuation policy that clarifies how their approach complies with such a framework.

- ○ Latest financing round – In my humble opinion, the best and most straightforward way to value a portfolio company is by marking it to the most recent fundraising round's valuation if the round was done within 12 months and applying a slight discount to be conservative if the market is hot. The more recent the round, the more precise the valuation will be. For example, if the fund manager had invested $2.5M in a company that was valued at $25M but then nine months later the company raised another round at a valuation of $100M, the stake owned by the fund manager should be marked up to $10M before applying any discount. If the round was older than that, then taking the original valuation multiple and applying that based on the new revenue or EBITDA number will provide a benchmark. To clarify, let's assume the company raises no more financing rounds, and it's been three years since the last round when it was valued at $100M. Suppose that prior round was raised at a valuation multiple of 4x revenue (the company had revenues of $25M when it was valued at $100M), and three years later the revenue has grown to $75M. In that case, the company's implied valuation is then 4 x $75M = $300M. The implied valuation of the fund manager's stake is, therefore, now worth $30M before applying any discounts to the valuation.

- ○ Two fund managers, two valuations – In theory, the same company held in two different portfolios should be valued the same, but that is rarely the case. You may have invested in two fund managers that are both invested in the same portfolio company, but they value the company differently. This allows you to see and compare which fund manager is more aggressive or conservative in their valuation approach. While that might sound like a rare occurrence, it does happen when an impact investor invests in several fund managers who are all in the same sector, such as education or healthcare.

- ○ Paper returns don't mean much – As much as you want to ensure the valuation approach is appropriate for compliance reasons, the reality is that all the "gains" that a fund manager shows on their portfolio mean little until those gains are monetized into realized returns. For example, if the fund manager thinks a portfolio company is worth $10M, but when they look to exit the investment, the market is only willing to pay $3M for the company, the number that really matters is the $3M. That is why marking to the most recent round of financing is the closest to the "market's" view on the company's valuation. So why do fund managers try to be aggressive with their valuations? It's all for marketing purposes, quite frankly. Fund managers raise multiple funds, so you'll typically see more aggressive valuation approaches when the fund manager is ready to go out to raise their next fund.

- **Write-downs and Write-offs** – Always ask about the deals that don't do well and how the fund manager handles writing down the valuation or even writing off the investment. Fund managers are very reluctant to mark their investments down since it makes their portfolio performance look bad, so your team may actually need to do it for your own books. I've been to many investment updates for funds I've invested in, and it always amazes me how even when the sky feels like it is falling, the fund managers see only rainbows! It's understandable that a fund manager doesn't want to scare their investors but being unrealistically optimistic will lose credibility with investors in the end. In addition to asking about their valuation approach, always dig into what lessons fund managers learned from underperforming investments. The good GP will be humble and discuss where they think the mistakes were made, while the not-so-good fund managers will be very defensive. No investor is perfect, and there will always be a couple if not more investments that don't pan out; the key is to see if the fund manager actually learned from their mistakes.

- **Leverage** – If the fund is a private equity fund, does the fund use leverage to juice its returns. There are risk and regulatory compliance implications if the fund manager uses leverage. Risk can be at the fund level or at the deal/company level. Leverage is more common for private equity or buyout funds since they invest in positive cash flow companies. Venture capital funds rarely employ debt as most of their investments are much earlier stage companies with negative cash flow. Using debt can significantly boost the return profile of an investment when things go well (think of the mortgage on your home and the equity value you have in it when real estate values are rising rapidly). However, the impact on the downside is also multiplied (remember the 2008 mortgage crisis). If the fund manager uses debt at the deal level, this is less risky than at the fund level since the exposure is specific to the deal. Most likely, the lender will lend specifically to just that deal rather than the whole portfolio. If the debt is raised at the fund level, there are tax implications for private foundations that need to be reviewed by your legal and tax advisors, not to mention the inherent risk for the fund as an investment.

- **Key Man Risk or Key Person Risk** – This is the risk that the leadership in the GP does not continue with the fund. The way to think about this is if the GP gets hit by a bus, who takes over that can continue to execute the fund's strategy. If the fund manager is a well-established firm with multiple funds and broad leadership, the risk is much lower since someone can likely step in. However, if this is a first-time fund with a sole GP or two co-founders, there is a significant risk that the strategy will not be successful if one or both leaders get hit by a bus or leave the fund. Accidents happen, the GP might have health issues, and many other potential problems can arise, causing the GP to be unable to continue managing the fund. Then there is also the potential situation where one GP may decide to leave the fund because they either disagree with their partner over compensation split, operating style or simply lose interest in continuing to manage the fund. Review the Key Person clause on what the terms are for replacing the GP and remediation options, including the right to exit the fund. Here are a few things to look for when evaluating the Key Person Risk:
  - How much GP Commit – This is the "skin in the game" factor for the GP to align their interest with the investors. Usually, this is 1 to 2% of the fund, but the primary benchmark is how much of the GP's wealth is tied to the fund. Some GPs are

first-time fund managers with little personal wealth and may not even be able to commit the 1 to 2% but whatever they can commit is very material relative to their overall wealth.

○ What else are the founders doing outside of the fund (permitted "Outside Activities") – when you hire the fund manager, you expect them to dedicate all their time substantially to the fund. So if the GP has ten side hustles, unless the fund benefits from those side hustles, that should be a red flag on how committed the GP is to the fund.

○ How old is the GP – While it isn't a direct correlation if the general partners are already near retirement age, do they still have the motivation and excitement to work hard and execute the fund's strategy? Again, I hate to sound morbid but also seriously do take into account the health of the GP and tastefully ask during due diligence how committed they are to the fund. Of course, it's illegal to ask how old they are! Some fund managers will include the age of its various partners and senior executives in the LPA.

• **Limited Partner Advisory Committee (LPAC)** – Typically, the LPAC comprises the largest investors in the fund, although not required. The LPAC serves as a governance body to approve conflicts of interest or other matters that need approval. Some examples of when the LPAC is engaged include approving: a deal that is invested by more than one fund within the same firm; fund servicing fees charged by the fund manager to the fund that is generally paid to an outside service provider; or deals that fall outside the typical parameters for the fund such as a larger check size than usual. The benefit of being on the LPAC may be having visibility into these potential issues that arise with the fund. However, other than the perceived "prestige" of being on the LPAC, the value of LPAC membership is low unless there is material concern about governance. If there are material governance concerns, it seems odd to even invest in the fund. The primary thing to focus on when evaluating the LPAC is their authority in decisions on conflicts of interest and whether the LPAC members are independent in their thinking rather than just rubber-stamping anything brought to their attention by the GP.

- **Most Favored Nation (MFN) Clause** – This is a legal term for being offered the same favorable terms to you that the fund manager might offer to another investor. This prevents fund managers from cherry-picking and favoring one investor who might be better at negotiating or someone they like more over another investor. It's typically hard to get the MFN unless a threshold of investment size classifies the investor as a "Major Investor" that automatically receives the MFN. For example, if the definition of a "Major Investor" is a commitment of at least $5M, all investors that commit $5M or more will automatically be provided the MFN, whereas anyone less will not. While that seems unfair, it is perfectly legal and encourages investors to meet the Major Investor hurdle as an incentive.

- **Co-Investment Rights & Parallel Vehicles** – One of the major benefits of investing in a fund is the ability to co-invest in deals that you might not be aware of or even have access to. The hot deals get oversubscribed quickly, so if the fund manager is a well-known investor that entrepreneurs want to have on their capital stack, they will get an allocation that can be shared with their limited partners. In theory, that would be a huge benefit, but it doesn't always work out that way. Let's assume you are the fund manager and have been allocated up to $10M to invest in a hot, oversubscribed deal. If your fund has sufficient capacity to make that entire $10M investment, why would you want to bring a co-investor it? A rational fund manager would take the whole investment themselves; no GP is in the business to be nice; let's be honest here. No, not even idealistic impact investors!

  Let's assume, however, that if the fund manager only has $5M left of capital to invest, it would make sense for the additional $5M to be offered to its limited partners for co-investment. Note that the fund manager cannot just pick one co-investor among its limited partners to offer the opportunity. The Major Investors will each get their pro-rata right of the $5M available, and the fund manager must solicit interest among them all. That example is the ideal scenario for a co-investment, but frankly, those are much less common. The more typical scenario is when a fund manager might have the right to invest in a deal with plenty of capacity in the fund but isn't willing to take the entire risk. In our previous example, let's assume the $10M opportunity is actually in a deal that the fund manager likes but isn't entirely confident. So instead of maximizing its total exposure to the investment, it commits only partially to the deal and invites other limited partners to co-invest with it. The fund manager will invariably put a positive spin on why the deal is an exciting co-investment opportunity rather than disclosing their actual reason.

In hindsight, I've turned down many co-investment opportunities that dodged some bullets, so the idea of Co-Investments Rights needs to be taken with a grain of salt. It's nice to have, but theory and practice are not always consistent. Do your own due diligence rather than relying completely on the fund manager when you have a co-investment opportunity because the fund manager will inevitably be biased when the opportunity is offered. One of my co-investments was written down by almost 90% when I relied on the fund manager's analysis and their justification for the high valuation that I had expressed material concern with during the due diligence. That was a costly lesson, even if that investment eventually turns around.

When a limited partner decides to do a co-investment, a separate vehicle is usually created. The co-investment vehicle might be created solely with just the specific limited partner for multiple co-investment opportunities, or it might be a vehicle formed just for the particular deal with all the co-investors participating in that vehicle. The fund manager will typically charge a 1% management fee and 10% carried interest for the vehicle (essentially half the fee of the main fund). The benefit of a special purpose vehicle created specifically to serve one particular limited partner is that the same vehicle can be used to co-invest in multiple opportunities for that investor. However, that limited partner bears all the cost on its own rather than spread across other limited partners in the vehicle set up just for one particular deal. The advantage of the investment vehicle set up just for a specific deal is the shared cost, but there must be a new vehicle for any additional co-investments. Therefore, additional costs will be incurred. Here are a couple of rules of thumb to keep in mind:

○ Negotiate with the fund manager about lowering or eliminating co-investment vehicle fees. They benefit as much as you do when you make a co-investment. Some fund managers will vigorously push back because they feel they are only getting paid for the commitment made into the main fund, so you're getting a free ride on the co-investment vehicle if there is no fee. While that seems reasonable, the reality is that they're nearsighted, especially if you plan to co-invest in a rare scenario rather than frequently. The happier a fund manager makes their limited partners, the more likely the limited partner will invest in their future funds, so it's an excellent way to show an alignment of interests.

○ If your firm plans to invest in multiple co-investment opportunities, it is probably better to set up a co-investment vehicle specifically just for your firm and take the total cost of formation rather than on a deal basis. That will give you flexibility and efficient responsiveness to co-investments when they arise.

○ The fund manager may have parallel funds created to co-invest with the main fund that is not specific to a deal or one particular investor. These parallel funds are usually formed to meet specific regulatory requirements for some investors who cannot invest directly into the main fund. The critical thing to focus on when such parallel funds are created is to ensure they do not get favorable treatment over the main fund. For example, if a deal opportunity arises, the main fund should get first dibs on the investment opportunity, if not the same priority – your legal advisors should be able to identify language that will solidify that prioritization and ensure the main fund is the core focus of the fund manager.

• **Exit or Withdrawal Rights** – This is the right for the investor to get out of the fund. Quite frankly, this is one of the most onerous terms to get a fund manager to agree to and often requires significant negotiations and structuring. Why is an exit right so important? First, some investors, especially an impact investor that invests into the fund as a PRI, have requirements for compliance. One of the requirements is that when the investment strays from the mission you originally invested in (meaning there is mission drift and the fund manager no longer aligns with the charitability purpose of the initial investment), you must exit that investment. Thus, from a regulatory standpoint, the exit right is for compliance. Secondly, you also want an exit right when there is a material brand risk – this is particularly important for major private foundations who do not want their brand tarnished (although it should probably be important to any investor). The lawyers will need to fine-tune what defines a "material brand risk," but it would have to be something pretty extreme that triggers the Exit Right clause in the legal agreement since the investor would not agree to it otherwise. I like to think of extreme examples of situations like the GP getting sued for sexual harassment or other egregious criminal activity that could show up on the front page of the New York Times. Philanthropic investors and major family offices are incredibly skittish about being associated with such reputational risks.

- Stake of Investment and Control Limitations – Private foundations are prohibited from controlling any business enterprise. As such, there are limitations on how much a private foundation investor can own of a fund when the investment is structured as an MRI. More specifically, the threshold is capped at a 20% controlling stake in a fund (or any business for that matter), at which point the private foundation would be subject to Excess Business Holding tax under Internal Revenue Code Section 4943. That is an area of analysis your legal counsel will need to provide guidance on if you get too close to the 20% threshold; most investors do not come close to that ownership stake.

PRI vs. MRI vs. Grants

Making a fund investment can be done through any asset class. For nonprofit funds and accelerators, grant funding or PRIs are available options since they are philanthropic capital best suited for investing in charitable entities. Any of the three types of capital can be utilized for traditional funds. It seems odd that you can provide grants to for-profit entities, which traditional funds are. If structured appropriately, the grant could be used as first loss protection to credit enhance (make less risky) a loan fund combined with a PRI investment into the fund, as we previously discussed. Typically an investment into a traditional fund will likely be structured as an MRI.

It is possible to structure a PRI investment into a traditional fund. However, the legal advisors will need to be very clear on documenting the charitability of the investment and how the traditional fund meets the charitability test. To demonstrate, I'll give an example of how this was done with one traditional fund in the fintech space. The fund manager was a first-time fund manager that raised approximately $50M in total committed capital, mainly from impact investors. The fund was an impact fund since it focused on the underbanked low-income consumers, but it targeted the typical returns of an early-stage venture fund. One of the impact investors was a large foundation where financial inclusion was a programmatic area, so it structured the investment as a PRI. A key term to demonstrate charitability included in its Side Letter with the fund manager was a capped return at 4%. Essentially the foundation investor would give up any return above 4% to another investor (a major family office). The family office investor provided a guarantee to the foundation investor on the charitability qualification in return for getting the excess return. That was a bit of an innovative approach to get the PRI investor comfortable that it would qualify and pass the charitability test. I have not seen anything similar since then, but the point is that with the proper structure, a PRI investment can be made into a traditional fund and probably without the complexity of the example I just gave.

Direct Investments

Now that we've covered fund investments, let's shift to direct investments. Many of the considerations for funds are also relevant to direct investments. This section looks at direct investments into early-stage companies more than mature companies, although the concepts will likely apply to both. The idea of investing directly rather than through funds may seem daunting for those who do not have a financial background. However, as this section outlines, you don't have to be a finance expert to execute a direct investing strategy.

Reasons for Investing Directly

While making direct investments may seem more complicated than investing in funds, the benefits of doing so may be well worth the effort. Furthermore, if the impact investing strategy is structured appropriately, the complications or concerns with investing directly could also be alleviated, which we will discuss shortly. First, let's go through the benefits of doing direct investment and its advantage over investing in a pure fund investment strategy.

- **Directly Engaged with Entrepreneur and Control** – When you invest in a company, you get the benefit of directly engaging with the investee; this may be a one-off opportunity to engage or, more formally, through joining the entrepreneur's board where you have influence and control. Entrepreneurs also appreciate interacting directly with the strategic investor who can bring value beyond just the check-in supporting them. For example, suppose you are an actively engaged type of investor. In that case, a direct investment will be significantly more practical than a fund investment, allowing you to build a stronger partnership with the entrepreneur, which can pay dividends in multiple ways. The entrepreneur can serve as a reference to other potential investees if you build a strong partnership with them.

- **Deeper Understanding of the Investee** – No intermediary filters the communication flows, so you know exactly what the entrepreneur is doing, how they are doing, and how you can be helpful. That allows you to truly understand the company's products and services much deeper than if you had to learn about the company through a fund manager. That deeper level of understanding also allows you to be smarter when you are providing updates to your Investment Committee, senior leadership, and the board. Furthermore, your ability to think through ways to integrate the investee across your organization for collaboration will be much easier; being in the flow allows you to be proactive with insights you would not have through an intermediary. Lastly, you will be in direct contact with the entrepreneur's innovations rather than one step removed in the case of a fund investment; this may stimulate your own ideas and initiatives within your organization where the products or services may align.

- **Build Network with other Direct Investors** – Unless you are the sole investor, which is highly unlikely, you will have the opportunity to collaborate with other investors who co-invested with you in the company. Not only does this expand your network, but it provides learning opportunities too. Some may be strategic investors, while others are financially driven or impact investors, and their perspectives and motivations can prove insightful. These co-investors may also be potential collaboration partners for other areas within your organization; for example, another foundation with a similar programmatic focus could be interested in participating in initiatives that your foundation focuses on.

- **Higher Potential Return** – The upside potential for a direct investment will be much higher for a direct investment than for a fund investment. While rare, the potential for a 10x return on your investment will be much more likely than in the case of a fund investment because it's a concentrated bet on one company rather than spread across a pool of investments. To achieve the same 10x return potential in a fund, every portfolio company within the fund would need to be a 10x return versus just one company in direct investment.

- **Shorter Commitment** – While exceptions do exist, your holding period for a direct investment will usually be shorter than a fund. Remember, the typical fund will be a ten-year commitment with a potential extension of one to two years after that. A direct investment holding period will typically be three to seven years before the company has a liquidity event. That means you will realize the investment's return (or loss) sooner; if there is a considerable gain, you will get to redeploy that capital to other investments earlier.

- **No Fees** – This is one of the most significant advantages of investing in a company directly in that there is no annual management fee you would pay to a fund manager. Over time, the annual fees can be a considerable drag on the net return of the investment. Furthermore, you capture 100% of the upside on the investment if the company does well for your dollars invested. There is no carried interest that you need to pay a fund manager.

- **Better Mission Alignment** – It is very rare to see a fund manager that is very well-aligned in its mission with a particular investor unless the fund is incubated directly by the impact investor for a specific programmatic initiative. A nonprofit fund like an accelerator could come close to the objectives for a particular impact investor (think of an accelerator that invests only in entrepreneurs of color being incubated by a foundation focused on racial equity); however, they are not traditional funds. Traditional funds typically have a broader investment strategy to attract enough investors and no "product" or "service" offering that is programmatically driven. However, a direct investment will allow the impact investor to specifically pick the company with a product or service offering that addresses the programmatic objectives that align with the investor's organization. It may be a bit of a stretch to say investing directly into a company has a more significant impact than investing in a fund. Still, the impact of your dollar is certainly more direct than through a fund since your investment dollars directly support the service or product of the entrepreneur.

- **More Accessible Impact Metrics** – As a direct investor, your ability to ask the entrepreneur to report on metrics that align with what your organization focuses on will be easier than a fund manager who has to get all their investees to do so. These primary reasons for making direct investments will be more important for some investors than others. It's up to your organization to prioritize them and whether they are sufficient to justify a direct investing strategy.

Disadvantages of Direct Investing

Just as there are disadvantages to investing in funds, there are also plenty of drawbacks to investing directly into a company. Based on your organization's priorities, these disadvantages may or may not be applicable, but we will summarize the key ones as follows:

- **Time Commitment** – To extract and leverage some of the benefits of making a direct investment, the time necessary to engage with the entrepreneur will be much higher than investing in a fund. In addition, some entrepreneurs are very needy and require much more attention than others, which as an investor, you may not be able to dedicate time to, nor want to even if you do have time. Areas of support that entrepreneurs may need help with include:
  - Fundraising support
  - Recruiting talent
  - Financial structuring advice

- ○ Pitch preparation
- ○ Strategic advice on the company business model
- ○ Operational advice
- ○ Product market fit analysis
- ○ Executive coaching & mentoring
- ○ Therapy and moral support

And those are just a few roles I've played in supporting the entrepreneurs I had invested in. The last one—therapy and moral support—seems odd, but you'd be surprised at how important that is. Of course, not every investor will need to be actively engaged. Still, entrepreneurs may expect to leverage their investors (particularly strategic investors) to support them beyond just the capital invested. If you are a passive investor who does not want to be actively involved with the entrepreneur, you can mitigate that by managing expectations during the due diligence process before the deal is closed.

- **Higher Risk** – As we discussed earlier, direct investment is a concentrated bet on one company rather than a pool of diversified investments through a fund. That implies a higher risk if the investment underperforms, offset by a higher potential upside if the investment does well. Note that if the investment was structured as a PRI and utilized grant dollars, that should not be any riskier than doing a grant where the total amount of the grant money is given away with no return. It's critical to remember framing when making a comparison of risk. That would not be the case if it were an MRI investment using funds from endowment dollars to invest.

  An additional area for the higher risk is reputational risk. Most companies are actively engaged in media releases and having their brand out in the market, while fund managers tend to be less active in the media. That could be a double-edged sword if there is bad press for the company and your organization is listed as an investor, especially when you have a board seat.

- **Complexity** – Making direct investments is arguably more complicated than investing in funds. Performing due diligence on funds is relatively standard compared to vetting companies directly. However, each company's culture, products, solutions, circumstances, and resources are unique, so analyzing a direct investment will require deeper expertise. Furthermore, investing directly into a company allows multiple structures compared to more standardized structures for funds. Of course, this also means you can customize the investment structure to better suit your organization's investment opportunity rather than accepting something prescribed.

- **More Monitoring Necessary** – Since early-stage entrepreneurs operate at a swift pace to build their businesses, a lot happens in a month. For that reason, they need to be monitored more carefully. It's not unusual for early-stage entrepreneurs to be in a situation where they may run out of money in three months! Being in the communications flow and continuously tracking the performance of the company's metrics will help mitigate risks before they arise or get out of hand.

- **Potential Mission Drift** – I mentioned one of the advantages of investing directly is the more substantial mission alignment potential with your organization. However, at the same time, it's also more likely potential for mission drift than a fund. Companies (especially earlier stage ones) are constantly adapting to the market and evolving their business model. How tightly you and your organization define mission alignment will impact what may or may not be considered a deviation from the mission as the entrepreneur adapts her business model and grows the company. For example, let's assume that a company you invested in might have a technology solution that serves low-income individuals quite well. The technology can be applied to a broader audience as the business grows. The entrepreneur might then start focusing the company on serving not only low-income clients but also middle-income or high-income clients to expand their offering and increase revenue. Or the entrepreneur may be expanding geographically into new markets beyond the geographic focus of a place-based impact investor's narrow target. Doing so is expected in the course of any company looking to grow and evolve. But for an impact investor who invested because of the company's focus on low-income clients and vulnerable populations, it could feel like a mission drift.

Despite these disadvantages, investing directly into a company can be extremely rewarding for professional and personal development as you get to support passionate entrepreneurs who are building products and solutions that can be highly impactful. In addition, the energy you get from partnering with an entrepreneur will be quite different from investing in a fund manager; there's just a level of involvement and sense of partnership that is much stronger with a direct investment.

Debt vs. Equity Investments Implications

If you decide to move forward on direct investments, should you invest in equity or debt? Sometimes you won't have a choice since the entrepreneur is not interested in one type of asset class or another. The fundamental questions to think through:

What does the entrepreneur want? If the company is only looking for debt investments, you will need to think through how to structure the debt that best accounts for the risk inherent in the investment.

- What investment options can your organization participate in? Not all impact investors will have the flexibility to do all types of asset classes, so you may be bound by what your organization's investment parameters allow.

- What is your risk appetite? Per our discussion earlier, debt is theoretically less risky than equity. Convertible notes are somewhere in between debt and equity.

- How long are you planning to hold the investment? If it is an equity investment, you will need to plan on a three to seven-year holding period, maybe longer. Debt investments can be much shorter such as a six-month bridge loan.

- What is your return expectation? The upside for equity investment is potentially unlimited, given the higher risk. On the other hand, debt investments have a capped return of the interest you get paid on the loan and repayment of the principal.

- What type of control do you expect to have, and how do you want to engage with the entrepreneur? For example, as a debt investor, you will not have the same type of board seat opportunity (and consequently control) as an equity investor in the company. In addition, the way an entrepreneur partners with an equity investor is quite different than how it partners with a lender;

equity investors are essentially co-owners as shareholders of the company, unlike lenders.

• What type of internal infrastructure do you have to support the investment? For example, if you made a debt investment that pays a monthly or quarterly interest payment and amortization of principle, do you have the system in place to track those payments to ensure they are on schedule? Furthermore, suppose the debt investment is structured as a PRI. In that case, regulatory compliance considerations for debt interest and amortization payments must then be re-invested as part of your payout requirements for a private foundation. On the other hand, equity investments typically do not have such cash flow streams (assuming no cash dividends) and require much less monitoring on that front.

• Are you comfortable with the terms of the investment proposed by the entrepreneur? Is the equity valuation too high? Is the debt investment structure appropriate for the level of risk you take in making the loan? Can you negotiate the terms, or are they set, and you have to take it or leave it with the entrepreneur?

There are many factors to consider when considering which asset class to use for the investment in addition to the factors I've just listed, and we will touch on them next. Before I do, it's worth mentioning that sometimes the entrepreneur doesn't know what they actually want, so they may ask you as the investor to propose the investment structure. Or they might think they want an equity investment when a debt investment is more practical. And lastly, just because they are raising an equity round doesn't mean that they may not want to entertain a debt investment from an investor with who they really want as a partner. That is the beauty of investing directly into a company versus a fund. You have the potential flexibility to structure something that can work for both your organization and the entrepreneur.

In addition to debt and equity, it should not be forgotten that if neither option is appropriate and your organization has grant-making abilities, you could potentially structure a grant to the entrepreneur if there is strong mission alignment. Of course, the grant would have to be structured as an expenditure responsibility grant, which is slightly more complicated than a standard grant, but it can be done. All that is to say, you have lots of ways to partner with an entrepreneur that is not limited to one asset class.

Key Structuring Considerations for Direct Investments

Unlike fund investments, direct investing is much less standardized when it comes to structures, depending on what you are hoping to achieve with the investee. Some key factors should help guide the structuring of the investment, and I'll walk you through them depending on whether they are an equity investment or a debt investment. Before delving into asset class specifics, some of the considerations for fund investments are just as applicable to direct investments. I'll summarize those here:

- **Leadership References and Background Checks** – Just as investing in a fund is essentially investing in the general partner to execute the investment strategy when you make a direct investment into a company, you are backing the entrepreneur to execute their business model. A basic Google search on the founder(s) may uncover things about the company and the founder(s) that could impact whether to move forward or not on a potential investment. Doing a background check (and reference checks at the very minimum) on the company leadership is probably the most critical aspect of due diligence. That is even more important than the business model. Companies fail more from poor leadership than they do from poor business models. Here is a list of what I typically look for in the leadership of founders and company management:
  - o Humility – This is such an undervalued trait. The biggest challenge of entrepreneurship is learning from mistakes. Mistakes are expected and normal. Founders who are overly confident (arrogant) will not accept and own the mistakes they make and, consequently, won't learn from those mistakes. Always ask questions about what the entrepreneur wished they could have done differently, personally and professionally; the example does not have to be specific to the company you are investing in. The goal is to gauge their humility. Humility is such a critical trait that signals the entrepreneur's willingness to listen to feedback and counsel from their advisors.

- ○ Integrity – Whether it's an impact investment or a traditional investment, backing a leader with integrity will indeed protect your organization from potential risks to your brand. Knowing that you can trust the leadership team to do the right thing will make it easier to sleep at night. Should the company fail, the cause of that failure should not be due to bad actors leading the business, which will be a much more significant concern than the investment not working out for more normal reasons. Unfortunately, no one has invented the perfect lie detector. Still, after doing enough deals and asking the right questions, you will be able to sniff out the bad actors when combined with reference and background checks.

- ○ Grit – Knowing that entrepreneurship is an arduous path to success, successful entrepreneurs have grit; they don't let setbacks hold them back or crush their drive. Businesses rarely run as planned, and setbacks happen... often. A successful entrepreneur will have a track record of overcoming personal and professional setbacks. They are endurance runners, not sprinters.

- ○ Adaptability – Every business adapts to market condition changes in order to survive and thrive. The entrepreneur must have that nimble ability to adjust their business model and make pivots when needed. That is where arrogance can kill a business as the entrepreneur stubbornly ignores necessary changes with market conditions and sticks to their own belief that they are correct, only to sink the business when it becomes evident that it's too late to do so.

- ○ Courageous Confidence – This may seem like the opposite of humility which I had listed as the top trait to look for, but they are not mutually exclusive. There is a fine line between stubborn ignorance due to arrogance and confident conviction to push forward on a strategy that others might not be willing to execute. A strong leader will not be afraid to take the path less taken but also inspire and effectively motivate team members to come for the ride.

- ○ Creativity – Like the adaptability trait, an entrepreneur must be a creative problem solver. By definition, entrepreneurship is essentially finding solutions to the problems that need to exist but currently do not, or at least better solutions than what now does exist. Entrepreneurs need to be innovative to continually adapt and refine their business models to stay ahead of the competition.

- ○ Operating Style – What is the entrepreneur's operating style? How does it align with how you will engage or not engage with the entrepreneur. For example, some entrepreneurs are very extroverted; some are pushy and demanding; others are more timid and quiet. Understanding the personality type will be critical in how as an investor, you may want to engage them if they are an investee.

Review the depth of the leadership team and understand where the gaps are. Then, ask the entrepreneur about where they believe the expertise gaps are and how they expect to fill them.

- **Advisory Board and Advisory Council** – Take a look at who the entrepreneur has on the advisory board. Sometimes they may also have an advisory council in addition to the advisory board. The main difference between the two is fiduciary accountability. An advisory board member is typically compensated with equity in the company (unless they are investors) for bringing their expertise and will be liable as the governing body overseeing the company's executives. On the other hand, an advisory council does not have governance responsibilities. It is typically created with a handful of individuals with the specialized expertise that the entrepreneur can tap when needed. They might be paid with a small retainer and some contingent compensation when they are brought in on a specific deal or company initiative where their expertise is highly relevant. When reviewing the advisory boards and council members of the company, ask the following questions:
  - ○ How long is the term of the membership, and how are they selected? It is very typical for the larger investors in the company to hold a board seat. Usually, existing and prior investors get diluted as new rounds of equity financing get done, assuming those investors don't participate in the recent rounds. This results in new investors with more significant stakes replacing the prior diluted investor's board

seat. Furthermore, I always expect to see at least one or two independent board members in addition to the major investors on the advisory board.

○ How is the board member engaged? How active are they with the company? Some board members are passive and just figureheads who lend their brand; others are just representing their company as investors for governance reasons. In contrast, others are actively involved with the company's leadership supporting them with the expertise that complements the skills of the entrepreneur(s). The board members should bring a diversity of skills and thought. They should not be just rubber-stamping recommendations when leadership asks for approval. They should not be micromanaging the entrepreneur but provide thoughtful outside perspective and guidance and serve as an expert resource for the entrepreneur.

○ What does the entrepreneur expect from each board member? I have often asked my investees to put together a matrix that shows what skills and expertise they need and compare it to how board members (or advisory council members) match those skills. Identifying gaps and helping to recruit board members to fill those gaps will be one area where an investor can add value to the investee.

• **Company's Capital Structure** – Entrepreneurs do what they can to build their business and sometimes finance the business in a way that is not optimal. Of course, beggars can't be choosers when financing options are not available. Review the capital structure of the company and the rounds of financing that have already been done. Does the company have existing debt, and at what interest rates? I've seen some young companies that have maxed out credit card debt charging 25% interest which is an incredible burden that drains the cash flow from being invested more productively. Helping the entrepreneur think through their capital structure will be useful to them and strengthen their confidence in you as an investor. More importantly, it will help position the company for success if you invest. It will also make future financing rounds much easier with a cleaner capital structure.

As a side note, I remember one entrepreneur who had never done an institutional financing round. His prior funding rounds were entirely through simple agreement for future equity (SAFE) notes with high-net-worth individuals (including some relatives), each with different valuation caps. Frankly, it was one of the messiest capital tables I've ever seen. The entrepreneur openly noted that some of the SAFE note investors were incredibly demanding and overly micromanaging him, making it very difficult for him to build his business. Thus, I structured my investment to be contingent on some of the SAFE note investors being taken out (refinanced/repaid) or restructuring their investment to the same terms as the round I was leading as the first institutional investor. Cleaning up the capital structure made the investment more attractive to other institutional investors to join the round as well.

- **Exit Right** – We discussed this previously on fund investments, and the same applies to direct investments. In the Side Letter, to comply with the PRI charitability requirements, if your investment is structured as a PRI, there needs to be a mechanism to exit the investment when there is mission drift.

- **What Does the Entrepreneur Want or Need From the Investor** – An investment opportunity may be very attractive, but it doesn't mean you are the right investor for that company. If the entrepreneur is looking for an actively engaged investor who brings a particular skill set, do you or your team member have the capacity to provide that value? If not, are there other ways that you can help the entrepreneur fill that gap? Furthermore, are there areas that you can add value to the company that might not be obvious to the entrepreneur? Assess the level of engagement early on and manage expectations so that there are no surprises once the investment is made.

- **Ownership Distribution** – Outside of the investors, take a look at the ownership distribution among the executive team and staff. When you ask the entrepreneur about staffing and turnover, the reason for digging into this will become apparent. You want to ensure the entrepreneur fairly compensates their staff to incentivize them to stay. Simply put, how much skin in the game do the team members have in the company so that they have a vested interest in the company's success in alignment with the investors. Equity ownership incentivizes the retention of key staff members. chapter 12 on Advanced Impact Investing Strategies will provide more detailed structuring advice on Options Pool to address this issue and the concept of founder share vesting.

- **Business Model Analysis** – Look at the financial projections for the company and assess its feasibility. While there are no guarantees things work out as planned, there are still important factors to gauge as a reality check. By nature, every entrepreneur has to be an optimist; otherwise, they would never take the entrepreneurial route. As such, it's not surprising that their projections in financial models are inevitably overly optimistic, making you wonder what drugs they were taking, given how unrealistic the projections are. Here are a few things to consider when vetting the projections presented by the entrepreneurs:
    - Total Addressable Market (TAM) – How big is the addressable market the company serves? The market size helps you understand how big the opportunity is for potential upside on the investment.
        - Ask how the entrepreneur defines the addressable market? Does it make sense that their products and services actually fit the TAM? Or are they trying to make the TAM appear bigger even though their products only serve a much narrower niche within that market opportunity?
        - How much market share does the entrepreneur expect their company to capture, and over what period? Does that sound reasonable based on who else is in the market? An entrepreneur suggesting their company will capture 50% of the market share in five years of a $10 billion market is clearly not being realistic if they are starting with less than $1 million in revenue. If the TAM is only $50M, then the company will need to capture a significant portion of the market share to grow top-line revenue (e.g., 50% market share just to reach $25M revenue). If the TAM is that small, the investor needs to seriously justify why they believe the investment

opportunity is worth pursuing even if the investee has a high probability of dominating that market.

○ Is the TAM expandable? Sometimes the addressable market can be significantly expanded by new products or services that the company will add to its capabilities; other times, it might simply be a geographic expansion of where the products and services can be offered.

○ Are the assumptions for growth reasonable? How fast has the company grown in the past, and how does that compare to what its projected growth rate is going forward? If a company has revenue projections looking like a hockey stick, the founder needs to be able to justify that acceleration and exponential growth rate. Usually, taking a haircut/discount on the growth projections ranging from 10 to 50% is not unusual depending on how aggressive the projections are. Venture capital firms typically like to see companies grow revenue at a rate of 200 to 300% or more yearly. In contrast, private equity firms focused on later-stage companies will be satisfied with 20 to 30% annual revenue growth rates.

○ When does the company expect to reach profitability? Are the profitability margins reasonable? What is causing the improvements in projected margin improvements? For investors focused on early-stage investing (Series Seed and Series A in particular), profitability is less critical than growth, so you must apply what's more relevant to your investment strategy. Of course, in an ideal world, the company has high revenue growth and high margins, but that is rarely the case; software as a service (SAAS) businesses seem to be the few sectors where that is more feasible.

○ What is the company's edge? How competitive is the landscape? There must be some advantage that the company has over its competitors to make it an attractive investment. The competitive advantage (its "edge") must also be defensible and often referred to as the "moat." Some examples of competitive advantages include, but are not limited to:

- Technology or patents – the technology or product is patented and hard to replicate
- The uniqueness of the business model – this could be due to patents it owns that are core to its business model, or the time it takes to build the business model may take too long to be worthwhile for competitors to try
- Talented team/staff – perhaps the people on its team are uniquely capable, and the market does not have many of those individuals
- Network and relationships – the company's deep relationships allow it to get beneficial access or favorable treatment
- Brand – the company is an innovative first mover or leader for what it does or produces and establishes a brand that the market knows

When looking at the company's competitive advantage, it's helpful to create a matrix that plots the company's capabilities against its competitors to understand the landscape.

○ Are the products and services the company seeks to offer in the future connected to its existing business? Or do they feel too much of a stretch? For example, if the company has traditionally been focused on offering software solutions in the education space but then plans to expand into the healthcare space, how feasible is that? If the shift is too far of a stretch from the company's core competencies, this would be a reason to exclude or highly discount any revenue projections that count the incremental revenue from the new segment.

- **Sales/Revenue and Concentration Risk** – Looking solely at the topline revenue number is insufficient in and of itself. Instead, an investor needs to dig several levels deeper:

○ The first level is looking at what drives revenue. Even if sales growth is attractive, where does the growth come from? Does the company plan to grow organically (meaning its own products and services generate the revenues), or are there external contributions (the company plans to acquire another company)? While more common for later-stage companies, some young companies do grow through acquisition.

○ Does a mix of clients generate the revenue, or does one or two contracts represent most of the company's sales? The younger the company, the more likely there will be concentration risk. Typically a client representing more than 10% of the company's revenue would be considered concentrated since a loss of that client would have a material impact on the overall revenue for the company. Imagine if a client represented 80% of the company's revenue. I had an entrepreneur who actually lost a client that represented slightly over 80% of its revenue just before its financing round was about to close. You can imagine the valuation for the round should have been substantially revised; when that didn't happen, I chose not to move forward on investment.

○ How predictable is the revenue going forward? There are one-off types of revenue; after a service or product is delivered, that is the end. Think installation or implementation of a software solution. A client is going to install the software once. These one-off types of revenue are core to topline growth, but they are less attractive because they are less predictable. Investors like what is called recurring revenue that is predictable and sticky. An example of a recurring revenue would be a software license; once a client signs up, they tend to keep renewing the subscription (e.g., your Microsoft Office 365 license) to use the product. Separating the recurring revenue from the one-off revenue allows you to get to a cleaner revenue projection. If any discount is applied to a revenue projection, the discount should be more on the one-off rather than the recurring revenue.

• **Churn** – Similar to looking at staff turnover, reviewing client churn will allow you to assess the stickiness and predictability of the revenue projection. There is no specific churn that is standard; you would need to benchmark churn for the industry and how the company's churn figures compare. Ask management what the reasons are (as far as they are aware) of the causes for the churn if the number feels high and how they plan to address it.

Dig deeper into the loss of larger clients to understand whether the reason for it was due to something in the company's control or was it an exogenous factor. For clarification, an exogenous factor might be a client deciding to build a solution in-house rather than leverage an outside partner's product. In contrast, an example of something within the company's control would be if the client canceled or did not renew a contract because they were not getting the customer support they needed or found a competitor's product better or cheaper.

- **Pipeline** – Assessing the company's projections requires a thorough understanding of the pipeline of potential opportunities the company is pursuing. The company should provide a list of opportunities it is pursuing and context of how likely those opportunities could convert to an actual contract/sale. Depending on how far along an opportunity has been developed (e.g., introductory call vs. finalizing contract negotiations), the sales pipeline should be probability-weighted on the likelihood of getting to a sale. For example, if the company says it has a pipeline of over $50 million, drill down into the significant contracts and put a probability weighting for each one that is a realistic estimate of converting to an actual sale; that $50M pipeline may only convert to $5 million in confirmed sales ultimately. Reviewing the company's prior sales conversion from initial conversation to actual sales will give a reasonable basis for estimating potential revenue from their current pipeline.

- **Cash Burn Rate** – Knowing the monthly cash burn rate will be critical to how much runway the company has before running out of money. In general, you'd want to see a minimum of 12 to 18 months of runway, and if the company is down to only 6 to 9 months, an investor should monitor the company's performance much more closely. To determine the runway remaining:

Runway =

$$\frac{(\textit{Next 12 months revenue} + \textit{cash on balance sheet} - \textit{short term debt coming due})}{\textit{Monthly cash burn rate}}$$

When the runway is getting close to 6 months remaining, the company needs to consider what costs can be cut and staff restructuring to reduce the cash burn rate and extend the runway while seeking additional funding.

- **Existing Investors and Potential Co-Investors** – Reaching out to the existing and potential new investors (with the company's permission) can help with two core data points. Firstly, existing investors will be able to give perspective on their relationship with the entrepreneur and provide context and feedback, so you go into the investment with more visibility into the entrepreneur's operating style. Always ask about the entrepreneur's strengths and where they might see gaps that need to be addressed. Gauge how the entrepreneur has leveraged them and whether there were any surprises since they first invested, both positive and negative. Secondly, existing investors and potential co-investors may also be collaborators outside of just the investment into the company, especially the strategic investors who are mission-aligned with your organization.

- **What didn't I ask that I should have asked?** – I have found it always helps to ask that question at the end of a due diligence process with a potential investee. I always put it in the context of "Is there anything about the company or about yourself that you would like to disclose that we didn't cover?" That allows the company to disclose a sensitive issue that the diligence process might not have brought out. Suppose the entrepreneur does reveal something that could be material, then as an investor. In that case, you can dig deeper into the issue to see if it changes your investment decision or whether you can still be comfortable moving forward on the investment despite that additional disclosure. However, suppose the entrepreneur doesn't disclose something material that you later discover before the deal closes. In that case, it should raise red flags about the entrepreneur's integrity and lack of transparency.

PRI vs. MRI vs. Grants

Given the many situations an entrepreneur is seeking funding, it will be up to the investor to determine which of the full spectrum of capital will best suit the objectives for the investment. We will discuss capital stacking in the chapter on Advanced Impact Investing Strategies. Meanwhile, how do you determine which tool to use for an investment?

While no hard guarantees exist on choosing between an MRI or a PRI structure, here are some quick rules of thumb that can guide you:

- **Legal structure** – If the organization is legally organized as a nonprofit, you can only make a PRI investment in the form of a loan or provide a grant since nonprofits do not have ownership and, therefore, no equity in their capital structure. On the other hand, social ventures established as public benefit corporations or L3C entities have equity and can accept all types of capital, whether PRI or MRI, as well as grants.

- **Which pot of money will the investment be made from?** Some organizations have abundant resources and can pick and choose whichever pot they want, while others might be more limited. For example, if your organization is on the smaller side, your grant or PRI budget might be pretty little, which affects when you would utilize those tools.

- **Program-related investments** – There is potential for financial return, but you focus on mission as the core driver for investing. By IRS definition and requirement, PRIs must be made for the mission as its primary purpose. Key factors to look for when considering a PRI

    o Stage of the company – if the company is a very early stage startup, the risks are inherently much higher. The critical decision here is whether to do a grant or make a PRI. Should there be a high probability of loss, it may be more prudent to make the investment as a grant, see how the company develops, and explore a PRI later.

    o Does the organization have a viable business model to pay back the investment? Look at the quality of the revenue stream when analyzing the business model as discussed previously. For nonprofit entities, look at the split between revenue from fundraising for grants versus earned revenue. If a significant portion of the revenue comes from earned revenue, then the entity is much more viable for a PRI than one highly dependent on grant funding.

    o How does the company want to partner with your organization? A grant relationship is quite different than an investment partnership. Discussing with the organization's leadership to understand the uses of funds and how they view the partnership can help clarify which tool makes more sense. While one would expect a nonprofit entity to prefer grant funding since that is essentially "free" money they never have to repay, I have seen some nonprofit entities trying to jump on the impact investing bandwagon by asking for a PRI instead of a grant. At times this makes a lot of sense given their expansion of earned revenue or even the creation of a social venture subsidiary, but other times they simply wanted to appear innovative to their funders. They were attracted by the "cool" factor of the tool.

- ○ Are there more impact metrics reporting requirements that you expect the organization to provide? As previously mentioned, PRIs will require more impact metrics reporting (to demonstrate charitability) compared to MRIs. As such, does your organization have the infrastructure and desire to require and track the impact metrics reporting.

- ○ Monitoring – As you may recall from our earlier discussion, PRIs are structured as expenditure responsibility grants, so they will require more monitoring and reporting than traditional grants.

- ○ The amount of legal work necessary – PRIs will require more cumbersome legal documentation (e.g., your institution may require a Legal Opinion for all PRIs made), so is the cost of structuring the PRI worth the effort and expense. For example, if you made a $50K PRI and the legal fees amount to $15K for the deal (not to mention any other diligence costs), that is very high relative to the dollars invested (30%). It becomes more reasonable if the investment was a $500K PRI with the same $15K legal fees representing only 3% of the transaction value.

- ○ Preserving the corpus – Organizations with smaller endowments may want to protect their corpus, so structuring investments as PRIs may generate potential financial returns that can increase the pool of grant capital available in the future without draining the corpus.

- **Mission-related investments** – The investment is expected to drive a market-rate return (or close to market rate) that also considers mission alignment. The advantage of an MRI is the less stringent requirement on mission alignment than PRIs, although it adds an additional factor to consider: prudent investor rule guidelines. Some rules of thumb to consider for MRIs:

  ○ Stage and probability of loss – If the company has a robust business model and is already at a stage with potential for significant growth, then an MRI could be appropriate. Note that just because you have confidence in the company's success does not automatically qualify (nor require) it as an MRI investment; you can still make the investment as a PRI if the primary purpose is to drive the mission.

  ○ Mission alignment – Should there be any concerns that the investment would not qualify as a PRI in demonstrating mission alignment, then an MRI would be more appropriate, all other factors being equal in that the investment has high potential (market rate) returns.

  ○ Does it satisfy the Prudent Investor Rule – While PRIs must satisfy charitability requirements, MRIs must meet a different threshold to overcome on the financial return side. As a fiduciary, would you recommend this investment to someone looking for market-rate financial returns (regardless of mission alignment)?

  ○ Jeopardizing investment – Another bar that lawyers will have to justify the investment as an MRI revolves around the concept of a "jeopardizing investment," which in laymen's terms simply means the investment could put the whole organization at risk of existence. I know that sounds very drastic, but at the end of the day, that's precisely the intent of classifying investments as "jeopardizing." I don't believe meeting this hurdle is that difficult when the investment represents a small portion of the overall assets of the organization. As an example, when the W.K. Kellogg Foundation carved out $100 million for its Mission-Driven Investments program, even if it had put the whole $100 million into one investment as an MRI, that investment still would unlikely trigger the jeopardizing investment classification since the overall assets of the endowment totaled approximately $8 billion (the $100 million would be just 1.25% of the total endowment). Of course, it would not have been a prudent investment had they done so, but the point here is that the bar for the jeopardizing investment rule would not be difficult to comply with.

- ○ Would you make the investment without mission considerations? Due to the market-rate return expectations, the investment must be able to stand on its own without mission as a consideration that could be compared with other traditional investments. Some of you may disagree with this framing, but if you are taking investment dollars out of the corpus/endowment for an MRI opportunity, it would be logical to expect a substantially similar potential return as the corpus investments. The IRS has provided guidance that a slightly below market rate financial return for an MRI is acceptable when considering other factors (e.g., mission impact) in the totality of return expectations.

- ○ Co-investors – If the goal is to catalyze traditional investors to co-invest, structuring the investment as an MRI will be more comparable for such co-investors to participate in the investment. That is not to say a PRI will not crowd traditional investors; in fact, I've structured quite a few PRIs that brought traditional venture capital funds into the deal, but the PRI was also more likely to attract other impact-driven investors.

CHAPTER SEVEN: DEAL SOURCING

"Good investments are everywhere.
You just need to know where."

If you want to make an impact investment, where are you going to find the deals? Deal sourcing is a topic that has been challenging for many impact investors, especially those who are new to the field and just launching their impact investing program. Given the current market being flushed with capital, deals are even more competitive to find, so having a good deal sourcing process will be critical to the program's success.

There are no hard and fast rules to apply for deal sourcing, and your organization will need to try and see what works best given its unique situation. I'll provide some sources of deal flow from my own experience, but these do not mean they will work for you, and perhaps your organization may have other means that were not applicable from my own experience. So let's first start with the key factors that drive deal sourcing:

- Brand and reputation,
- Network,
- Niche or area of specialization,
- Track record, and
- Outreach

These factors are not ranked in any particular order. Brand and reputation refer to whether your organization or your impacting investing staff (especially the individual leading the program) has built a brand that the market knows about. A brand can be good or bad – if you have a good reputation in the market, others will want to come to you, and a bad one will steer potential investees away unless they are desperate and have no other investors interested. That is why managing your brand is so critical to the impact investing program's success.

Your network (supplemented by your consultant's network) also materially impacts your deal flow. People in your network will expand the reach of deal flow access, either because they are investing in similar deals and looking for co-investors or simply get shown investment opportunities that may not be a fit for them, so they will forward the opportunity to someone else, most likely the folks who they like. If I had to rank the factors for deal sourcing, the network would certainly be in the top three, if not the leading factor in deal sourcing.

What is your organization known for? Brand and reputation may seem redundant here, but the niche or domain expertise that your organization or impact investing strategy focuses on can be a more efficient driver of deal flow. Brand and reputation are much broader in how that is defined, whereas your specialization is something that narrowly helps separate you from other investors. For example, there are many investors in the education space today, some focusing on K-12, some focusing on postsecondary education, and others concentrating on workforce training. Then there are some investors focusing on all education-related investments. Add to that mix are education investors who focus on specific geography only. Understanding which area of specialization an investor focuses on helps the investor narrow their pipeline and the entrepreneur target who to reach out to. If you are an entrepreneur doing corporate training, you won't waste your time trying to get an education venture capital fund focused exclusively on investing in K-12. As you build your impact investing strategy, you will need to A) figure out if you want to be specialized and 2) if you are to specialize in a particular niche, what would that be? These are initial questions that lead to additional layers of questions, but they will help you differentiate yourself from other investors. The more specialized your strategy is, the fewer the investable pipeline will be, but it will also reduce the time wasted on opportunities that would not fit your strategy. If you don't have a specialization, it will be more challenging to differentiate yourself as an investor from other investors. Weighing the cost-benefit for where your investment strategy sits along that spectrum ultimately drives the brand and reputation you will build.

Your track record within your existing organization or predecessor firms will follow you. Just because you are launching a new impact investing strategy at your current firm does not mean you are starting from ground zero. People in your network will know what you've done before, and that track record can either help or hinder your success depending on whether the track record was positive or not so great. If you are starting with a strong track record already, it can help accelerate your brand and others' confidence in you, attracting deal flow. On the other hand, if you start with a track record that isn't as strong as your previous firm, you might need to explain how the new strategy differs from the prior one to essentially shift that last perception. Furthermore, being at a new firm with a refined strategy allows you to potentially invest in the high-performing companies from your previous firm that fit the new impact investing program's criteria while leveraging the lessons learned.

Lastly, but just as importantly, outreach is vital. Sitting behind your desk all day waiting for deals to come is like a fisherman waiting for a fish to jump into the boat—can it happen, yes, but will it happen? Highly unlikely. To find deals, you must reach out to build your brand. Let the market know your investment criteria and what differentiates you from other investors. That is critical in the early stages of building the impact investing strategy. The more you outreach do upfront, the less critical that will be later on as the market learns your investment strategy.

With those factors in mind on deal sourcing, I'll now describe the sources of deal flow that had led to some of the investments I've made. My own experience ranks these, but yours may differ if you employ the same sources. The important thing to remember is that deal sourcing will be most challenging in the early days of building the program but gets much easier once the strategy matures.

Network Referrals

By far, the best source of deals came from my network. I had the benefit of prior background on Wall Street, so my network from traditional finance combined with philanthropy provided a relatively broad network to leverage for deal flow. The key is to continue to develop and grow your network. The broader the network, the more deals you will see. The deeper the network, the more aligned deals you will see. To clarify, you may get sent lots and lots of deal flow from a broad network, but most will not fit your investment criteria. But if your network is deep in a particular niche or specialization that your organization focuses on, chances are good the deals will be more likely to be a better fit. For Lumina Foundation, being specialized in postsecondary learning and credentialing significantly narrowed the investment pipeline of opportunities, but any deals that fit the narrow scope will likely get referred to Lumina Impact Ventures (LIV), its impact investing arm. It became the go-to impact investing partner of choice for other investors in the education space who had a deal in the postsecondary education or workforce niche. Ideally, your network is both broad and deep.

Let's hone in on the network impact of deal sourcing. When I say network, these are the specific components:

- **Investors** – These could be impact investors, traditional investors, strategic investors, or even grant funders who may or may not co-invest with you.

- **Internal staff** – There are individuals directly in your impact investing team, but other staff members within your organization are also essential networks. If they understand your investment strategy and criteria, they can be a potential source of deal flow. The key is making sure they know your investment thesis and criteria. You may get bombarded by grant colleagues who don't understand what can be an investment that fits and what doesn't. So make sure you help educate and clarify to your colleagues exactly what would fit so they don't waste their time or yours in sending you the wrong types of opportunities.

- **Portfolio investees or grantees** – These entrepreneurs you've invested in are probably the best ambassadors for your program to other potential investees. They can be an invaluable advocate for your organization as an investor, sometimes helping to differentiate you from other investors. As an investee, they'll know you from the perspective that other potential investees will find very useful and relevant.

- **Stakeholder partners** – You may have collaboration opportunities with various stakeholders who can refer deals to you. These could be consultants that you work with or even brokers who are in the business of advising entrepreneurs on fundraising or mergers & acquisition. Associations like Mission Investors Exchange can also be a source of deal flow, given their network of members.

It's critical to ensure your network fully understands your investment strategy and criteria to provide better-aligned deal referrals. For example, if your approach focuses purely on investing in funds, then make it clear so that entrepreneurs are not reaching out to you for direct investments. Co-investor referrals tend to be the most likely source of deals that have a higher probability of aligning with your investment criteria, simply because the co-investor will know your strategy better than a referral source that isn't as informed.

One of the ways I have found useful in expanding my network is trying to be helpful whenever possible. As an example, for entrepreneurs who didn't fit my investment criteria, I'd forward them to the folks in my network that I thought was a better fit. The entrepreneur might find their investor through that referral, and the investor will be grateful for a deal they are excited about. That strengthens my relationship with both of them. Staying in touch and reaching out to your network regularly will ensure that you are not out of sight or out of mind. Outreach is such a critical part of relationship building and successful networking.

Conferences & Speaking Events

There are numerous conferences on impact investing (at least there were pre-Covid pandemic), and getting the opportunity to be highlighted as a speaker will help build your brand. Sometimes conferences have a pay-to-play model where funders sponsor a specific topic for a session and get to be a speaker for that session. Other times if you have specialized expertise that the conference focuses on, the organizers may want to bring you in as a speaker. At that point, you get the opportunity to provide a brief overview of your organization's impact investing strategy. The visibility from these conferences can accelerate the brand and reputation of your impact investing program. Furthermore, if the conference focuses on a niche that your impact investing strategy is focused on, there could be potential investees in the audience. I found a couple of my investees through that process.

Since you can't attend every conference, reach out to your network to get recommendations on the ones that make the most sense to participate in. You may rotate which ones to attend each year rather than the same ones every year. Some conferences are expensive, costing $3,000 to $4,000 for the conference ticket alone. When you add in hotel costs and airfare, it can get very pricey so if you do attend one, go with a very set objective and be strategic about how to spend your time. Some may release the attendee list in advance, so you may reach out to those individuals before the conference to schedule a meeting with them. Never do more than half an hour for an intro meeting. You can always do a follow-up call or meeting for a more detailed discussion if it's worthwhile. That allows more efficient use of time to work the conference to get the most bang for your buck, as they say. Divide and conquer if you have internal colleagues or your consultant with you attending the same conference; there is no need for both of you to hear the same pitches. You can always debrief after.

I remember the first time I attended one of the biggest education-focused conferences held by ASU – GSV with nearly 4,000 attendees where literally meetings were being scheduled for only 15 minutes each because I got bombarded by entrepreneurs before I got to the conference requesting meetings. It felt like a conveyor belt of entrepreneurs coming to my table that I had staked out at the coffee shop to make their pitch. Despite the conference being known for attracting big-name speakers like Bill Gates, I attended none of the conference sessions. While 15 minutes might seem like too short of a time to do an intro meeting, the reality is that you should be able to pick out enough critical details about the company to know whether you want to do a follow-up call or not.

Accelerators and Incubators

These early-stage funders/investors can often be good stakeholder partners for the deal flow pipeline. Major funders provide these accelerators with grant capital since A) they are programmatically aligned with a specific focus area of the funder, or B) they can develop a specific initiative for the funder. For example, Lumina Impact Ventures supported several accelerators with grant funding:

- Camelback Ventures – minority-led accelerator specializing in supporting entrepreneurs of color, whether nonprofit or social ventures
- LearnLaunch – an education-focused accelerator that also held an annual conference
- Village Capital – accelerator with various focus areas, including education as one of the verticals

In doing so, these accelerators may have entrepreneurs in their cohort that may be well-aligned with the criteria that LIV sought and would make the introduction to LIV. This is not to suggest that you need to fund an accelerator to get them to refer deals to your organization; accelerators are happy to help their entrepreneurs whenever they can. You just need to build a relationship with them so they know which entrepreneurs to connect to you. It would be mutually beneficial for all stakeholders.

Not all accelerators are the same, so if you do fund an accelerator, be strategic about which ones. From the LIV example, even though all three accelerators were in the education sector, they each had something unique. Funding all three accelerators broadens the potential pipeline of deal opportunities.

In addition to stakeholder partners that may be a source of deal flow because they focus on companies that are too early for your program, it's also important to have relationships with investors that focus on deals later than your strategy. For example, a venture capital fund that focuses on Series B investments may come across deals that are Series A or Series Seed rounds simply because they are in the market, so they may refer downstream to you. Just as an accelerator refers deals upstream to you, you may eventually refer deals upstream to the investor in the later stage. Having both sides of the funnel is an incredibly helpful value add to an entrepreneur since you are "capital staging" by supporting the investee with an off-ramp once they reach maturity outside your investment criteria.

Intake Forms

Another way to source deals may be through having an application link on your website. To make sure you don't get bombarded by entrepreneurs that don't fit your investment criteria, require enough information to be gathered with gating questions that automatically filter out deals that can't meet that hurdle. Unfortunately, the aggressive entrepreneurs will figure out how to answer the questions to get through the filter just to get their information submitted, but the majority of entrepreneurs know it wouldn't be a good use of their time to do that. Some examples of gating questions/criteria include:

- Type of investment sought (grant vs. investment capital, debt vs. equity)

- Size/amount of investment sought
- Revenue last year and projected
- Geographic focus
- Demographics served
- Asset class
- Sector focus

These are not exhaustive, and each organization will need to fine-tune the gating questions appropriate to their investment strategy. An intake form will never be the core driver of sourcing deals, but it allows unsolicited submissions from entrepreneurs who might not know how to reach you and your investment team. In essence, it helps to democratize access without bias.

Market Scans

Leveraging your consultants to do a market scan can also provide deal flow in theory. Depending on the consultants, this could be fruitful or a total waste of money and time. If your investment strategy is reasonably broad, the likelihood of finding a deal that fits through a market scan will be higher. However, if your investment strategy focuses on a particular specialization, unless the consultant already has deep expertise and a deep network of relationships in that same area, they are not likely to uncover deals that you would not already know about. That is especially true if you and your organization are already deeply networked in that sector. The consultants will need to get up to speed and leverage your network while they do their research. However, if you are not as deep in the sector already, then leveraging a consultant to support you in getting up to speed and understanding the landscape would then be much more helpful. But it should be a consultant already knowledgeable about the sector and well-networked within it.

If you have subscriptions to research databases such as Pitchbook, Crunchbase, Capital IQ, or Bloomberg, they can usually set up customized screens for investment opportunities that fit your criteria with automated updates on financing rounds that can serve as an efficient mechanism for knowing about opportunities. They may even send out sector-specific newsletters that you can subscribe to for free by getting on their distribution list. Unless you are a large organization without the financial constraints that most organizations operate under, each of these proprietary resources is quite expensive to subscribe to, as discussed in a previous chapter. If you are doing less than five deals a year, it may not be a good return on investment, so leveraging consultants who have access to such databases where they can spread the cost across their various clients would be a better option.

Tracking & CRM

To close out this chapter, one of the most important things to do in deal sourcing is keeping track of all the deals that come through your pipeline, both the deals you decide to invest in and the ones you passed on. You don't need some fancy customer relationship management (CRM) system to do this; a simple excel spreadsheet will do. Of course, if you already have some fancy CRM system in place, then certainly make use of it, but I wouldn't spend much time or money trying to build some sophisticated CRM infrastructure for this. Things to track in particular which will be incredibly useful long-term:

- When did the deal come in
- Source of deal flow (who referred it) or was it an unsolicited inbound
- Stage of company and type of capital sought
- Amount of raise
- Sector and Geography
- Revenue (last twelve months actual and recurring)
- Comments/Notes about the company
- Invested or pass (if passed, note the reason in the comments)

That should provide just about enough information for you to analyze over time. As more and more deals get tracked, you'll be able to gather insights on your screening to deal closing (conversion) ratio. You'll see where your primary source of deal flow comes from, and for the deals that were passed, you can revisit those a year later if the reason for passing before was due to the stage being too early. That allows you to reach out, assuming most early-stage entrepreneurs raise a financing round every 18 to 24 months.

The hardest part about having this tracking sheet is keeping it up to date. The list of key information noted is just enough details that will be useful later but not so onerous that keeping up the tracking will be too time-consuming and will get left by the wayside. I've certainly made that mistake of wanting to track so many granular factors about a deal that the tedious effort to keep it up to date became too much work that the tracking sheet kept falling behind further and further until it was just not worth keeping up with. So for those who like to track lots of details about a deal, just know that you have to be honest with yourself on what you really need and will keep up to date versus all the information you would like to track. Of course, you could assign your consultants to track the pipeline for you, but that doesn't always work out so well either, as I've learned from my consultants, who ended up asking me for all the details of the deals to fill out the tracking sheet.

CHAPTER EIGHT: CHOOSING AN OUTSOURCED PARTNER OR CONSULTANT

"If you try to do everything, you may achieve nothing."

If your organization decides to hire a consulting firm, finding the right one can really accelerate your program development. At the same time, the wrong one can also set you back significantly if the program's credibility is hurt by poor advice. When I entered the impact investing sector, there was barely any impact investing advisors available, given how new the field was. Today, many hang up their shingles as impact investing advisors, so how do you pick the right one?

Choosing the Right Consultant

Some pointers to keep in mind when selecting a consulting firm:

1. Is the need a one-off project, or will this be a stepping-stone to developing a longer-term relationship and partnership? If it's a one-off project, then the needed expertise for that project is all you focus on. In contrast, a long-term partnership will require forecasting future needs beyond the project and whether the consulting firm brings such expertise. Balancing near-term needs with the potential evolution of the impact investing program needs may not be feasible, but something to keep in mind, if at all possible.

2. The expertise and track record of the consulting firm should be at the top of the list for vetting potential advisors. Every consultant will present themselves in the best light as to be expected when pitching for business; sadly, some present themselves to be more capable than what they can actually deliver. So how do you shift through the pitch to find the substance? First, look at what the consultants have done—their track record should speak for themselves. Do they have real expertise in the areas that

your organization is seeking support on? Don't be afraid to ask tough questions bluntly, and ensure you are comfortable with the responses. If the consulting firm is relatively new, does that mean they lack expertise? That is not necessarily true if you look at the backgrounds of the principals at the firm and their resumes. Or on the opposite end, if the consulting firm has been around a long time, does that mean they are highly qualified? I'm aware of one well-established consulting firm everyone seems to pick because of its longevity. Still, when it comes to expertise, the firm is much better to partner for fiscal sponsorships rather than having depth in impact investing expertise. Organizations want to pick the "safe" bet (like going with an IBM for technology needs, even if it might not be the best option for a specific role) since it's a lower risk when things don't work out. I don't blame anyone for doing so but understand that picking a firm on that basis may not be optimal for the objectives of your program. These superficial filters are reasons why some organizations often select the wrong advisory firm, sometimes without even knowing it. Some key questions to ask when interviewing potential consulting firms:

a. What would the firm consider its strengths and core competencies?

b. What relevant experience does the firm have for the type of need we are looking to fill? Provide specific examples and your role in those examples?

c. Who will be dedicated to servicing the project? What are their capacity and workload? Please share their resumes.

d. What are the types of clients that the firm likes to work with? What engagements are "typical," and what would be out of their comfort zone?

e. Has the firm failed to deliver on a project, and why?

f. Can they provide sample work products they've done for other clients?

3. Do quick background checks and get references before hiring the consulting firm. That is a critical step that some organizations skip, but it is probably the easiest way to ensure alignment of what the consultants pitched with what they delivered or can

deliver. You might be surprised by what can come up when you do a simple Google search of "lawsuit" and the firm name. That's not to say you immediately drop the firm if something comes up that might be concerning. You just need to dig into it and ask the firm to clarify or elaborate if something concerning does come up from the quick search. Every consulting firm will likely be able to give you their list of three to five references who absolutely will provide them with glowing reviews. Of course, those references wouldn't be willing to be referenced if they were going to be negative, so I take those references with a grain of salt.

What is more valuable are the unsolicited references. This takes a little more digging, but the effort and time invested can shed a lot of light on the consultant and verify the information presented. One example of an unsolicited reference check is to find a client that the consultant didn't offer and reach out to that client with the caveat that you have to be transparent about why you are reaching out to them. Another reference might be a company that had been due diligent for an investment by the consulting firm; ask that investee how they felt about the process, how thorough the diligence was, and how that compares to other investors. Yet another reference check could simply be finding mutual contacts on LinkedIn who you can reach out to that might have additional information about the specific individuals that would be servicing the project from the consulting firm.

4. Cultural fit is another critical factor when vetting the consulting firm. At the end of the day, will you feel comfortable working with the firm? Is the firm's style and culture a good fit for your team and organization? Some consulting firms are very talkative and like to think conceptually; others will dig deep into details and just get work done. Some consultants are less direct about their feedback and put a positive spin on things; others just tell you the facts and might not offer emotional support. At the end of the day, do you feel comfortable with the firm, and can you trust there is strong alignment in what your organization is trying to achieve with what the consulting firm can deliver? Does the consulting firm give you confidence as a partner that you can rely on? For one-time projects, this is less critical, but if you

expect to partner with the firm, you might as well make sure it's a firm that you enjoy working with, can trust to have your best interest at heart, and have the expertise to deliver on time and budget. Just like marriages don't always work out, sometimes the consulting firms don't work out, and it's okay to change; doing your homework upfront on the firm will mitigate the risk of that happening.

5. Not surprisingly, the cost of the contract proposal should always be a factor, but it needs to be evaluated appropriately, both on an absolute and relative level. Some consultants bill on an hourly rate and provide an estimate of what they anticipate the total hours for the project to take that would ultimately give you the overall project budget. Other consultants bill purely by deliverables rather than an hourly rate, although there might be some implied comparable hourly rates. It's effortless to look at the budget proposed by each consultant and just pick the one that seems to be the cheapest, but the old saying that you get what you pay for holds true here. As mentioned previously, for consultants that bill by hourly rates and have a proposed budget for the total anticipated, it would behoove your organization to ask how often projects have gone as expected in terms of time and budget. Sometimes a consultant might provide a low-ball proposal just to win the project, but the actual cost and time will be more evident when it comes to execution. One way to avoid that is to ask for a guarantee from the consultant that their proposed budget is realistic and specify details of how invoicing is done. That is why a retainer or deliverables-based proposal is preferable since the consultant can spend a lot more hours than anticipated, but the project cost will not be impacted. Both parties' interests are aligned since the consultant would want to be as efficient at delivering as they can be. When comparing proposals and their costs, here are a few things to keep in mind:

   a. Just because the billing rate is high does not mean the proposal is more expensive. For example, suppose a consultant has a high billing rate but has deep experience in the areas your organization is looking for advisory on. In that case, they may be much more efficient as being lower total cost compared to a consultant that may need time to get up to speed. Furthermore, their higher fees and deeper experience may also reduce the potential risk of errors or bad advice that won't need to be addressed in the future.

b. Always negotiate. You might be surprised to find that a consultant may provide a discount if your organization is a nonprofit. Or perhaps if the intention is to use the first project as a "test" run, but there is potential for a longer-term partnership, the consulting firm may also offer a discount.

c. How many staff members from the consulting firm will be dedicated to the project? Suppose there is only one individual who will service your organization at one firm with a very high billing rate, but another consulting firm may dedicate two individuals, each with lower billing rates that, when combined, is higher than the single individual of the other firm. In that case, it's important to compare total billing rates, not individual ones.

d. If consultants bill by hourly rate, ask for the total proposed budget for the project anticipated and a guarantee that costs would not exceed that amount.

e. Confirm availability and capacity, a consultant might be well-qualified, but their capacity and availability may not align with your organization's needs.

Having the right consulting firm as a partner allows your organization to leverage them in a way that functions as an extension of your team. It should be relatively seamless working with the consulting firm; they should be mission-aligned and, just as importantly, reliable and fun to work with. To close out this chapter, Figure 17 summarizes the core factors when selecting an outsourced consulting firm. As shown, the ideal advisory firm should be at the intersection of mission, knowledge, network, and experience.

Figure 17: Factors for Selecting Outsourced Advisory Firm (Kind Capital, 2022)

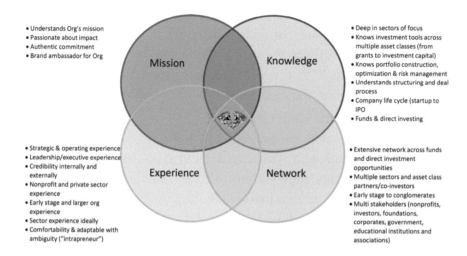

- Understands Org's mission
- Passionate about impact
- Authentic commitment
- Brand ambassador for Org

Mission

Knowledge

- Deep in sectors of focus
- Knows investment tools across multiple asset classes (from grants to investment capital)
- Knows portfolio construction, optimization & risk management
- Understands structuring and deal process
- Company life cycle (startup to IPO
- Funds & direct investing

- Strategic & operating experience
- Leadership/executive experience
- Credibility internally and externally
- Nonprofit and private sector experience
- Early stage and larger org experience
- Sector experience ideally
- Comfortability & adaptable with ambiguity ("intrapreneur")

Experience

Network

- Extensive network across funds and direct investment opportunities
- Multiple sectors and asset class partners/co-investors
- Early stage to conglomerates
- Multi stakeholders (nonprofits, investors, foundations, corporates, government, educational institutions and associations)

However, it may be aspirational rather than realistic to find a consulting firm that fits at the intersection of all these core factors. Knowing what might be weighted higher in the priority given your organization's resources and existing capabilities can help determine which elements may be less critical.

How to Work With your Consultant

As noted previously, the right consulting firm you partner with should feel like an extension of your team. The primary difference is that hiring or firing them for performance will be much easier. You may even become good friends with key individuals at the consulting firm, not much different from your teammates internally.

- **Set expectations** – To get the most out of your outsourced partner, make sure to set clear expectations for deliverables. Document specific needs and deliverables in the contract. Doing so helps avoid misunderstandings and miscommunications that could lead to awkward conversations later. If the quality of the product does not meet your standards, be honest with the consultant so that it can be addressed. At the end of the day, their products are reflections of you and your team when they get utilized, and you are paying the firm to deliver a quality product. These tough conversations are essential to have early so that adjustments can be made; just as you would have an internal staff member put on a performance improvement plan, you may need to do the same with your consulting firm. Sometimes consulting firms get too comfortable with a client they have had for a while and spend the extra effort on new clients rather than maintaining quality for existing ones; that is simply not acceptable when you are paying them to deliver. You may even want to put together a simple performance evaluation for the consulting firm at the end of each year.

- **Review and adjust the contract annually** – Even if you are partnering with a consulting firm for the long term, best practice requires reviewing the terms of the agreement annually and adjusting the fee if appropriate. Have an open and honest conversation with the consultant about their fees and expected work for the year. For example, you may need to increase the contract size if more work is expected (your team expects to do twice the number of deals from now on compared to the prior year). Or you'll need additional areas of support that were not part of the initial contract. On the other hand, if your organization decides to put a hold on deals in the future, the consulting firm should be more than willing to reduce its contract fees. The key is to ensure that both parties feel the costs and expectations for the amount of work needed are fair. If the consultant does not feel like they are fairly compensated, the quality of their work may suffer, or their prioritization of your firm may be lowered relative to their other clients.

- **Leverage the consultants for their expertise** – This should be obvious but doesn't always happen. If the consulting firm does not have experience with a particular need of your organization, find another one that does. You may feel like you might hurt the feelings of your existing consultant, but frankly, that is irrelevant, and if they were genuinely aligned as partners, they would understand. Good consultants know what they are good at and will be honest with you about what they do not have expertise in.

- **Don't use the consulting firm for high-level internal discussions unless you have a fully outsourced model** – There are reasons for when you'd want your consulting firm to present and lead discussions internally, but it comes at a cost. For example, let's assume the due diligence on an investment is completely outsourced, and your impact investments team internally is only peripherally involved. In such a scenario, the consulting firm should present the deal to the investment committee for discussion. Still, the internal staff should provide context and recommendations for why the investment is recommended. The internal impact investing staff needs always to be front-facing since, ultimately, your team will be responsible, even if you were not actively involved in the diligence. Over-reliance on the consulting firm for internal discussions will also lower the confidence the leadership team and the board will have in your internal team. An excellent consulting partner will do their best to make you and your team look great internally and externally. Their job is to make you look good rather than their firm. If that is not the case, it may require revisiting who you want to have as your consulting firm.

- **Thought partners and bouncing ideas** – The consulting firm should be a trusted partner from whom you can ask questions and seek advice without fear of being judged. They are paid experts who can provide honest feedback to help your team and your organization. If they don't have the answer, they might know someone in their network who does. Doing practice runs for important meetings or presentations can also be helpful, such as a board or senior executive update meeting. That can also be helpful to the consulting firm who may participate in those meetings, but their participation should be kept to a minimum, as noted in the last point. Sometimes even in meetings where the consulting firm is not asked to be actively engaged, I have found it helpful for them to listen in so that they can provide feedback and constructive advice from what they had observed.

- **Schedule regular check-ins** – While this is pretty obvious, some organizations don't do it; either they don't believe it's a good use of time and should only be scheduled as needed, or they don't want to incur the hourly bill. However, suppose the consultant is unaware of what is happening at your organization. In that case, they can't be helpful, so the check-in allows you to update them on the priorities and status of specific focus areas. In addition, this regular cadence sets a disciplined progress check that will enable you to stay on top of mind for the consultant so that you remain a priority – as the saying goes, out of sight out of mind.

- **They are not therapists** – This may sound odd, but some clients get so attached to their consultants that they let it cross some boundaries of professionalism. Of course, bouncing ideas and getting feedback are expected and encouraged with your consulting firm. Still, calling them repeatedly to vent because something did not go well personally or professionally unrelated to your engagement with them is awkward. It makes it difficult for the consulting firm. It's not that different from romantic relationships in the workplace; if the relationship doesn't work out, things get very awkward. The same goes for your consultant should you decide to terminate the contract.

- **Ask for constructive feedback** – Some consultants are afraid of giving feedback to their clients even though, as an outsider, they are in the best position to provide you and your team with constructive feedback. Furthermore, their feedback has no bearing on your internal performance review. Therefore, always encourage your consultants to be honest and provide you with feedback; this is incredibly useful for professional development for you and your team. Naturally, the consultant will give positive feedback but really push them to get their input for areas for improvement.

- **Use them in negotiations but don't let them lead the negotiations** – Some individuals are not as confident with negotiations and want to rely on their consultants to drive the deal terms. That is appropriate if the consultant working on the deal is highly skilled in negotiations and truly understands your organization's priorities and deal breakers. However, there are disadvantages when the consultants drive the negotiations. Firstly, it's rare the consultant would know your team's priorities better than you and often have to defer to you for guidance. For the consultant to do so during a negotiation slows down the process and may also lose the confidence of the other party who feels they are not negotiating directly with you. Secondly, being directly involved with the negotiations allows you to understand how the other party thinks, reacts, and their operating style before the deal closes; that direct insight may be invaluable as to whether they will be a good partner to work with as an investee. If you must use a consultant to lead your negotiations, here are a few pointers to keep in mind:

- Always participate in the negotiations even if you are not driving the process

- Prepare in advance the key terms that are considered deal killers that you must get or you will walk versus the terms that are "nice-to-have" but willing to compromise on; walk through those in advance with your consultant so they know which levers to push during the negotiations

- Prioritize and discuss what terms you are willing to compromise on with the consultant

- Set the context at the beginning of the discussion that your consultants will drive the negotiation so that the other party understands who is driving it.

- If you feel the consultant has not negotiated a term the way you expected, jump in and clarify at the point of discussion, don't wait. That will mitigate the perception that you are changing the terms if you come back later to explain.

- Strategically prepare to jump in on key points when prompted by your consultant (this is something that can be prepped).

Lastly, don't hesitate to use your consultants as the "bad cop" in negotiations if that is helpful to the process. That allows you and your team to be the good guys as the investors, and therefore, even if the other party dislikes the consultant, you are starting off on good terms with the entrepreneur once the deal closes.

CHAPTER NINE: PORTFOLIO MANAGEMENT

"There are no bad investments, just bad investors."

Once you start making investments, the next critical step will be how to build out the portfolio. What you choose as your first investment will have implications on how your portfolio needs to be built out. Before we begin, I want to clarify that this chapter is NOT about the portfolio construction strategy a traditional investor would execute for their endowment. Many books exist on portfolio theory and asset allocation that can get much more technical on optimizing financial return and risk mitigation. Instead, this chapter should provide some concepts of how you should build your impact investing strategy. Some of the suggestions might be counter to a traditional portfolio approach, and that is intentional. The impact investing portfolio is not meant to be traditional.

The first investment sets the tone. Some consultants and practitioners may recommend you just need to learn by doing, so just jump right in and make that first investment. While that may be true for some organizations, understanding the importance of the first investment will shape how you think about your subsequent investments. To be clear, I am not suggesting the theory of jumping in and learning by doing is flawed. I'm merely reinforcing the point that there are ramifications for doing so, as I will explain shortly.

The Impact Investing Policy Statement, as we had discussed previously, guides the overall investment strategy. Portfolio construction is the application of that policy. Therefore, an investment criteria document that has been well defined will ensure compliance with the IIPS. As a reminder, here are some factors to include for the investment criteria that may be included as part of the IIPS or simply as a separate document:

- Asset class – Which asset class can your organization invest in? Debt? Equity? Mezzanine? Is there a preferred asset class even if you can invest across the full spectrum of capital? In other words, just because you can does not mean you will necessarily do so. In practicality, you may focus on just debt or just equity investments.

- Direct or fund investments – Will you invest only directly? In funds only? Both?

Stage of investments – What stage of investments will you focus on? Startups? Growth? Venture?

- Average check size – How much will you invest per company? What are the minimum and maximum check sizes? Do you make follow on investments?

- Active or passive investor – Will you take a board role with the entrepreneur?

- Geographic focus – Are there specific geographies you target? Regional? National? Global?

- Sector – Which sector(s) do you invest in?

- Lead or Co-invest – Can your organization lead financing rounds, or do you only follow as co-investors? Is there a preference for either, if you can do both?

- Reporting requirements – Do you require impact metrics reporting? If so, how frequent?

- Priority – Are investments driven by impact/mission-first? Financial returns? Or are both equally important considerations?

By having these factors clearly defined, effectively focusing on the right opportunities will be much easier to execute. You could literally create your intake form with some of these factors as the gating criteria when an entrepreneur submits their information for considering an investment.

Diversification

In traditional finance, the concept of diversification is core to portfolio construction to mitigate risk. However, diversification is unlikely to be feasible or practical for an impact investment portfolio, especially a newly established program. The opportunity set of investments for traditional portfolios is very large, and selecting the components to build a diverse portfolio is achievable and desirable. Again, the objective is to meet return targets while mitigating risk. Diversification across asset classes, geography, duration, and riskiness are among many aspects that a traditional portfolio manager will focus on, and they'll have numerous options in terms of investment instruments available to fit a specific purpose within the portfolio. Imagine you have a gigantic box of Lego pieces (the investment products), so you essentially can build whatever structure you want (the portfolio).

Now in the case of an impact investment portfolio, that box of Lego pieces becomes significantly smaller, so what you can build from the available pieces becomes substantially more limited. There lies the challenge of trying to construct a diversified portfolio for impact investing; the number of Lego pieces is growing, but it's nowhere near those available in the traditional markets. New products are coming to market that will help, but currently available products are insufficient for building a truly diversified portfolio.

Even if there are ways to achieve diversification similar to that of a traditional portfolio, it begs the question of whether that should be an objective of an impact investing portfolio. If the goal for the portfolio is to drive impact, regardless of where along the spectrum of financial return the target for the portfolio is, diversification would not appear to be well-aligned with that objective. Perhaps diversification focused on nonfinancial goals would make more sense. The idea of diversification along the lines of impact needs further analysis, but here is one approach I've implemented in my prior roles in the education sector:

- Short-term impact – These tend to be low-cost, high-volume impacts driven by the investment. An example of this would be increasing the number of low-income students getting access to tutoring resources in community colleges.

- Long-term impact – These are much more challenging to achieve and require more investment. An example would be increasing the graduation rates of low-income students. Because achieving these types of impacts takes longer, the volume/quantity will be lower than short-term impacts.

- Nonquantifiable impact – Sometimes, there are no quantifiable measures to capture the investment impact even though the anecdotal evidence is there that connects the investments made to the outcomes achieved. Policy changes and systems changes are examples of such impact.

Building out an impact investment portfolio, it makes more sense to diversify across these different types of impact. Clearly, a traditional portfolio would not be concerned with this diversification aspect.

Another aspect of diversification to consider could be programmatic focus areas. This would only apply to organizations with more than one programmatic area. For example, if your organization is focused on saving sea turtles in Costa Rica, I'm afraid that probably doesn't allow for much flexibility. But if your programmatic focus is broader, such as in sectors like healthcare or education, there are multiple aspects within each to be able to diversify. In the case of education, as an example, there are K-12, postsecondary and workforce subcategories. Within healthcare, there are pharmaceuticals, biotech, healthcare services, and healthcare IT as just some examples.

Lastly, diversification can also focus on the stage of investments to balance risk. For example, your portfolio may include some later-stage investments that are more mature in their business model evolution. At the same time, you also include some earlier startups that may be at higher risk but could be more innovative and have higher return potential. Similarly, the balance between direct investments and fund investments may be another approach to diversification when it comes to balancing risk.

The key takeaway from this section is how your impact investing program should think about diversification will be materially different from how a traditional portfolio will think about diversification due to the current limitations of investable opportunities within the space. That may and likely will change as more impact products come to market in the future, with the sector continuing to grow. Until then, the idea of diversification, in the traditional sense, should be a lower priority when building out your impact investing strategy relative to other objectives.

Target Return

Earlier I mentioned that your first investment would impact the buildout of your impact portfolio. This can be attributed to the expected return for that initial investment, the stage of the investment, and where along the impact spectrum that initial investment fits. Additional investment will therefore need to consider the first investment's characteristics and how that impacts the buildout for the rest of the portfolio.

Suppose there is a target rate of return for the portfolio, which inevitably there should be once your IIPS is finalized. In that case, the portfolio construction needs to mathematically achieve that target portfolio return when weighting each investment with their probability of expected return in the time frame for that target return. The table in Figure 18 provides a sample of a $3 million impact investment portfolio targeting a 10% return. The sample investments span the full spectrum of low-risk assets (the bank deposit with the lowest return potential but highest probability) to highest-risk investments (the direct investment into an early-stage company with the highest potential return but lowest probability). The expected return is effectively what the asset class projects for the return. Debt instruments like a bank deposit or a loan are the easiest since they pay a specific interest rate, but equity investments, be it a fund or a direct investment, will be much less precise. For example, an equity fund may target an IRR of 20% but how likely that will be achieved is not certain. As an investor, you will need to weigh the probability of that investee being able to achieve the target return they projected. In Figure 18, you can see that the projected returns were discounted for both funds to be only 80% probability they will achieve their target return. The direct investments were discounted even more. How much to discount each investment will be based on your experience and track record for the asset class and the specific investee rather than applying some rule of thumb.

Figure 18: Probability Weighted Portfolio Return

Portfolio Target Return   10%

Investment	Amount Invested	Expected Return	Portfolio Weighted Return	Probability of Return	Probability Weighted Return
Bank Deposit	$500,000	1.0%	0.2%	100.0%	0.2%
Debt Impact Fund	$750,000	6.0%	1.5%	80.0%	1.2%
Equity Impact Fund	$1,000,000	20.0%	6.7%	80.0%	5.3%
Direct Investment Company 1	$250,000	30.0%	2.5%	40.0%	1.0%
Direct Investment Company 2	$500,000	30.0%	5.0%	50.0%	2.5%
Total Portfolio	**$3,000,000**		15.8%		10.2%

While the sample portfolio in Figure 18 shows a target return of 10%, it would be better to have a target range rather than an exact return threshold. For example, instead of 10%, the portfolio target return should be in the range of between 7 to 10% in the IIPS. That gives your organization some flexibility. For example, imagine if the portfolio achieved a 9.8% return; instead of celebrating that you're on the higher end of the return target range of 7 to 10%, you may end up trying to defend why your portfolio did not hit its return target!

What is your target portfolio return? I get this question asked numerous times, and most impact investors I've spoken with who get asked the same question try to pivot and avoid answering it or claim there is no target return for their strategy. That strikes me as rather odd when you are making investments because every "investment" will have some return component by definition unless you apply the investment term to include grants, which would be inappropriate, in my humble opinion. Grants have no financial return expectations, so unless your entire portfolio consists of grants, there will be some return expectations for the non-grant deployment of capital. Perhaps the portfolio returns are not achieving the target return, and those individuals are embarrassed by that, but frankly, even if that scenario is true, there shouldn't be any embarrassment. Investing is not easy, and not every investment pans out; learning is key. There is much value in taking the lessons learned from investments that didn't pan out. Perhaps the target portfolio return was set too high to begin with and unrealistic, which may be the real reason for why the target return was not achieved.

Given that context, what should your target portfolio return be? Every organization will have factors driving what they want their impact portfolio return to be, but I think there are a few drivers to keep in mind to guide how to set the return expectations. Let's start by looking at how a private foundation's core traditional portfolio (the endowment) thinks about its target return. To sustain its endowment into perpetuity, the foundation endowment needs to achieve a minimum threshold of return driven by several factors:

- Annual payout requirements (average 5%),
- Operating expenses (average 1-2% so we'll assume 1.5%)
- Inflation (average 2%)

Based on the components noted, to achieve a rate of return to allow an endowment to continue in perpetuity (no decrease in assets under management), the minimum target portfolio return for a traditional portfolio is calculated:

Minimum Endowment Return = Payout Required + Op Exp + Inflation

= 5% + 1.5% + 2%

= 8.5%

Note that the 8.5% is the minimum return for an endowment, not necessarily the target return. That number may vary a bit depending on the circumstances of the private foundation. For example, the 5% payout requirement is fixed, but some foundations may pay out a higher amount. Secondly, assumptions for inflation may be higher or lower depending on the CIO's perspective, and the endowment's operating expenses may also vary based on how efficiently the organization operates. The point of this is simply to give you a context of a reference point for setting the impact investment portfolio target return when you understand how the traditional portfolio thinks about its target portfolio return.

If we assume that 8.5% is the target return for your organization's traditional portfolio, given that your impact portfolio has an additional bottom line, then logically, the financial return should be lower for the impact portfolio. Furthermore, the impact investment portfolio does not have a payout requirement, so the target financial return may be materially lower if you strip out the 5% payout requirement leaving 3.5% as the target portfolio return. Adding further that your investment universe will be much more limited than a traditional portfolio, which can also justify a target portfolio return should be lower for the impact investing portfolio. One large foundation had set 4 to 6% as its target portfolio return for its impact investing portfolio. That may seem low for some finance professionals, but when you take into account the factors noted previously, it becomes much more reasonable in that context.

CHAPTER TEN: PERFORMANCE EVALUATION

"Every fool thinks their performance was good without knowing what good is."

Core to any impact investing strategy is the need to measure performance. Performance on both dimensions of financial return and impact need to be considered. This chapter will provide an overview of both and the framework for social metrics. More specifically, we will discuss:

- Financial return
- Impact return – social metrics and measuring impact
- Learning return
- Total return framework

In the last chapter, we've already discussed financial return targets for an impact investing portfolio, so we'll mainly focus on the impact metrics.

Financial Return

In the last chapter, we discussed the framework for setting the target portfolio return range for an impact investing portfolio. Financial return from a purely technical standpoint in traditional finance is well defined, and we won't dwell on this. However, how to think about financial returns based on the type of asset class is briefly covered below:

- Private investments – Recall from chapter IV the discussion on internal rate of return (IRR) and multiple on invested capital (MOIC) as the two main metrics when evaluating financial returns on an investment in private equity or venture capital.

- Public market returns are even easier since you can literally just compute the change in stock price performance over some period, including the stream of dividends if any.

- Debt returns – Debt returns can be a little more complicated. Conceptually when you provide a loan at some interest rate, the return on the investment is simply the repayment of the principal plus the interest earned. In normal circumstances, the loan is repaid fully, and all interest would be paid when due. That is really simple, but when you get into public bonds and more advanced structures such as callable or puttable features built into them, the interest earned may not be what was expected. The bond's price may be higher or lower than when it was issued (par value). Getting into the technically complicated bond math discussion is beyond the scope of this book. But suffice it to say, debt return essentially comprises the return of principal, and total interest received upon the exit of the investment, whether a loan is repaid or a public bond is sold.

- Convertible notes – These hybrid securities have debt and equity components, so the financial returns are much more variable. As a result, they are less risky than a typical equity investment but also have a higher return potential than a regular debt investment, given their convertibility into equity.
  - Unconverted – If the convertible note never gets converted because conditions do not justify the conversion, the return is no different than a typical debt investment where the principal and accrued interest are fully repaid.
  - Converted – When the convertible bond is converted to equity, the return becomes an equity return because the fixed income instrument is now an equity investment. What you paid for the equity (accountants refer to this as the "basis" or cost of the investment) is simply the implied per share cost of the stock when the total value of the bond and accrued interest are converted based on some conversion ratio in the structure of the bond. Your return is then simply the price you sold the shares for minus the price of your basis.

There are plenty of books discussing financial return calculations and getting deep into the various technical calculations, especially for securities with exotic features like callability, if you want to geek out on those topics. For our purposes, we simply need to know the basic concepts of how to think about financial returns for different types of instruments, so we'll leave it there.

Impact Return – Social Metrics and Measuring Impact

The core reason we do impact investing is to have a positive impact through the various investments we make. As you may recall in earlier chapters, the spectrum of impact varies among investors. Where your organization fits along that spectrum will ultimately drive the level of risk tolerance and investment opportunities available. Let's start by reviewing some of the more common frameworks and tools in the market today.

- **IRIS** – Created by the Global Impact Investment Network (GIIN) and launched in 2013, the Impact Reporting and Investment Standards (IRIS) has gone through many interactions over the years, with the most recent release in 2019 of IRIS+ (https://iris.thegiin.org/). IRIS is a crowdsourced catalog of impact metrics taxonomy. Standardizing taxonomy for impact metrics helps to ensure comparability of how each organization thinks about impact.

- **United Nations Sustainable Development Goals (SDGs)** – After the conclusion of the 15-year anti-poverty Millennium Development Goals in 2015, the United Nations launched on January 1, 2016, the Sustainable Development Goals to drive its next 15-year mission the 2030 Agenda. This more comprehensive framework considers broader impact areas with 17 Goals, as shown in Figure 19.

Figure 19: UN Sustainable Development Goals (United Nations, 2015)

The SDGs provide a very high-level set of impact themes or priorities but do not get to a level of granularity that some investors perceive to be more necessary to avoid impact washing. As a result, it would be easier for corporations to claim impact by aligning with the SDG than to comply with more granular and rigorous frameworks.

- **Operating Principles for Impact Management** – Launched in 2019 by International Finance Corporation's (IFC), these 9 Impact Principles provide a framework for investment managers to set up their impact measurement systems and implementation that will ensure impact considerations are integrated throughout the investment life cycle. (IFC, 2019) The critical component of this framework is the need for independent verification, unlike other purely self-reported frameworks. These nine principles are summarized in Figure 20.

Figure 20: IFC Operating Principles for Impact Management (IFC, 2019)

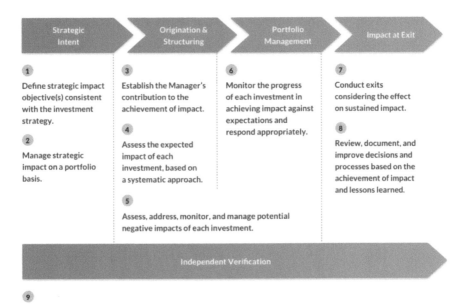

Over 150 investment manager signatories have signed on to comply with these nine principles. While still early, it could provide a mechanism to mitigate impact washing by fund managers.

- **The Impact Management Project (IMP)** – Incubated by Bridges Insights and launched in 2015 among a consortium of investment managers, the IMP has gained traction as the framework for investors to take into account their impact. With over 2,000 organizations globally in its community, it reached a consensus that impact can be measured across five dimensions, as summarized in Figure 21.

Figure 21: IMP Five Dimensions of Impact (Impact Management Project, 2022)

The IMP reached global consensus that impact can be measured across five dimensions: What, Who, How Much, Contribution and Risk	
Impact Dimension	**Impact questions each dimension seeks to answer**
What	• What outcome is occurring in the period? • Is the outcome positive or negative? • How important is the outcome to the people or the planet experiencing them?
Who	• Who experiences the outcome? • How underserved are the affected stakeholders in relation to the outcome?
How Much	• How much of the outcome is occurring - across scale, depth and duration?
Contribution	• Would this change likely have happened anyway?
Risk	• What is the risk to people and planet that impact does not occur as expected?

While these five dimensions may appear simplistic, the overarching intent of each dimension provides guidance on how to approach your organization's impact. Starting with this template will allow thoughtful strategic prioritization of the impact objectives of your impact investing program, which can then guide the more profound tactical components of the actual measurement of impact.

One key observation of these five frameworks is that they may be complementary, but each is not mutually exclusive. For example, a fund manager may be a signatory for the Operating Principles of Impact Management and, as a result, may apply the IMP framework and the IRIS taxonomy to comply as a signatory. Another observation is that currently, there does not seem to be a clear mechanism for benchmarking. How do we know one fund manager is more impactful than the other? Even though the Operating Principles signatory requires third-party verification, there is not necessarily a requirement that the third-party verifier will be standardized in their assessment. All that is to say, there is still a long way to go in the impact measurement space as it continues to evolve to meet the needs of the impact investing sector.

Now that you have a sense of the different frameworks that exist, I'll explain the framework of what to measure that Kind Capital uses, which was developed at the W.K. Kellogg Foundation during my time there. First, impact needs to be measured across both quantitative and qualitative factors. When we look at the quantitative impact, that can be categorized further into short-term and long-term effects. These measurable metrics allow for calculating the dollars invested to achieve the result and potential comparability within specific categories. For demonstration, Figure 22 shows how Lumina Impact Ventures applied the framework with education metrics.

Figure 22: Lumina Social Metrics Framework

Metric	Impact Type	Sample Metric
Quantitative	Low cost, High volume (shorter term)	• Increase in applications to post secondary programs
	High cost, Low volume (longer term)	• Increase in graduates with post secondary degrees • Quality jobs obtained
Qualitative	Leverage	• Outside capital attracted • New partners aligning with mission
	Influence (direct & indirect)	• Systems changed • Policies influenced

$ invested per impact comparable *within* these categories, but not across categories

Notice that shorter-term impact tends to be much lower cost to achieve while also much easier to attain, and therefore likely to be higher in quantity. In contrast, the longer-term impact, such as graduation rates, take more investment financially and time to achieve and, therefore, will be lower relative to the shorter-term impact. The apples and oranges on the right of Figure 22 simply suggest that it would not be pragmatic to compare a longer-term impact with a short-term impact if you were trying to benchmark the dollars invested to achieve that impact. Instead, comparing one short-term impact with another short-term impact on the dollars invested would be more relevant.

Qualitative impacts may not be as measurable, but they are no less important to consider. Most impact investors focus on just the quantitative measures and don't devote enough time to collecting the qualitative impact of their investees. Imagine if you can influence policies because one of your investees has data and insights that support or prove the need for specific initiatives. Policy changes literally drive impact at scale, so any influence to further that would be a significant impact. Reporting on qualitative impact tends to be more anecdotal, but that should not suggest they are less meaningful than quantitative metrics. Furthermore, storytelling and anecdotes of qualitative impact from an investee can be compelling and easier to digest when provided in impact reports and updates to senior executives and the investment committee. Having a mix of both would be ideal. The downside of qualitative impacts is that you won't be able to show a trend the way quantitative measures can be plotted over time.

When trying to measure and track impact, there needs to be a balance between practicality and collecting enough data from investees (or grantees, for that matter) to understand how your investment dollars have contributed to those outcomes. Unfortunately, some investors and funders get overzealous about collecting so much information that it burdens the entrepreneurs who are already resource-constrained. The number of impact metrics to collect and the level of granularity required should be driven by:

- How meaningful is that data point?
- How hard will it be for the entrepreneur to collect that information?
- Can the investee even collect that information that may be subject to privacy restrictions? For example, if restricted due to privacy requirements, can you accept aggregated summary information, or will that not be sufficiently meaningful?
- How frequently will the data be collected?
- Is the entrepreneur already collecting data similar to what you want to know; if so, is that sufficiently similar enough that you don't need to add another layer of information request?

Don't require impact metrics for the sake of collecting data, be thoughtful about why you need that metric. Your investee will be much more willing to collect the data and appreciate your thoughtfulness. You should always discuss with the investee and get to an agreement on which data to collect to get their perspective and include those in the Side Letter before the deal closes. The granularity of the data should be driven by how meaningful that data point is for your organization. Simply put, you want to ensure the metric is not so high level that it isn't meaningful but also not so granular that getting the data may be so difficult that the entrepreneur would not be able to gather the needed information.

It may be helpful to phase in the data types to collect rather than requiring all the data immediately. To clarify, imagine an investee is a relatively early-stage company that provides supplemental education support in high school math. The company just got a contract with a new school district. A typical metric may be easily collected by counting the number of students using the software and how that number grows quarter over quarter. The second metric could be based on the grade improvement for students who use the software. However, that second metric would not be a data point that can be tracked until two quarters have passed to be able to compare the change in grade improvement. Thus, even though the second metric was included to be tracked, the data may not be available until the company's solutions have been implemented long enough to generate the metric. As an investor, knowing that a particular metric might be crucial to have may be justification for being flexible on when that data becomes available if the investee has the potential to gather such information once they have enough years of development and client traction.

Kind Capital's general rule of thumb is to collect between five to ten impact metrics per investee, and among those impact metrics, at least half are standard across all investees. At the same time, a few might be more customized based on the investee's products, services, and sector. One of the challenges of collecting so many different metrics across each investee is how to report on an aggregated basis if there are no overlaps. For example, imagine having ten investees, each with ten different metrics. Your portfolio would be reporting on one hundred impact metrics for each reporting cycle. Trying to track all those metrics and extrapolate insights from them will be significantly more challenging.

Learning Return

Early in the W.K. Kellogg Foundation's mission-driven investments (MDI) portfolio, the concept of a learning return had been a significant factor in the investment decisions. In the early days of the impact investing strategy, we knew that social impact was the core reason for creating the mission-driven investments program but without compromising on financial returns. But given how early impact investing was at the time, the learning return had more weight than later on in the program, mainly because we had so much to learn in the program's early days. MDI was pioneering and innovating on how an impact investing program should or could be. The learning from investees and the investment process provided rich opportunities to evolve and share with peers. We called it the learning return but frankly couldn't systematically have a method of quantifying or capturing it other than hiring consultants to write case studies for us. Ben Thornley, who was at Pacific Community Ventures then, wrote a case study on the MDI program. In addition, David Bank wrote a case study on one of MDI's community development bank investees Southern Bancorp. For MDI, building the impact investing ecosystem or, as philanthropy commonly refers to it, "field-building" is one of the mission areas of the division, so capturing and sharing lessons learned effectively served as the learning return documentation.

The learning return can be categorized into a couple of components. First is the investment process and knowledge learned from simply building out the impact investing program and investment portfolio. The knowledge update includes a vast array of investment processes, deal structures, new financial terms, etc. Secondly, there is the learning return coming from the investees. When you make an investment, there are technologies, solutions, and data from the entrepreneur that might be able to be leveraged by the grant-making team through collaboration. If there is such a potential, documenting the learning opportunity in the investment memo will help add another factor to weigh in the decision-making process. Lastly, there is the portfolio level learning return coming from the aggregate portfolio in which investees learn from each other within the portfolio, as well as the overall learning from the portfolio that could be leveraged for systems change such as influencing policies. As the most challenging return to measure, the learning return is likely the least considered by investment committees. Still, in my humble opinion, it should be one of the most critical factors to include in analyzing an impact investment. It would be naïve to assume the marginal increase in learning return decreases over time because there will always be something to learn from new investments. No learning return implies the program is operating flawlessly with deep expertise, and the new investments are not providing any additional insights, which would be highly unlikely.

Total Return Framework

Having now gone through how to measure financial return, impact return, and learning return, how do they all connect? Conceptually, we could summarize the total return as

Total Return = Financial Return + Impact Return + Learning Return

Stepping back, this formula simply says that for every dollar invested, what are you getting back in terms of money, the impact you've generated, and what you've learned from making that investment. As we noted earlier, the learning return is not something you can quantify, and some of the impact return (policy change) is also not always quantifiable. Nevertheless, the concept of a total return framework allows us to disaggregate the components that may influence how the investment committee should weigh their decision on approving or disapproving potential investments.

Let's unpack this point by returning to the Total Return formula.

Total Return = Financial Return + Impact Return + Learning Return

> Let,
>
> R_T = Total Return
>
> R_F = Financial Return
>
> R_I = Impact Return
>
> R_L = Learning Return
>
> Therefore, $R_T = R_F + R_I + R_L$

If we step back and think about this framework and how to apply it, we can use an example with a target return of 20% for a direct investment, which is the standard IRR threshold that most investors would target, and we will set that as R_T. Now let's assume that you are about to bring to your investment committee a startup that realistically will get you a 15% financial return (R_F). Since your total target return is 20%, one would typically reject the investment in a traditional investment scenario, given the target return is not met. But in the impact investing arena, we would incorporate the other components. If we assume that the potential investee has the potential to scale more rapidly with your investment and thus, accelerate the impact it has by 4% relative to if you did not invest, then we set the impact return to that 4% (R_I). Note the additionality of impact, not just the impact the company would have had without your investment. The last piece is the learning return which we noted could not be quantified; this last component is essentially just a bogey that you could set to some percentage. If there is significant learning potential, perhaps that is set at 3%; if it is lower, then set it to 1%; and if there is no expected learning, it could be set to zero. For the sake of our example, we'll set the learning return (R_L) to 2% because the company has a strong potential to drive lots of learning. We now have the key components for the formula:

$$R_E = R_F + R_I + R_L$$

Let R_E = Expected Total Return

$R_T = 20\%$

$R_F = 15\%$

$R_I = 4\%$

$R_L = 2\%$

$R_E = 15\% + 4\% + 2\% = 21\%$

$R_T < R_E$

By incorporating the other components, we now see that the expected return is 21% versus the target return of 20%, so this investment should be recommended and pursued. Framing and clarifying why the impact return and learning return should offset the lower target financial return allows the investment committee to consider factors that traditional investments would not typically consider. How much those two components should compensate for a lower financial return needed to pass the sniff test. For clarity, if your total target return is 20%, but your expected financial return is only 5%, is it reasonable to justify 15% of return from the impact and learning components? Using those two components to plug the wide gap might be viewed as fuzzy math to justify an investment that shouldn't have been made in the first place. There is no rule of thumb here, but something to consider if you utilize this total return framework when discussing return expectations for an investment with your investment committee.

The discussion on total return had been from an introspective position and how to frame the conversation with the investment committee, but let's now look at total return from a broader impact capitalist perspective. If you were purely a venture capitalist, your only concern is financial return. However, for philanthropic funders, your objective is focused only on impact. Impact investors (I prefer the term "impact capitalists" since we essentially use capitalist tools to drive impact) combine both objectives. Still, there is also the third component that captures the value-added by the investor. Recall our formula previously in estimating the total return for an investment:

Adding the term "expected" to each of the terms is simply the projected return for each of the components. Instead of a Learning Return component, however, we add the concept of "alpha" for the value-add from the investor.

Total Return = Financial Return + Impact Return + Alpha

$$R_E = R_F + R_I + a$$

What exactly is alpha? Alpha can be split into two components: financial (a_F) and impact (a_I). Without getting too complicated or technical, think about it this way: where can you have added value to the investee? Well, the impact alpha (a_I) would comprise all the ways in which you as an investor help the entrepreneur increase the impact that they would have beyond what the company would have achieved on its own without your investment. How is this different from just the Impact Return that we had just discussed? When you invest in the company, your capital allows the company to do what it could not do were it not for the funding, so your purely financial investment into the company allows it to grow its impact incrementally. That is what Impact Return comprises. But let's say, in addition to the capital you invested, you actively help the company think through how its products or services can grow even more rapidly through partnerships that you introduce to the company. These partnerships expand the investee's reach to even more vulnerable communities. Your active engagement is the impact alpha (a_I) you've generated for the company.

Financial alpha (a_F) is simply everything else you do that adds value to the company to make it more valuable; in theory, this could get broken down into more granular components, but we can keep it simple by aggregating them into one. Some examples of financial alpha include helping the company gain new customers and helping leadership and the founder with strategic planning. Advising the company on establishing an institutional-quality core infrastructure for operational efficiency and risk mitigation or simply helping the company connect to new investors can also be a financial alpha. These are all incredibly valuable to the company and its leadership, driving incremental upside for the company that may not have been achieved were it not for your engagement.

As you might have guessed, the alpha concept would mainly apply to more actively engaged investors. If your investment approach is to write a check and wait for an exit, then alpha would effectively be zero. Of course, there is nothing wrong with having zero alpha. It is merely just a different investment approach and philosophy. A good comparison is around the topic of an actively managed fund where the fund manager thinks she can outperform the market versus an index fund that effectively just tracks a particular index. Studies have shown that most active fund managers underperform the broader index, particularly when you consider the fees paid to the active fund manager. You will find experts on both sides of the issue. Some are die-hard proponents of index funds, such as Peter Lynch, author of A Random Walk Down Wall Street, with the thesis that stock prices are random and therefore cannot be predicted. On the other end of the spectrum are hedge fund managers who charge very hefty fees believing they can pick the best stocks and outperform the market. In particular, the ones employing an activist strategy where they actively engage company management after taking a substantive stake in the company and getting onto its board to push for significant strategic changes to increase shareholder value. In essence, the activist hedge fund manager creates alpha through their engagement with company leadership, in theory.

Whichever philosophy your investment style adheres to, if you are an actively engaged investor, the total return framework for an impact capitalist can be summarized as follows:

Total Return = Financial Return + Impact Return + Alpha

$$R_T = R_F + R_I + a$$

$$a = a_I + a_F$$

$$R_T = R_F + R_I + (a_I + a_F)$$

Total Return = Financial Return + Impact Return + (Impact Alpha + Financial Alpha)

For traditional investors and Chief Investment Officers reading this, my proposed total return concept that integrates impact and its alpha may cause some angst to digest when you've been taught to focus purely on financial returns as a fiduciary and apply the Prudent Investor Rule. However, if we are to evolve our thinking about investments and consider the total stakeholder considerations, the Prudent Investor Rule may need to be amended or rewritten. The investment drives a financial return for the investor. But what about its impact on society, the community, the planet? This comprehensive stakeholder consideration approach is why we must include impact return and impact alpha when trying to get to a total return framework.

Let's add more angst (just a little) to this total return framework by extending the impact return and impact alpha discussion to include harm and negative impact. We've been talking about alpha as positive. But it is also imperative to think about negative alpha, just as there are negative financial returns (you lose money on an investment). Imagine if you invested in a chemical company that made you a 30% financial return, a massive return that any investor would be thrilled to achieve. But let's say the chemical plant dumps pollution into the water on the river. It is killing wildlife and polluting it to the point where fish species commonly found there no longer exist. Furthermore, studies have tied significantly increased lung cancer occurrences among the local community since the company launched production. To add insult to injury, let's assume that you're involved with the company's board as an active investor. While not required, the company management proposes more stringent clean manufacturing practices by implementing specific technologies that would have significantly reduced pollution and creating a multi-million dollar pool of funds to support the community affected by the health issues. As a board member, you know these proposed strategies would significantly hurt the company's profitability and therefore lower its valuation, thus reducing your financial return potential, so you voted against it. These extreme assumptions show where negative impact return and negative impact alpha should be applied. If you assume a negative impact return of 15% for all the harm done to the community and nature and an additional negative impact alpha of 10% for your active opposition to solutions that would have been helpful, you've essentially reduced the total return to 5%:

$$R_T = R_F + R_I + a$$
$$= 30\% - 15\% - 10\%$$
$$= 5\%$$

When you put the initial 30% financial return into this total return context, the excitement for the investment becomes materially less attractive. For investors looking to divest assets from existing portfolios that are potentially harmful and counter to your organization's mission, this total return framework can be applied to think through the analysis. I cannot provide a rule of thumb on how much to quantify a negative impact return or negative impact alpha; the examples provided were intentionally extreme to demonstrate a point. Still, at least the concept of taking into account negative impact will help your discussion with your investment committee and board members.

CHAPTER ELEVEN: LESSONS LEARNED AND OVERCOMING OBSTACLES

"Wisdom comes through suffering." Aeschylus

I have made a lot of mistakes over the years, as well as watched the mistakes of others. This chapter summarizes a few key areas, some of which I had already alluded to in previous chapters. Hopefully, you won't repeat any of these or at least learn to recognize them before they become a more significant issue.

Tearing Down the Wall – Internal Politics and Creating Cross-Functional Buy-in

Impact investing has grown and developed quite a bit over the last ten years, so this will likely be less of an issue than it was before. However, some traditionalists still believe that grant-making and investing should remain bifurcated functions, as has historically been the case. Stereotypically the grant-making side of foundations may think anything that makes money is pure evil and greedy. And the investments side perceives the grantmakers as idealistic do-gooders who have no practical sense of how they think about sustainable organizations. When you bring in impact investing as the bridge between those two factions, you'll be hated by both sides of the house since you don't fit on either side. These are extreme examples, but I have seen this directly.

One former program officer I had worked with was so appalled that we were going to make an investment in "a company that was making money off poor people" without truly understanding the business model—the mere fact that the social venture made any money was enough for him to put up a wall and immediately perceive the organization evil compared to his angelic grantees who were doing good making no money. In reality, the organization served low-income people with their product, but the business model didn't charge those individuals for their services; instead, it had contracts with organizations (hospitals) that had these low-income patients. Had the program officer just taken the time to understand the business model and see what the company actually did and the positive impact their product had on low-income patients, his original perception may have changed.

So how do we tear down that wall? In the example I gave, it didn't help that this happened early in my impact investing journey having just left Wall Street for a small Midwestern town of 50K people. There were already perceived horns sticking out of my head when I arrived and lots of suspicion about my motives. To folks who had lived all their lives in Battle Creek, Michigan, I was the epitome of an elitist Ivy-educated evil banker encroaching on their turf. It might not have been as bad had I been relocating from Ann Arbor or Chicago, but I was moving from New York City, exacerbating their stereotype. I knew that if I couldn't overcome that perception, they definitely were not interested in making my job easier if not ensuring my complete failure. So I created a three-step plan that ultimately changed their perception (most of the people anyways, can't win them all): Listen, Learn, Lead.

The **3L Approach** can be summarized as follows:

- **Listen** – Early upon arrival, I became a sponge. My goal was to absorb and learn as much about each individual as possible and their motives. What drove them, what made them who they were, and what would potentially be how they might benefit from what I could bring to the table. Furthermore, I also listened to what people disclosed about the political dynamics and figured out who were the intelligent leaders that everyone respected versus those who held senior titles but didn't have the respect or admiration of staff or executives. I recall one director who had been offered ample opportunities to be promoted but chose not to because he loved his job and role. He already had the respect of staff members, and executives and the board members loved him even without the title. Unfortunately, the downside of someone with that power and admiration also attracted envy from more senior executives who didn't enjoy that status despite their more senior titles. Learning that information was invaluable because that director happened to be my boss at the time!

- **Learn** – I had no philanthropic experience other than serving on a charter school board before arriving at the foundation, so my knowledge of philanthropy was candidly starting from ground zero. So, in addition to being a sponge for learning about people, I also became a sponge for learning about philanthropy, the organization I had just joined, the various departments and how they work separately, and how they work together. Doing so would allow me to identify gaps where I could add value and where the impact investing tools could be applied.

- **Lead** – In order to lead, one must have credibility and respect. I had to become an expert (well perceived to be one) in impact investing that would allow the department to be recognized as a leader internally and externally for being innovative and impactful. Some of this was done by speaking at conferences, providing grant funding to support field-building infrastructure in the impact investing ecosystem, and making investments in ways others might not be as open to or even considered. For example, grants were made to associations that ultimately became Mission Investors Exchange, to the Global Impact Investing Network (GIIN), to CDFI association Opportunity Finance Network (OFN), and to support new tools like social impact bonds when it first entered the U.S. market. Taking a multiprong approach from grant-making to investing across the full spectrum of capital helped establish the department's brand as a leader in the space. Of course, it also meant there were higher risks of funding things that would fail, but we got executive leadership comfortable with risk, primarily thanks to my boss at the time, so I want to give credit where it is due.

Capacity Building of Staff and Leadership

In applying the 3L approach, I did a couple of things. Firstly, I scheduled coffee and lunch meetings with different people within the organization so I could learn about them, their roles, and the department they worked. That may be harder to do during the Covid pandemic but connecting with colleagues is critical. Secondly, I read up on things in philanthropy and impact investing, and asked lots and lots of questions to people with more experience, both internally and externally. And then, once I had enough confidence that I had something

I could share, I scheduled "lunch & learn" sessions where I would teach different topics to staff around impact investing. These topics range from discussing the role of the impact investing department to an impact investing 101 sessions walking through the various tools in basic terms. Using jargon and financial terminology puts a lot of folks to sleep and on the defensive when they don't understand them. So every presentation I made was done as if I was explaining it to a middle school child because the concepts needed to be kept as simple as possible. In addition to staff, board members were invited to some of the sessions if they were interested in learning more. Sometimes the concepts need to be presented multiple times before they sink in; this isn't because people are incompetent but simply that it's not their normal area of focus or tool they had used. It's like learning a new language that you don't practice every day, so you need a reminder whenever you learn a new vocabulary.

One of the most important aspects of holding these lunch and learn sessions included bringing in the founders of the companies we had invested in to speak and talk about their companies. The message may be the same, but the messenger makes a big difference in how the message is received, even if both are saying precisely the same thing verbatim. Having the entrepreneurs speak at the sessions allows the investments to be more tangible and real, not just some dollar amount invested shown on a slide. I have found these passionate entrepreneurs talking about why they created their companies, the impact their companies have on people's lives, and how the impact investing team had helped them just makes them incredibly powerful in getting staff to understand what the impact investing function does. The entrepreneurs would often say things that almost seemed like we had planted the answer for them before the session (we didn't!). Even though we did not prep them about what to say, they genuinely gave their authentic perspective about the impact investing team's role. When the grant-making team can better understand these portfolio investees, it may also drive potential collaboration opportunities.

These activities allowed me to show folks my authentic self and genuine motives that helped disarm their perceptions of the evil banker. It also allowed me to give tactical examples of potential collaboration where the impact investing tools could help accelerate the initiatives previously solely funded by grants. I should note that the lunch and learn sessions were open to all staff, not just grantmakers or executives; this inclusiveness also helped to show people that we are all here for the same mission of the organization; we just have different tools. Unfortunately, there was this classist bifurcation between front office (grantmakers) and back-office (operations) roles, whether real or just perceived. Still, I can tell you from personal experience that when I got the trust of the back office people, including the cafeteria workers, it was evident they felt a class separation from the front office folks. That is somewhat ironic since we are talking about a private foundation environment, not Wall Street!

Another way to build the capacity of staff and leadership is to bring them along on on-site visits or let them participate in some of the due diligence calls. Seeing some of the ways you work and meeting entrepreneurs who are passionately driven with their products or services makes it much easier to understand your work. Furthermore, your colleagues may have other thoughts and contribute to the process that you might not be thinking about. When appropriate, putting an internal colleague from a different division onto the board of an investee also helps to strengthen the internal collaboration potential, depending on the entrepreneur's need. For example, someone from the Finance Team, Legal or even programmatic areas could add value to the entrepreneur without taking the board seat yourself, saving you time and giving your colleagues an opportunity they likely rarely get.

To be clear, I made good traction in tearing down the wall, but it was not completely torn down. There will always be some folks who religiously oppose anything that makes money. I've tried including grantmakers on due diligence calls and site visits for deals where their area of expertise could be beneficial. They would also be able to see and meet the entrepreneurs to understand these social ventures have impact motives just like grantees but may have the potential to scale even faster. The uptake by some was incredibly helpful to leverage during investment committee meetings, where they joined the discussions to provide their perspectives and why they supported the investment. Unfortunately, others could not get over the fact that the business model made money, and those are the people you should leave behind because they will drain your energy and time no matter how much you try to convince them to open their minds.

Cross-Functional Committee

Another tactic I tried that had mixed results was creating a cross-functional team to pre-screen investment opportunities. This committee didn't have any governance authority (although some members were part of the investment committee), and their purpose was to get a preview of deals in the pipeline that they could provide input on. In building this committee, I made sure there were representatives from Legal, Finance, Technology, Grant Making, Operations, and Communications. It gave other divisions within the organization visibility into what the impact investing team had been focused on in terms of investments that were coming through the pipe while also getting their input. The original intent of creating such a committee made logical sense. However, the challenge was getting everyone's availability to meet when you have such a big group of committee members to coordinate schedules with. Secondly, some deals were very time-sensitive, so the luxury of taking several weeks to schedule a meeting is impractical. In retrospect, there are probably ways to make it work. Still, the way I had structured it in my prior role, some circumstances prevented it from working out the way it was intended, both logistically as well as other dynamics within the organization added to the challenge. If you do create a cross-functional committee, key things to keep in mind are:

- size of the committee,
- who will actually attend the meetings once they are set,
- who are critical input you want from, and lastly,
- should some of them be investment committee members that might want an earlier look at deals before it gets to the investment committee?

Keeping those factors in mind may make your pre-screening committee more effective. The second factor seems odd, but it was not uncommon for people to accept meeting invites and not show up.

How to Handle Deals That Don't Work Out

Inevitably there will be some investments that don't work out. If every deal worked out, either you are extremely lucky, or you are not truly "investing" by taking enough risks. In my view, anyone who brags about having a portfolio with no investments that didn't work out raises more questions than credibility. Let's assume you have a few deals that did not pan out in your portfolio. You have two stakeholders to consider: the first is internal, and the other is external (the entrepreneur). Before we jump into how to deal with a bad deal, let's make sure we review some ways to mitigate the impact of having a deal go south.

- **Manage expectations** – From the onset of creating your impact investing strategy, always manage expectations about losses being expected in any investing strategy. You will likely need to repeat this over and over again when you provide updates to your executive team and investment committee.

- **Monitoring and updates** – Always keep the investment committee informed during the quarterly updates when you provide an overview of the portfolio. Companies do not fail overnight; they usually show signs of trending towards it before things get really drastic. I used to classify investments as doing well (green), doing ok (yellow), or underperforming (red) so that at a glance, there is a sense of how the overall portfolio is performing. By tracking the underperforming companies, you can see what steps can be taken to turn them around. And if they ultimately fail, it would not be a complete surprise.

- **Build trust with the entrepreneur** – It's not surprising that entrepreneurs do not want to disclose bad news but are happy to share the good news. That is just human nature. The problem is that if you do not know the bad news, you can not take the necessary steps to help mitigate or even solve the issue potentially. Having the entrepreneur's trust is so critical, and allowing them to be fully transparent without being judgmental when things don't work out will be helpful to avoid finding out the bad news when it's too late to fix.

When every effort made by the entrepreneur seems not to work, and the investee looks like it's heading into a bad situation, you can either try to salvage the situation or make things worse by blaming the entrepreneur. I can assure you the entrepreneur will likely feel much worse than you do if their company is not doing well because most of their wealth is probably tied to the company's success. Not only is their livelihood in dire straits, but also their reputation for leading a company to failure. When deals are not working out, these are some pointers to consider:

- How will the co-investors handle it? This is where a good relationship with other investors will allow for transparent and honest discussions on what each is willing to do to move things forward:

  o Some existing investors may want just to dump the investment and move on

  o Some existing investors may be willing to provide additional capital for liquidity or even recapitalize the company entirely, which will significantly dilute existing investors who do not want to participate and the entrepreneur's stake. In essence, the investors that look to bail out the company may buy out other investors' stakes 10 cents on the dollar.

- Are there new investors who may be interested in putting money in, given the significant write-down of valuation?

- Are there potential acquirers who may want to buy the company at a significant discount (either for cash or through a stock swap)? For example, perhaps one of your other portfolio companies may be a natural acquirer that can be mutually beneficial.

- Calculate the runway left before the company runs entirely out of money, taking into account significant cost-cutting and restructuring to extend the runway as long as possible, so you have a sense of how much/little time there is before the company is completely out of money. Require the company to provide weekly cash flow updates and cash burn rates.

- Work with the entrepreneur and other investors, not against them. It's very easy to get caught up in the emotion of frustration when things don't work out, and assigning blame becomes the focus that ultimately serves no benefit to any stakeholder and possibly expedites the downward spiral. Encouraging the company's leadership to think through the best turnaround or wind-down strategy and getting other investors to align will be critical to ensuring the best possible outcome given the situation. When everyone is emotionally charged, that can be very challenging, but if you can get as many stakeholders on board as possible, then the outcome need not be as bad as it can be. Most importantly, you protect your reputation with the entrepreneur and other investors.

- Inform your finance team, do not surprise them. The finance team will need to make accounting adjustments on your organization's financial statements when/if the investment ultimately fails.

- Loop in legal and communications team – Your internal legal folks should be informed and consider obtaining guidance from outside counsel on potential risks and liabilities. Sometimes pre-emptively getting their advice on how to engage the entrepreneur, especially if things have the potential to get contentious, understanding the risk and exposure related to potential litigation can be super helpful. While unlikely, the Communications Team may also be looped in just in case any public releases are required.

- Write down all the reasons why the investment did not pan out. It's essential to document this while things are still fresh so that you can learn from it and share it with your team. Then, compare those reasons to the risks discussed in the investment memo during the initial investment committee meetings that approved the deal. Were those risks noted in the original investment memo, or were new risks that hadn't been considered during the due diligence process? If the risks had been identified, you can be confident that your underwriting process was done correctly. On the other hand, if the risks are new, this may be a good learning opportunity to tweak your due diligence process, whether done internally or through an outside consultant.

Record Keeping and Documentation

It might seem like common sense, but I can't emphasize how important a clean record-keeping system will save you a lot of headaches down the line. It is so critical for compliance reasons, not just operational efficiency. For example, if there is ever an IRS audit, you know exactly what documents to send and where to find them. Your organization's auditors will likely want to pick a couple of the impact investing deals annually to review as part of their work, so you can just send them a link to a folder that they can access. As someone who is a bit more anal about keeping things organized, I certainly have been grateful that when anyone ever asked about a deal, all the records are readily accessible.

Keeping your files organized is much easier if you're someone who is meticulous about it, but it is a much bigger issue when you've got colleagues who are not quite as…meticulous. Unfortunately, one of my former colleagues had no consistency in where to store files, how to name them, etc. Let's just say, as brilliant as the individual was, being organized is undoubtedly not his strength. That made trying to find documents incredibly difficult. And if he ever gets hit by a bus or leaves the organization, the person taking over would be left to sort through trying to decipher everything. It got so bad that I had my assistant create a standardized file naming system and asked her to organize our online files in a way that was consistent across every team member.

This disciplined approach forced every team member to have a uniform filing and storage process. That may sound like overkill, but I will point out that after I left my role, the person who replaced me actually reached out and told me how grateful she was for how detailed and organized the information was! For someone new to an organization, it would be such a nightmare to dig through years of data that others had created if it was not organized well. Being organized is much easier when you start out than trying to clean up a huge mess later, so I would strongly encourage you to create a standardized naming and filing system that everyone sticks with. Something so little can significantly impact your ability to respond to requests for information and give you comfort and confidence that you have everything in order.

Get the Deal Killers On the Table Early

One of the worst things about working on a deal you get super excited about is finding out at the later stages of the process that you have a term or condition that cannot be compromised. Not only does that waste time and resources dedicated to the diligence process, but it will also hurt your reputation and leave both parties highly disappointed. To prevent that, or at least mitigate that risk, put together your list of deal killers and be transparent about them when you initiate conversations with potential investees early in the process.

When I started conversations with potential investees during my time at Lumina Impact Ventures, my pitch was: we are cheap on valuation, we are slow in our process, and we may be more difficult to work with given the requirements for our investments as an impact investor.

That certainly does not sound like desirable traits that would endear potential investees to pick Lumina as an investor, but the intent of the messaging provided transparency and set the rules of engagement with the entrepreneur early. As a result, they will not be surprised when specific terms are required in the Side Letter or if the diligence process takes three months to get from an introductory meeting through investment committee approval.

Every investor will have its own set of deal killers. A few that were particular to me when I started a diligence process for a potential investment include the following:

- **Mission-alignment** – If the leadership team, especially the founder, is not aligned when it comes to mission fit, the purpose of the investment would be moot. Gauging mission fit is always the first gate that a potential investment must get through before vetting any other areas in diligence.

- **Impact measurement** – The investee must be willing to report impact metrics; even though the specific metrics have not yet been determined, the willingness to adhere to this requirement can set expectations for what will be required for the investment to proceed.

- **PRI-specific compliance requirements** – These include the put rights and exit rights discussed previously for both mission drift and reputational risk.

- **Time frame** – If the entrepreneur is looking to close a deal within three weeks, but your normal diligence process takes three months, it's just not going to work. Being clear on timing expectations will avoid disappointments later, and consistently updating the entrepreneur on the process will help along the way. It's possible that a round may be kept open to accommodate investors who the investee feels are critical for strategic partnership.

- **DEI and diversity requirements** – If your organization is highly committed to diversity and has a mandate requiring a clear, measurable representation of commitment to DEI, the investee may not be aligned nor interested in aligning on such initiatives.

- **Geographic focus** – For a local family foundation that only invests in place-based opportunities within the local or regional community, an investee that has little focus on the target geography could be a significant barrier to considering the investment unless there are other strategic reasons (e.g., learning opportunity) for making such an investment.

These are just some examples of potential deal killers but are not comprehensive. The critical point is to ensure your organization's deal killers are clearly communicated early.

CHAPTER TWELVE: ADVANCED IMPACT INVESTING STRATEGIES

"The right deal can go wrong."

I've already covered many of the strategies for direct investments and fund investments. This chapter will provide a few additional tactical strategies that may also be useful to consider in your impact investing program.

Utilizing Grants

We discussed grants as a way to provide credit enhancements through loan guarantees or even first-loss protection. I've often been asked how to structure a grant to a for-profit company, so I wanted to add some more context. The first way is to fund a nonprofit entity that might benefit from using the for-profit company's product or service. We can demonstrate this with an ed-tech company that provides tutoring or coaching (we'll call the company 2torMe for simplicity) services to college students, mainly focused on community colleges as the core client base. 2torMe has a roster of over 1,500 mentors available 24/7 covering over 400 subject matters, and charges an hourly rate for its service. If you are a funder who is concerned about giving a grant to a for-profit company, even if it is a social venture, then you could provide a grant to a community college that might want to use 2torMe's service by paying for a set number of hours, say 1,000 hours for the year. The community college could then allow its low-income students to utilize the 2torMe service from the prepaid hours. As the grantmaker, the grant could be structured to specify that the community college can only use the funding to serve low-income students, specifically through tutoring services. It's important to note that you cannot explicitly require the community college to use 2torMe as the service provider with the grant; the community college should be able to use the grant with any provider as long as the grant's intent is met. Of course, since the community college most likely already expressed interest in using 2torMe's service when it applied for the grant, the risk is low that they would use a different provider.

You could also make the grant directly to a for-profit company if the structure of the grant can be shown to be charitable and not explicitly to benefit the company. In the example of 2torMe, let's assume that the company is only offering its service in English, but your organization happens to focus on Spanish-speaking low-income students, specifically located in Bentonville, AR. You could structure an expenditure responsibility grant to 2torMe with the following requirements:

- Support recruitment of Spanish-speaking mentors for math and literacy support
- Offer 1,000 hours of free access to students located in community colleges in Bentonville
- Tracking utilization of service and academic improvement correlation

This grant would be charitable since it would be unlikely that the company 2torMe would have done the charitable activity that the funder was trying to support programmatically. But, of course, your legal advisors would need to vet the structure of a grant to a for-profit entity for charitability. Suffice it to say, expenditure responsibility (ER) grants may be a little more complicated than a standard grant, but they can be surgically deployed to drive a programmatic initiative in partnership with a for-profit company with an innovative product or solution.

Another way that grants have been applied to for-profit companies is through supply guarantees. For example, let's say your foundation focuses on increasing access for lowest-income populations in emerging markets to vaccines. Those demographic and markets are neither attractive nor profitable to biotech companies traditionally focused on commercially more profitable developed markets. So your organization could guarantee some volume of vaccine purchase, ensuring a revenue commitment for the biotech firm as an incentive to expand into the specific market you care about. Using such a structure mitigates risk for the biotech firm and may also catalyze other investors to invest, knowing that some level of revenue is already guaranteed.

Capital Stacking

Capital stacking is one of the core areas where an impact investor can leverage the full spectrum of its tools to further its mission. We've just discussed how grants can be used to support nonprofits as it has traditionally been done and to support for-profit entities. Combining a grant with a PRI is more typical than other combinations, but it is possible to combine all three tools, as I will demonstrate with an example shortly. Knowing when to consider stacking capital will potentially reduce risk while optimizing mission objectives. It makes the deal more complicated when there are different tranches of capital but allows for stakeholders with different objectives and risk tolerance to participate in the slice that is most appropriate for them. This is best explained through an example, but we'll just make up fictitious names and terms to protect the deal's confidentiality. This was a real deal that I had led. We'll call the deal the Dairy Good Fund, and here are some background parameters:

- Mission focus – increasing healthy food access to low-income communities and food desserts; advancing the food ecosystem in the State of Wisconsin
- Investors – ranging from philanthropic entities to traditional banks
- Size of the fund – target raise of $30 million capitalization
- Asset class – debt

A prominent funder that was very strong in the food sector had hired a consultant to scan the market to understand the challenges in the food ecosystem for low- and moderate-income (LMI) communities and food deserts. The research confirmed the hypothesis that food entrepreneurs (grocery stores, restaurants, small farm owners, etc.) lacked access to investment capital due to the perceived risk in the sector. Thus, if a debt investor could provide loans to these entrepreneurs, the ecosystem could develop to support the targeted communities, especially if the loans were not charging exorbitant rates and the terms of the loans were not so demanding to make it nearly impossible to obtain. That led to the initial concept of the Dairy Good Fund, which took almost two years from the initial market scan to fully doing deals and deploying capital.

Options Pool and Ownership Distribution

In the direct investing section, we discussed the importance of having ownership distribution that will incentivize the leadership team and drive staff retention. Some founders own over 90% or more of the company when they look for their first institutional round of financing (Series Seed), while others may already be much more diluted. While there is no rule of thumb for what percentage of ownership an entrepreneur should have, the goal is to ensure both the founders and the executive team have the right alignment of interest with the investors. Two specific considerations when structuring the investment: Options Pool and Founder Revesting.

• **Options Pool** – The options pool allows the entrepreneur to attract and retain talent by granting stock options that give an ownership stake in the company. Typically the options pool is equal to a 10 to 20% stake on a fully diluted basis of the company, and the grant has a vesting period. When a company does its first institutional round of financing, I expect the entrepreneur to create this options pool if they don't have one already. How big the options pool should be will depend on how big the existing leadership team is and what additional critical talent is needed to round out the management team's capacity for the company to succeed. Not surprisingly, the bigger the options pool, the more dilution the entrepreneur will have to accept of their stake in the company, so it's natural they would push back and want a smaller options pool. On the topic of greed, Wall Street has a saying: pigs get fat, but hogs get slaughtered. Helping the entrepreneur understand the intent of the options pool is critical so they don't feel like they are taking unnecessary dilution. If there is significant pushback to creating an options pool from the entrepreneur, the investment may be one to pass on.

The options pool may be calculated pre-investment or post-investment. If the pool is created post-investment, this means that as an investor, your stake will be diluted, not just the entrepreneur's. If the options pool is created pre-investment, then only the existing investors will be diluted (mostly the entrepreneur, who likely will be the largest owner). Given that context, as the investor, it might feel obvious that choosing the pre-investment option is the right path, but you will need to get the entrepreneur to accept it, which may not be possible. You may be a fantastic negotiator and get the entrepreneur to accept the term, but bear in mind that you are in a partnership with the company as an investor, so do you want to go into the investment with the entrepreneur feeling like they got cheated or taken advantaged of? That is why structuring and negotiating an investment is very much an art rather than a science. Furthermore, if the entrepreneur's stake in the company is already quite diluted before the financing round, a more considerable further dilution by requiring the pool to be calculated pre-investment will potentially disincentivize the founder, which would clearly not be the intent. Adding to the complexity, if the financing round has other co-investors participate, then those investors will also need to agree on the size of the options pool, especially if it is calculated on a post-investment basis since their stake will be diluted pro-rata.

- **Revesting Founder Shares** – One of the biggest sticklers in negotiating an investment, particularly for early institutional rounds (Series Seed rounds mainly, although I've seen in some Series A rounds), centers on the requirement for founders/ entrepreneurs to revest their shares. Let's start by explaining what revesting means. Usually, when stocks grants or options grants are given, they have a vesting period, typically ranging from three to five years. To demonstrate with an example, let's say you get 100,000 shares as compensation with a five-year vesting period and one-year cliff. This means that you get 20% of the amount for every year you stay with the company; after the first year, you get 20K of those shares. After the second year, you get an additional 20K shares, etc. So if you left the company at year two, you only get 40K shares of the initial grant. The one-year cliff simply means that if you stayed for less than a year (say eleven months), you get none of the shares. Typically these incentive stock compensation structures have a one-year cliff and quarterly or monthly pro-rated vesting. If you stayed one year and three months, you would be entitled to 20K shares for the first year and 5K shares prorated for the second year for a total of 25K shares. The vesting schedule drives the retention of key staff who are given stock grants or options grants.

The same concept applies to the founder's ownership of the company. If the founder leaves the company before the vesting period is over, the unvested shares they own will revert to the company or the investors. Understandably, founders who have never done an institutional round may feel offended when they are asked to vest their shares in the company they created, having put their money, sweat, and tears into it. However, adding a vesting requirement for the founder's stake is insurance against the founder leaving to do something else. And yes, it does happen; one of my entrepreneurs left the company he founded to take a CEO job at a prestigious foundation! Some ways to structure the founder share vesting requirement include:

○ Minimum three years vesting period – Ideally, you would want the vesting period to be the same as all other employees, but having a shorter period for vesting the founder's shares is acceptable.

○ Vesting based on controllable triggers – It is unfair to an entrepreneur if an exogenous event out of their control causes the entrepreneur to no longer be able to serve in the leadership capacity, so they should not be penalized for such a scenario. For example, the vesting period should terminate if the founder gets hit by a bus or is terminally ill. The core goal of the vesting schedule is to ensure the entrepreneur doesn't leave voluntarily. But, of course, if the entrepreneur does something egregious that results in their termination for cause (e.g., a lawsuit for discrimination), then the vesting schedule still applies.

○ Only some portion of the founder shares needs to vest – It would be unreasonable to require all the founder's shares to be subject to a vesting schedule, but some significant stake would be sufficient (25 to 50%). When entrepreneurs are sole founders and genuinely committed to building the company, they should be less resistant to such an arrangement, especially when the vesting schedule is three years. However, if you have multiple co-founders, the likelihood of one leaving the company is much higher, making vesting the founder's share even more important.

○ The concept of revesting is literally what it implies. Imagine being the entrepreneur who had been required to vest their shares in the company's Series Seed round and then asked to revest those shares again when they raise their next round of financing, adding an additional three more years to earn back those shares. It's less typical, but it happens if the investor(s) are concerned about the entrepreneur leaving the company. Again, this is more of a concern when there are multiple co-founders where one key executive may leave rather than when there is just one sole founder with substantial ownership of the company. Of all the terms an investor asks for in negotiations, this one would be the most contentious for most entrepreneurs to accept.

Side Letters

As discussed in earlier chapters, the Side Letter is the agreement explicitly laying out the terms of the investment between your organization and the entrepreneur, which do not apply to all investors. For example, you might require social metrics reporting while a traditional investor would not care nor require it. Things to make sure you push for are summarized below:

- Impact Metrics Reporting – As an impact investment, this should be an absolute requirement for the entrepreneur. The number of metrics and what the metrics are will be more negotiable. Pushback from the entrepreneur for having this requirement would be a good gauge of the mission alignment of the company. Mission-aligned entrepreneurs will be more amenable. For PRIs, unwillingness to report impact metrics should be considered a deal killer and something that should be brought up very early in conversations with the entrepreneur, even before due diligence begins. These deal-breakers help ensure you don't waste time on a company that isn't as mission-aligned. They are DOA…dead on arrival.

- Exit Rights
  ○ Put Right For Mission Drift – As a requirement for PRIs, including a put right for mission drift in the Side Letter will be critical for demonstrating charitability as a complement to the social metrics reporting requirements. The key issue

for this particular requirement is defining what "mission drift" is; the more narrow the definition is to be considered a breach, the easier it would be for the entrepreneur to accept. For example, let's say the company you are potentially investing in provides software that helps children learn math faster and more effectively through gamification of concepts. You could define a breach as where the company pivots to providing casino games with no educational value as its new business model. This example is pretty explicit on the trigger and makes it clear enough for the entrepreneur to accept.

For PRIs, there is a more onerous requirement than the exit right for mission drift: a put right to sell your shares back to the company, not just to sell the shares to someone else. This nuance is more problematic for an entrepreneur to accept, but there are reasons for this requirement by the IRS. If you put yourself in the entrepreneur's shoes (no pun intended), your company must buy out the shares from the investor who claimed you've had a mission drift. Since the company is likely to be resource-constrained as an early-stage company, this extra level hurdle can be really scary to the entrepreneur since a triggering event could put the company out of business! You (or your legal advisors) will need to explain this requirement to the entrepreneur and their lawyer, who will most likely balk at it if they are unfamiliar with PRI requirements under IRS tax codes. Make it clear that this is not your or your organization's requirement; it's the IRS for PRI investments.

To make the entrepreneur comfortable, here are a few things you will need to clarify when explaining the put-right requirement.

- If the triggering event happens and both you and the entrepreneur agree there has been a breach, there are opportunities to fix/cure the breach.
- If triggering the event forces a financial obligation on the company that would put it into a precarious financial position or potential failure, you as the investor can structure a plan of redemption with the company that can

ease that burden. To clarify, while the IRS requires the company to repurchase your investment, it also forbids you to put the company into a dire financial position or out of business. The IRS also does not provide any requirements on the timing for the exit process once it's triggered. As long as you provide documentation for when the triggering event was, the remediation processes, and the exit strategy, this should sufficiently address that requirement. Your lawyers may need to get updated requirements on this, but to date (January 2022), that has been how I've structured Side Letters for PRIs. The entrepreneur should be relieved to hear these additional details and be more open to the put right.

- **Exit Right for Reputational Risk** – While the Put Right allows you to get out of the deal for mission drift by selling back your shares to the company as required by the IRS, the more general exit right for reputational risk is not a requirement by the IRS. Foundations, in particular, are much more sensitive to reputational risk, and adding this requirement into the Side Letter allows the foundation to get out of the investment when a triggering event that the foundation does not want to be affiliated with occurs. Similar to the Put Right, defining what is considered a triggering event will make negotiating with the entrepreneur less confrontational if you can be more specific. Some general examples may include events such as the company being found guilty of sexual harassment, discrimination, or other illegal activities. This form of exit right simply allows you to sell your shares and does not require the company explicitly to purchase them back, making it easier to facilitate. Not every investor is concerned about reputational risk, but having that right is one way to ensure the company does not carry out any activities that might cause such a breach.

- **Co-Investments – Real Benefit or Steer Clear**

  Fund managers will often dangle co-investment rights as a carrot for investors willing to write larger checks to qualify as a "major investor" who gets these special rights. As you may recall, we discussed previously other special rights, such as the most favored nations (MFN) clauses which are genuinely real benefits. However, the co-investment right is not exactly as great a benefit as fund managers may have you think. I touched on this briefly before, but let's review it here because it is pretty important to keep in mind when negotiating deal terms. There are times when co-investment rights will truly be beneficial since you want to cherry-pick the deals most aligned with your organization's mission to double down on. Unfortunately, that is not usually the case when a fund manager offers you a co-investment "opportunity." I mentioned earlier that the agent-principal problem sometimes exists due to asymmetric information access. Let me refresh your memory: a fund manager will have much more information on the deal, having done deeper due diligence than you would before offering the co-investment opportunity. For example, suppose the deal is highly sought after and oversubscribed. In that case, the fund manager will naturally want to take all of the deal rather than bring in co-investors since the higher return opportunity will make the fund perform better. On the other hand, if the deal is a bit riskier than the fund manager is comfortable with, he may bring in co-investors to fill in the allocation rather than take the entire amount himself.

So how do you know if your fund manager is actually giving you a co-investment opportunity rather than trying to offload some risk? First, scrutinize how "oversubscribed" the deal really is. Secondly, grill the fund manager about why he thinks the deal is truly an opportunity and why he is offering it as a co-investment. Lastly, do some basic back-of-the-envelope math. If the fund manager can right a $5 million check and the deal allocation is $15M, then clearly, the fund manager doesn't have the capacity. Still, if the allocation is only $3M, you seriously need to ask yourself why the fund manager isn't taking the total amount for the fund himself. There may be completely legitimate reasons for a fund manager not taking the entire allocation when they have the capacity. But you definitely want to ensure you understand those reasons well. For example, perhaps a strategic investor for the deal will be highly beneficial to add to the capital stack aligned with the investee. Or maybe the fund manager just wants to build a better relationship with you to get you into their next fund.

Ultimately, co-investment rights are nice to have, but I would not fight as hard for them compared to other terms in the deal. Here's one reason: if you didn't have co-investment rights, in theory, you could simply reach out to the entrepreneur and directly invest in the round separate from the fund manager's allocation if you didn't have co-investment rights. Doing so would also avoid paying a co-investment fee that the fund manager would charge if you did it through the fund manager.

- **Most Favored Nation (MFN) Clause** – We've discussed this in previous chapters, but worth repeating here. The MFN Clause essentially protects you as an investor from getting worse terms than another investor who might be able to negotiate more favorable terms. It virtually guarantees you the same terms as any other favored investor, hence the term "most favored" in the definition. MFNs are typically reserved for the major investors in a fund investment, and naturally, there is some threshold in terms of the minimum dollar amount required to meet the definition of a "major investor." However, if you are an important investor, especially a strategic, or have an excellent relationship with the fund manager (perhaps you've been an early investor in their first fund, and this is now their 4th fund), you may be able to negotiate to get the MFN even if you don't exactly meet the minimum dollar investment threshold. For example, if you are the first (or only) major foundation investor, that could give you some leverage if the fund manager is looking to diversify its investor base.

- **Other Investor-Specific Issues** – Depending on the type of investor your organization is, some more esoteric clauses may need to be considered. A couple worth mentioning here include:
  - Mitigating UBTI – As discussed previously, if the fund utilizes leverage at the fund level and your organization is a private foundation, you could be subject to unrelated business taxable income (UBTI). Your legal advisors will likely have the appropriate language that could either A) forbid the fund from utilizing leverage at the fund level (less of an issue at the deal level with investees), which most likely will be

incorporated into the main Limited Partnership Agreement; or B) specifically address it in the Side Letter where your investment may be protected from UBTI through the fund manager creating "blocker corporations" for investments that may generate UBTI. Of course, leverage at the fund level is not the only cause of UBTI, but the point here is that if you are a private foundation, your legal counsel should include language regarding mitigating UBTI.

- **Non-US Tax Exposure** – If the fund manager makes investments outside the US, you will want to include language that mitigates your exposure as an investor to foreign taxes. Sample language could be "The General Partner agrees it will use commercially reasonable efforts to structure investments in companies issuing securities from a jurisdiction outside the United States so as not to cause the investor to become directly subject to income tax in any such jurisdiction...etc." Of course, your lawyer will have much better language, but that should give you a sense of the intent of the clause.

Active vs. Passive Roles

One of the critical factors for your impact investing strategy is whether to be an investor that is actively engaged or one that is more passive. They are fundamentally different approaches that will impact the types of entrepreneurs you will invest in. Note that this is most applicable to direct investments; it would be a rare scenario for an active role when investing in a fund. However, with smaller impact funds, it could happen as they may need more support and involvement from their investors.

If you are taking a more passive investor role, you are essentially investing in an entrepreneur with a track record that you are genuinely confident in and who won't need much support. Alternatively, perhaps you believe the company already has other investors who can bring the skill sets and support it needs, so there isn't a need for what you or your organization can bring to the table. Furthermore, another reason for being a passive investor may simply be bandwidth capacity. You may not have the time or staff to engage actively with the entrepreneur. Nevertheless, being a passive investor does not mean you should completely let the investment go on autopilot since all investments need to be monitored. Attending the quarterly updates is the minimum amount of interaction you should expect to have with the entrepreneur. Not surprisingly, with such limited interaction, your relationship with the entrepreneur will not be as strong.

Having an active investment role where you become a true partner to the entrepreneur is very time-consuming, but the rewards of being considered a partner by the entrepreneur have lots of upsides. As we discussed, the more you understand the business model and strategy, the more potential integration you can explore in collaboration opportunities with other parts of your organization. Furthermore, being in the flow gives you visibility into the business direction and risks earlier. A few suggestions I would highlight if you took an active investor approach:

- Being an active investor does not necessarily mean that you have to be the individual sitting on the board of the company (board observer role); it could be a colleague from other parts of your organization, depending on what the entrepreneur needs.

- Rotate the board role – Knowing that you typically can only be effective on at most three to five board roles at a time, as your portfolio grows, rotate others from your organization into the board roles of the investee. I typically try not to be on the board role for more than two years with each investee; this gives the entrepreneur access to more than one individual from my organization while still being able to reach out to me when they need my specific input. Of course, you have to make sure the entrepreneur is comfortable with whoever you put to replace you on the board so that it's mutually beneficial.

- Be clear about what you bring to the table – Entrepreneurs who are not seasoned repeat entrepreneurs will need much more guidance. Always try to understand what they need, sometimes they will tell you, and it's clear; other times, they don't know what they don't know, which is just as important a role to provide guidance on. However, there has to be a balance between being actively supportive and overly controlling. Never micromanage. Realize that you are an investor and shareholder, you are not the founder, and you won't know the business as well as they do. Unfortunately, I've seen arrogant fund managers who seem to think they are supremely knowledgeable and try to micromanage the entrepreneurs, steering them in directions that have had disastrous results.

- Set expectations early with the entrepreneur – When you enter a relationship through the investment, it is best to set the rules of engagement so that each knows what to expect from the other. For example, you may want to set a regular check-in with the entrepreneur on some frequency, or you may prefer to have more ad hoc interactions when needed. In addition, be clear about how you like to be engaged by the entrepreneur. Ultimately you want to be a trusted partner.

- Come prepared to meetings – This sounds like a no-brainer, but unfortunately, not all investors attend meetings having thoroughly prepared in advance, and it becomes painfully apparent during the meetings who those individuals are. Entrepreneurs are betting everything on their company, so every minute they spend not building the business is time not creating value for their investors. When meetings are set, ensure they have clear objectives and you have read any materials necessary before so that the meetings are productive. Sometimes entrepreneurs send materials too late for you to have time to digest, so this is where setting the rules of engagement are essential on how much time in advance materials need to be distributed before a meeting.

- Get to know other investors – In addition to partnering with the entrepreneur, there is significant value in getting to know your fellow investors and what they bring to the table. Identify who are the actively engaged investors and who are more passive; you'll want to understand the active investors and how they can be partners in helping to support the entrepreneur. When things go well, everyone is happy, but when things don't go well, how can the investor's partner steer things back in the right direction? Ironically, sometimes you may need to help the entrepreneur navigate the investor base as well, especially when some less-than-helpful co-investors add negative value (yes, there is such a thing!) with their input or input micromanagement.

Aligning Interests with Investees

As an impact investment, the mission alignment of the investee drives the investment thesis. Early in the diligence process, you need to gauge whether the investee's leadership, particularly the founder, has a strong alignment. Probe their character; frankly, most entrepreneurs will tell you what they want you to hear so that they can get the investment, making it harder to assess their authenticity to the mission. We've discussed Side Letter terms that could help ensure mission fit through Exit Rights.

Beyond mission alignment, does the investee operate in a values-aligned manner, and is the founder going to make decisions for the company that benefits all shareholders and investors, or will some of the decisions help only the founder and executive team. An example of this would be some type of financing decision that may benefit a specific class of stock that could harm other classes of shareholders; another example could be business decisions that have near-term benefits but are longer-term harmful to the company's value creation. We've previously discussed options pool structures as another mechanism to attract and retain the right talent; observing how options are granted to existing and potential employees provide insights on alignment.

Structuring executive compensation to align with performance on objectives and goals is another method to ensure strong alignment between the company and investors. There must be a balance of what metrics to set and how realistic the bar is to meet. A bar set too low will not incentivize the investee executives sufficiently, but the same is also true if the bar is set too high that achieving the metric is unlikely. Creating a bonus pool for executives and employees can incentivize behaviors aligning with mission and investor objectives. Some areas to set as performance goals include:

- **Company performance** – Not surprisingly, these are the fundamentals of the investee, so it is critical the company actually delivers on its strategic plan. There can be revenue targets, financing targets, client diversification targets, or profitability targets. These will be the easiest and more standard for performance evaluation.

- **Impact** – Unlike traditional investments, the fact that they are impact-oriented makes it logical to put at least one performance metric around the impact achieved.

- **Culture** – With the growing focus on ESG and DEI, adding a metric around corporate culture will complement the more fundamental traditional company performance metrics. Some examples of metrics on culture include employee satisfaction, staff retention, diversity, etc.

The dollar amount can be allocated based on the importance of each performance metric. For example, if DEI is a big area that needs improvement, perhaps it could be weighted 25% of the bonus pot while profitability may not be as critical, so it only gets weighted 10% of the total bonus pool. Note that there should not be so many metrics that the intent of putting them in place gets lost and interpreted as micromanaging the company; you simply want enough performance targets to steer the company in the right direction and reward them accordingly.

Regrettably, sometimes things don't work out as intended, so the founder may need to be removed. This could be a situation where the Exit Right Clause does not get triggered, but it's clear the leadership of the investee needs to change either due to the company underperforming more generally or simply that the company has reached a stage where a new leader needs to be in place which has more experience to take the company to the next level. Removing the investee's leader, especially if it's the entrepreneur founder, is awkward and can get contentious, although it doesn't always have to be if you have a rational founder. That is where the importance of ensuring a good partnership with the co-investors will be helpful. Here are a few suggestions regarding leadership changes with the investee:

- **Get the co-investors aligned** – you need a united front that investors all agree to the change. Otherwise, the entrepreneur may leverage the other investors who are loyal to them to prevent the forced transition.

- **Document explicitly the reasons for the forced removal** – if there were consistently underperformance, the entrepreneur should not be surprised about the change in leadership requested by the investors. That will also reduce the potential legal liabilities should the transition become contentious.

- **A leadership transition does not mean an exit** – just because the entrepreneur is no longer the right leader for the company does not mean they need to leave the company, assuming the transition is not contentious. In fact, a good transition scenario is to allow the individual to take a different role within the company and continue to support its strategy under new leadership.

- **Allow the entrepreneur to save face** – in a friendly transition, create a communications strategy internally and externally that makes it positive. If the individual steps into a new role that continues to support the company, this will go a long way to demonstrating it was the entrepreneur's decision rather than forced. Strategize with the entrepreneur on how to communicate the transition.

- **Provide an incentive to make the transition smooth** – This can be done through an earn-out, meaning that there is a period by which the entrepreneur continues to show good faith support of the company as a condition for receiving the compensation. If the transition is contentious, then the payment may be more of an incentive to leave quietly and without disparagement.

- **Frame the transition as mutually beneficial** – even if the entrepreneur is transitioned out, they will still likely have substantial ownership in the company, so it is in their best interest that the company is successful in preserving the value of their ownership. On the other hand, if the transition is contentious, it may be best to offer to buy out the entrepreneur's stake entirely to allow the individual to cash out and move on. That will be a bit more complicated as it gets into negotiating the valuation of that stake that both parties can agree on.

- **Hope for smooth, prepare for contentious** – while a smooth transition would be ideal, it is often hard to predict how someone will react when the news is delivered. Be prepared for an adverse reaction and have a plan for what to do if that happens. For example, does a board member need to step in as an interim leader? Or has another executive within the company already been selected to take over the CEO role? Discuss with legal counsel to be fully aware of the liabilities and steps to mitigate them before implementing the transition process.

The list of suggestions is not comprehensive but should help with most leadership transition situations.

Mitigating Risk

We've already discussed some of the areas of risk mitigation related to mission drift in the legal structuring of the investment. Now I'll provide some additional tips that are business tactics rather than legal structuring. I'll summarize them here:

- **Would you rather be king or be rich?** – One key question I ask the founder of a company during the initial due diligence process is, "Do you want to be king, or do you want to be rich if you had to choose?" Their response can be telling of what happens during a leadership transition. When the entrepreneur chooses to be king as their response, it indicates that control will be more important to them. That is not the response I want to hear as an investor because it means being in control is their top priority. Ideally, you want the entrepreneur's answer to suggest they would be open to stepping out if it was in the best interest of the company's success. That is the alignment you need to hear since it shows self-awareness and humility, critical factors I always screen for in a leader. That helps mitigate risks down the line when/if you need to transition the CEO out of the role.

- **Tranche disbursements** – When a company is at a very early stage and does not have a lot of traction yet, you may want to structure the investment in a way that allows you to tranche your investment based on milestones. For example, if your company provides a revenue projection that you are not as confident in, one way to test how realistic that projection is with the entrepreneur is to tie the release of some portion of the investment based on achieving a specific revenue target. When you do so, the entrepreneur is going to be much more realistic with the revenue projections if they want to be able to access the funds you intend to invest. The milestones for the release of tranched investments could also be based on the number of new clients, reduction of churn, improvement of margins, or any other key performance indicators that are important to you as an investor.

- **Probability weighting** – As previously noted, entrepreneurs are almost always overly optimistic when it comes to projections. When they provide you with a pipeline of opportunities, always ask them for their probability estimate that the pipeline opportunity is realistic, and then discount it some more. You want to balance their optimism with your conservatism. Pipelines don't always come to fruition for many reasons: sometimes it's timing delays, other times it might be a change in strategy or even changes in the point of contact at the potential clients that changes the strength of the relationship the entrepreneur has with the potential client. Simply put, many reasons exist for the pipeline not to convert to actual revenue for the company. So probability weighting each one, especially the bigger ones, will be important in ensuring realistic revenue projections.

- **Under-promise, over-deliver** – When setting targets, make sure they are realistic and achievable. That applies in multiple areas. For entrepreneurs, set realistic expectations for the timeframe. If your organization typically takes six months to get a deal done and the investment round closes in two months, ensure the entrepreneur is aware and fully transparent. You do not want to string an entrepreneur along thinking you can meet their timeframe. In most circumstances, if the entrepreneur values a particular investor, they will do whatever they can to ensure there is the potential for that investor to participate in the round. In some cases, they may ask other investors for permission to hold a round open longer to facilitate such a scenario. With your executive team, be sure to anchor expectations for returns at the lower end of potential returns and constantly remind the investment committee of possible losses, even if the portfolio is performing exceptionally well. Inevitably some investments will not perform as expected. It's much better to exceed expectations than not to meet them.

- **Diversify** – It may sound hypocritical that I'm mentioning diversification when in previous chapters I had noted that diversification is not practical for an impact investing portfolio like a traditional portfolio. To be clear, that remains true, but you can still diversify by investing in different geographies, stages, mix of fund vs. direct investments, and asset classes. Furthermore, recall it is also possible to diversify based on the types of impact you are looking to drive, quantitatively and qualitatively.

- **Monitoring** – When you have a small team and lack the infrastructure and staff, you must devise an effective monitoring strategy. Having less than five investments in your portfolio may not be as difficult to monitor. But when you have 20+ investments, there is just only so much time you can spend on each portfolio company. So there are significant opportunities to miss red flags that may allow you to pre-emptively address any potential issues that can become even more significant issues if left unattended. Again, you can rely on your consultants, assuming they have the proper infrastructure and dedicated staff to help you with your portfolio. Additionally, you may also leverage technology that gives you sufficient information to know how each of your portfolio investees is doing. It doesn't have to be the most sophisticated or most expensive technology solution, but it has to serve its purpose of ensuring you have complete visibility of portfolio performance. Unfortunately, at the time of writing, I have not seen any current solution that does a good job of it, and one of the reasons why Kind Capital is developing an impact investing solution called Compass to serve that very need. When I was at Lumina Foundation, I recall we had used Salesforce and Fluxx, spending embarrassingly enormous amounts of money on them for customization. And even then, despite that investment, they still didn't serve my needs satisfactorily. People don't realize that the cost of the annual licenses may be relatively low (both under $5,000), but the cost of customization may be in the hundreds of thousands of dollars or more, depending on what your organization needs the software to do. Know what you want and find the most cost-effective solution that gets you there. Monitoring is not fun but critical for mitigating risk and optimizing portfolio performance.

- **Shared/Sharing Knowledge** – We had discussed the learning return previously, and part of the benefit of learning is sharing it with others to ensure the same issues do not repeat themselves. If one investee is underperforming and you can isolate the problem and the solutions for that issue, sharing that experience with other portfolio companies to foster growth rather than embarrassment will encourage other portfolio companies to do the same in other matters. This was such an essential aspect of building a portfolio of shared success.

CHAPTER THIRTEEN: CASE STUDIES AND DEAL EXAMPLES

"Imitation is the sincerest form of flattery..." Oscar Wilde

Throughout this book, you have been given many different concepts and strategies. The best way to understand some of the concepts is through examples. This chapter will provide some examples of investments made by the two major foundations: W.K. Kellogg Foundation and Lumina Foundation. In a perfect world, we could dig into the details of each investment so you can see the actual deal documents and structure. Unfortunately, due to confidentiality concerns, the information provided will be kept high level, or the investee will be kept anonymous. I will provide one example of each of the following:

- CDFI Deal Using Capital Staking
- Fund Investment
- Direct Investment
  - Debt
  - Equity

The purpose is to give you some key takeaways of how these investments align with the mission and why they were made without going into too much detail that would breach confidentiality concerns.

CDFI Case Study (Capital Stacking) – Michigan Good Food Fund (https://www.migoodfoodfund.org)

- Purpose and Mission Objective: Increase healthy food access
- "Fund" Size: $30 Million (at launch)
- Investor: W.K. Kellogg Foundation (WKKF)
- Investee: Capital Impact Partners – A national CDFI

- WKKF Investment Amount: Confidential
- Asset class: Loan and grant funding

Overview Summary

The W.K. Kellogg Foundation has a long history of programmatic work in the food space. That is not surprising that food access would be one of the pillars of programmatic work, given the founder being Will Keith Kellogg, who established the Foundation and was also the founder who built the cereal and food conglomerate. Kellogg had been looking to improve healthy food access in Michigan, taking the lessons learned from efforts in other states, including Pennsylvania and California. The Mission-Driven Investments (MDI) Team worked cross-functionally with Michigan statewide, Food, and Detroit program grant leads on creating the Michigan Good Food Fund from the ground up.

Here are a couple of points to highlight before going into the actual investment details. Firstly, MDI had existing loan investments to Capital Impact Partners, the national CDFI that had also been the administrator for a similar food access initiative in California, as well as multiple other loan investments in partnership with Capital Impact Partners, including several charter schools. This point is relevant to mention to understand why Capital Impact Partners was the chosen CDFI investee—Kellogg already had a long partnership/collaboration with Capital Impact Partners. Furthermore, the CDFI has a solid track record in the food space relative to the many other CDFIs that MDI had made investments in. At that point in time, there were no local CDFIs with the same track record and established capacity, even though it would have been preferable to have a local CDFI serve that role. Over time, that could shift as local CDFIs' ability develops. Secondly, the term "Fund" was a loose term and not a standard fund structure. The Michigan Good Food Fund was called a fund but, in actuality, was more of a collaborative investment vehicle rather than the usual general partner/limited partner structure of a fund. It was intentionally structured that way from lessons learned from other states' food financing initiatives that were structured as funds that did not end up executing as well. We will continue to refer to it as a fund to keep things simple. Lastly, it is also important to highlight that a market study had been done before structuring the Fund; the landscape research assessed the need for healthy food access and the types of businesses that needed funding. One of the simplest mistakes made in philanthropy is the perception that if you build it, they will come, thinking you already know the solution before understanding the problem. With the Michigan Good Food Fund, Kellogg's grant team funded research that provided a better understanding of the need for healthy food access in the State of Michigan, the types of capital that the market was not providing, and the type of technical support needed by the small businesses.

Extrapolating the insights from the market research, it was clear that many of these small businesses in the food space lacked access to loans because existing lenders were not willing to provide them, provide them at exorbitant interest rates, or they were just not ready to be investable, given how early some of those businesses were. Thus, the Michigan Good Food Fund needed to be structured to address all those issues for small businesses. Secondly, there were certain geographic areas where healthy food access was not available or highly limited, so incentivizing a food entrepreneur to bring in a grocery store or other food business to those areas provided another factor to incorporate into the Fund. In addition, the research provided some background on the amount of capital needed, which drove the initiative to target a $30 million vehicle. As you can see, each component of the Fund was structured very intentionally with data to support the rationale.

The multi-tranche investment by Kellogg had been structured in three tranches, each intended to complement the needs of the fund with the stacking of capital.

- Market rate loan – mission-related investment
- Catalytic capital in the form of very low-interest loan – program-related investment
- Grant funding

The market rate loan piece that had been a commitment to Capital Impact Partners, similar to other investments the MDI team had made focusing on food and education space investment opportunities. In essence, the commitment allowed Capital Impact Partners to co-invest MDI's loan into opportunities where there may be a funding gap. In addition, the PRI was a very low-interest loan to Capital Impact Partners with an extended maturity date; it was meant to provide additional loan capital that could reduce the weighted average cost of loans to small businesses with the blended rate. Lastly, grant capital funding came from Kellogg's grant-making team that funded technical assistance and provided credit enhancement for loan losses, further increasing the catalytic impact of the PRI investment. Figure 23 provides a schematic overview of the development phase through the execution phase and the key stakeholders involved.

Figure 23: Michigan Good Food Fund Structure

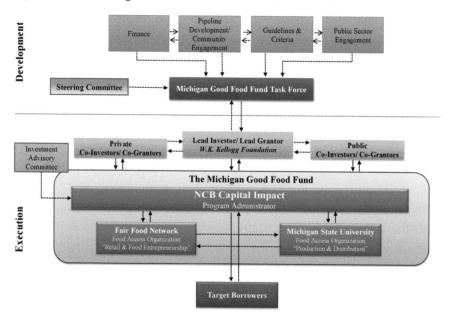

The Fund is one of the more complicated public-private-philanthropy partnerships developed, but the complexity is also one of the reasons it was successful. It took a very collaborative approach to build something that would be sustainable and scalable beyond Kellogg's initial funding. Many partners were involved across the community and allowed each to bring their expertise to the table to support the singular mission of improving healthy food access.

Kellogg's role in creating the Michigan Good Food Fund was not in itself innovative. But the way it thoughtfully did so by engaging the community and successfully bringing together such a broad group of stakeholders for the collaboration was incredibly admirable and rare, especially staying behind the scenes rather than trying to highlight itself. Secondly, taking the humble approach of funding research and the landscape scans before creating the Fund might not seem very special. Still, you'd be surprised how many funders go into an initiative believing they already know the solution before even understanding the problem. Thirdly, taking the lead in structuring the Fund and the various tranches across the capital stack allowed Kellogg to accelerate the syndication of the investment opportunity to other investors and funders. Each funder or stakeholder seeking to participate in a particular tranche or multiple tranches already had a prescribed set of terms that Kellogg made with its own capital, thus streamlining the legal negotiations and process for the Administrator of the Fund Capital Impact Partners.

Fund Investment Case Study – Fund Name Confidential

- Mission Area: Fintech fund focusing on the unbanked or underbanked population
- Fund Size: $45 Million
- Investor: W.K. Kellogg Foundation, Mission-Driven Investments Team
- Investee: Confidential Fintech Fund I
- WKKF Investment Amount: Confidential
- Investment Structure: Limited Partner
- Asset Class: Equity
- Geographic Focus: United States

Overview Summary

The Family Economic Security grant-making team broadly focused on initiatives ranging from job creation, financial inclusion, and workforce training objectives. Programmatically, investing in a fintech fund that would improve access to credit for low-income individuals aligned well. Just to give some context, unlike today, where technology has significantly improved where you can scan a check with your cell phone and have it deposited into your checking account, back in 2012, the ability to cash a check often cost individuals as much as 15% of the check value and had to be done in person. In addition, payday loans were charging low-income individuals exorbitant rates. If there were solutions that could improve access to credit, lower the cost of borrowing or even simply help low-income individuals improve their credit score, MDI wanted to find them and support their development. Thus, an early-stage fintech fund focused on innovations that improved financial inclusion filled that need quite nicely.

The fintech fund was a first-time fund led by two general partners. The fund's strategy was to invest in early-stage fintech opportunities that would serve the unbanked or underbanked population. The founder did not have a strong track record of prior investing experience; in fact, his primary investing experience was leading the accelerator/incubator at a renowned nonprofit association focused on serving the unbanked. The initial concept for the fund was actually a spinout from that nonprofit association.

Kellogg decided to make a commitment to the fund because the mission alignment was strong given the focus on the unbanked population, which dovetails well with its family economic security programmatic work. Because of the high risk of the fund, the commitment amount was at the lower end of its range. Most of the other investors were also philanthropic in nature, further strengthening the argument that the investment was mission-driven rather than profit-driven. Interestingly, Kellogg structured its investment as a mission-related investment while some other philanthropic investors structured their investments as program-related investments. In retrospect, the Kellogg investment could probably have been better off structured as a PRI given the strong mission intent of the fund. The inexperience of the GP as a fund manager was apparent in the fund's early years, even though they had extensive domain expertise. It took some guidance from the investors to help steer them in the right direction, learning when to pull the plug on underperforming investments and what investments are more attractive to back.

While most of the terms of the fund were relatively standard, a couple of crucial structuring points are worth noting. First, given the high risk of the fund and the mission focus, Kellogg wanted to have a role in the Limited Partners Advisory Committee (LPAC) that would provide governance and strategic guidance to the GP. First-time fund managers usually need more engagement from their investors, and the LPAC would play a much more important role than in more-seasoned funds. Secondly, there was a compensation structure that tied the impact achieved to some variable compensation for the GP. That was probably the first time an impact fund manager's compensation had been structured this way. Each year there was an Impact Committee consisting of the several limited partners. They would vote on the impact metrics achieved and translate it to the variable compensation component earned by the GP. This structure helped ensure that mission was core to the fund's strategy and not left by the wayside as an afterthought. Lastly, Kellogg also negotiated to have co-investment rights. MDI reviewed a number of the fund's portfolio companies for co-investment, but ultimately, none of them made it to an investment. That is not to say that the co-investment rights were a waste; on the contrary, performing due diligence on some of those opportunities allowed MDI to get smarter about the underbanked market. The learning return from the fintech fund investment proved to be relatively high, even though the investment in the first fund was mediocre. The GP successfully raised additional funds that performed better than the first fund, having leveraged lessons learned from the experience in the first fund. That is precisely why many institutional investors steer clear of first-time funds, but philanthropic investors can play a catalytic role in supporting those emerging fund managers.

Direct Investment Debt Case Study – Confidential Charter School

- Mission Area: Education
- Company: Charter school located in a low-income community in New Orleans
- Investor: W.K. Kellogg Foundation, Mission-Driven Investments Team
- Investment structure: Term loan
- Security/collateral: Unsecured
- Use of Funds: Operating capital for the charter school to reach a self-sustainable scale
- Interest rate: Confidential
- Exit strategy: Charter school refinancing with a public bond issue or early repayment

Overview Summary

One of Kellogg's pillars of programmatic focus was in the education sector, particularly around early childhood. Charter schools are publicly funded like typical public schools are funded with per-pupil revenue but operate more independently. Most charter schools start up with one grade level (Kindergarten) and then grow each year by adding a new class, as shown in Figure 24.

Figure 24: Charter School Revenue Model

Classes	Year 1	Year 2	Year 3	Year 4	Year 5	Year 6	Year 7	Year 8
Kindergarten	50	50	50	50	50	50	50	50
1st Grade		50	50	50	50	50	50	50
2nd Grade			50	50	50	50	50	50
3rd Grade				50	50	50	50	50
4th Grade					50	50	50	50
5th Grade						50	50	50
6th Grade							50	50
7th Grade								50
Total Students	50	100	150	200	250	300	350	400
Per Pupil Revenue	$8,500	$8,500	$8,500	$8,500	$8,500	$8,500	$8,500	$8,500
Total Revenue($K)	$425	$850	$1,275	$1,700	$2,125	$2,550	$2,975	$3,400

As you can imagine, in the early years of the charter school's development, revenue is low in the early years due to how few students the charter school serves, making it very difficult, if not impossible, to obtain financing for operations, let alone to build the charter school facility. Charter schools were also typically located in the lowest-income communities providing an alternative to some of the underperforming public schools serving those communities. Nearly 100% of charter school students receive free or reduced lunch. Parents interested in having their children attend a charter school would enter their names into a lottery system, given the high demand for them.

You may wonder why charter schools don't just start with all seven grades at once so that they immediately have the scaled revenue. A simple explanation is that the operational and financial complexity of recruiting and adding staff and students would be complicated; starting with one grade level is hard enough. Secondly and the more critical issue is that the charter school has a positive culture, mindset, and methodology that it wants to create with its students. Starting from the very beginning is much easier than changing some of the bad habits and mindsets learned from other schools when students transfer in from later grades.

In 2012, MDI invested in the New Orleans charter school through a commitment/co-investment with a national CDFI with a long history of financing charter school development. The school was a new geographic expansion of a leading charter school network with existing charter schools in the Northeast. The loan would be structured as a seven-year term loan secured by the building, and the interest rate was the market rate for a senior secured term loan. The seven-year maturity date was set to give the charter school enough time to reach the revenue scale necessary to be able to obtain other financings. Another structural aspect was no prepayment penalty should the school decide to pay off the loan early. For MDI, the objective was to allow the school to get to self-sufficiency, so the sooner it could happen where the school could repay its loan, it would be considered a positive development rather than undesirable by traditional lenders. Typically, charter schools with at least five to seven years of operating track record refinance through a bond offering that locks in longer-term financing at a lower cost, which is the mechanism that most use to pay off their prior loans.

It should be noted that MDI had a strategic partnership with the CDFI due to its leadership and experience in charter school development. The partnership allowed MDI to rely on the national CDFI to source charter school financing opportunities where it could co-invest. For example, if the CDFI planned to invest $1.5 million into a new charter school, MDI would get the option to take up to 50% of that amount ($750K) of that as a co-investor. The CDFI would perform most of the due diligence and underwriting, handle all the loan agreements, and MDI would invest through a Participation Certificate of that loan, having the same rights as the CDFI in terms of the loan to the charter school. The strategic partnership essentially tacked an additional spread onto the loan paid to the CDFI, say 25 bps or 0.25%. For instance, if the loan were priced at 6% to the charter school, MDI would be paying the CDFI 6.25%. The money first went to the CDFI, who then transferred it to the charter school. The CDFI handles all the monitoring and operational aspects of the loan given its lending infrastructure and saves MDI the hassle. MDI invested in several charter schools that way, in addition to investing in a national charter school financing fund as a limited partner. Even though MDI staff had over five years of experience serving on a charter school board, such an approach and partnership with the CDFI allowed MDI to leverage the charter school financing expertise of the national CDFI as well as access to deals that it would not have been aware of. The CDFI benefited from the incremental fee it gets from MDI and having additional capital to lend beyond its own balance sheet.

Direct Investment Equity Case Study – Credly

- Mission Area: Skills-based Credentials
- Company: Credly Inc
- Investor: Lumina Impact Ventures
- Asset Class: Preferred Equity
- Stage: Series Seed Venture Capital
- Amount: Confidential
- Exit Strategy: Recapitalization or acquisition

Overview Summary

Lumina Foundation is the largest private foundation focused exclusively on postsecondary credentialing. The foundation has a long history as a leader with significant domain expertise in postsecondary education and workforce training. In 2015, it launched Lumina Impact Ventures as its venture arm to leverage impact investing as a tool to further its mission. LIV would invest in ed-tech companies and solutions using programmatic dollars (PRIs), complementing its existing MRI portfolio of funds.

Credly was an early-stage ed-tech company at the forefront of the digital credentialing space, led by experienced entrepreneur Jonathan Finkelstein. The company created digital badges for its clients to represent specific verified skills. Being in the credentialing space, Jonathan was very aware of Lumina Foundation and the strategic value that having LIV as an investor could bring to Credly. In addition, Credly's investors already included two of Lumina's MRI funds, so having a direct investment from LIV would further strengthen the connection to Lumina.

As LIV was just created, the first investment would set an anchor and represent the types of investments it would make in its strategy. Therefore, the first investment was materially going to shape how it would message the strategy internally and externally for LIV, adding additional pressure to get it right and why the Credly investment made sense as its first investment. The structuring of the investment can be summarized below:

- LIV participated as a co-investor in the Series Seed round (as well as in follow-on rounds with its pro-rata share). That meant that the lead investor predetermined the deal structure and terms for the valuation, so LIV would have to accept the terms if it were to invest.

- LIV took a board seat with the investee as part of the investment. Although it was a board observer role (meaning LIV did not get a vote), given the strategic value of Lumina, the level of engagement and leverage LIV had with Credly was no different from other investors who had voting board roles. LIV would never take a voting board seat owing to the liability. Frankly, if it could get the same influence and leverage being a board observer without the liability of a fiduciary role, that was even better. Furthermore, because Lumina had two MRI funds invested in Credly, there was additional leverage through those investors, which was quite unusual.

- Direct investment into Credly rather than through a co-investment vehicle set up by the MRI funds. This is a critical point to highlight because it has implications for fees and governance. Recall in the prior discussion that usually, when a fund manager allows its LP to co-invest in a deal, the LP will typically pay the fund manager fees related to the co-investment amount (1% management fee and 10% of the carry). LIV was adamant that it would not be willing to set up such a structure, made it clear to the investee and the MRI funds, and was ready to walk away from the investment as a deal-breaker. Unsurprisingly, this did not endear LIV to the MRI funds, but it set the rules of engagement with them on how LIV would operate. In normal circumstances, if LIV relied on the MRI funds for diligence and monitoring, structuring the co-investment vehicle would have been more acceptable. But LIV would do its own diligence and monitoring and want a board observer role directly with Credly, which may not have been feasible otherwise through the vehicle.

- Required social metrics reporting – Credly would agree to report specific impact metrics as required by LIV.

- Required PRI Side Letter terms given Lumina was a private foundation and structuring the investment as a program-related investment – Credly understood and accepted the requirements of PRI terms that were documented in a Side Letter.

As a strategic investor, LIV sought to support Credly beyond just the dollars invested. One example was connecting Credly to Lumina's grantmaking team focused on credentialing to explore collaboration opportunities there. The grantmaking side of the foundation benefited from leveraging Credly just as much as the company did from Lumina. One significant grantee of Lumina was the American Council on Education (ACE) which ultimately entered a strategic partnership with Credly for its ACE Credits. LIV also launched and hosted an annual invite-only conference called the Lumina Investing in Future Talent & Education (LIFTEd). LIFTed brought together various postsecondary learning stakeholders; at the event, LIV showcased Credly on a panel as a portfolio investee, giving it exposure and brand credibility. Additionally, beyond providing strategic advice through the board observer role, LIV made multiple introductions to Credly, ranging from strategic partners and investors to potential investors.

On average, LIV targets a holding period of three to five years for its investments, which is probably on the shorter end for early-stage investments. However, being solely funded by the foundation and not a typical fund structure with limited partner investors, it can be a patient investor without the time pressure typical funds face. In January 2022, Pearson PLC publicly announced it would acquire Credly for $200M, representing a very successful exit for Lumina Impact Ventures' very first investment (https://plc.pearson.com/en-US/news/pearson-acquires-digital-credentialing-leader-credly).

CHAPTER FOURTEEN: SUMMARY CONCLUSIONS AND TAKEAWAYS

"I have a bachelor's from Yale, an MBA from Kellogg, and a Ph.D. from the School of Life."

No fancy degrees from a top business school or undergraduate program can teach you what the School of Life teaches from experience. I have learned a lot over a decade in impact investing that I want to share, so hopefully, they can help you avoid the same mistakes I made. These are just a few things I wished I had known earlier when I started my impact investing journey.

- **Don't be afraid to walk away from a deal** – I've noted that when you start to get emotionally attached to deals, that is when you make irrational decisions. Sometimes the irrationality can be in the form of chasing deals with high valuations rather than being disciplined with what your analyses would justify. Other times it may lead you to compromise on terms of a deal that you would not usually feel comfortable giving on. Never do a deal because you've already spent too much time on it if you start seeing red flags. You may feel you missed out on an opportunity, but frankly, it is much better than having buyer's remorse when you've made a bad investment that will haunt you long term.

- **It is better to be lucky than to be good** – That is something I've learned from one of my former bosses Tom Reis and that wisdom would be great if there were a consistent way to bet on luck, but there isn't. So be grateful when you are lucky, but never bet on it. Gambling is not the same as investing.

- **Be humble** – When things work out, it's easy to mistake that for skill and not simply luck. However, it is just as important to reflect on what drove the successful investment so that it can be repeated; the same analysis should be done for deals that didn't work out so that those lessons can help avoid future errors. Having the self-awareness and humility to differentiate luck from skill will provide more consistent performance.

- **Learn by doing** – No matter how much you read, while the intellectual knowledge may be there, the execution will always be a better teacher. Think of it this way, would you want to be operated on by a surgeon who has only read about how to perform surgery? That would be pretty scary! Likewise, investing is a muscle that needs to be exercised to gain strength; purely reading about how to do something gives knowledge but not experience, and you need both to be confident and successful.

- **Don't go it alone** – That African proverb that "if you want to go fast, go alone, but if you want to go far, go together" applies quite well in impact investing. There are many others either farther along on their programs or just starting out their impact investing programs, but all can benefit you as much as you can be helpful to them. I've never hesitated to help others on their impact investing journey or learn from others. The field continues to grow, evolve, and innovate. Having fellow practitioners along the way will make the journey much more exciting, impactful, and lower risks while helping to accelerate your professional development and the growth of your program.

- **Don't reinvent the wheel** – I can't reiterate this enough. In the field of philanthropy, I've often seen organizations try to build something that already exists so that they can put their brand on it. That is frankly a terrible waste of time, money, and intellectual resources! Unless you have something authentically unique that addresses an issue or gap in the market that existing solutions don't seem to be doing very well, leverage what has already been done by others. Partner and focus your resources on things that truly are innovative that you can put your brand on.

- **Your time is valuable** – Some leaders have a hard time delegating because they think they can do it better. But the critical question a leader needs to ask is: how valuable is your time? Is your time best spent on this specific activity versus something else? Sure someone might not do as good of a job on a particular task, but they can learn. Always know what the best use of your time is. If it would be more efficient to delegate to a colleague or to hire an outside advisor/consultant to do a time-consuming task that takes you away from something of higher value for you to focus on, then you shouldn't be doing that task.

- **Thoughtful mistakes are just learning opportunities** – Those who have never made a mistake have no knowledge of how to fail. A good investor needs both knowledge of how to succeed and how to fail. Forgive yourself and don't dwell on having made a mistake; take the opportunity to learn from it, and you'll be better for it.

- **Trust but verify** – It is easy just to believe what someone tells you; that should be how things work in a perfect world. Unfortunately, we don't live in an ideal world, and not everyone will be as transparent or honest as others. If there are data points that just feel a bit off or someone tells you something that seems unrealistic, do a gut check by looking for supporting evidence to confirm. The more investments you make, the better your gut check will be able to sniff out real facts from what Kellyanne Conway calls "alternative facts." Sometimes people may genuinely believe what they are telling you, and it isn't intentional nefarious lies. They just have a different level of confidence in a projection or are so emotionally tied to an investment that everything has a positive bias.

- **Have fun** – This work is not easy, so it can get extremely frustrating if you aren't passionate about it and not having fun. Unless you are having fun, you'll have more bad days than good when you deal with internal obstacles, demanding entrepreneurs, underperforming investees, long hours, and unexpected situations that are highly stressful. Life is too short, and you should invest your time and energy in things you have fun with and are passionate about. Surround yourself with people you enjoy being around who will celebrate your successes, but also be supportive when things don't work out. I have a personal rule where if more than 40% of my time is spent doing something I feel is a waste and no longer fun; it is an indicator that the time has come for me to move on. In any job, there will always be at least 25 to 30% of time spent doing something that you'd rather not be doing, but just a necessary part of the role. It always amazes me that some people are willing to accept 80% of their time or more being miserable at a job when they have options to leave. Have the confidence to change roles when you are reaching your threshold of frustration where the current position is not fun anymore, whether it's an internal transfer or seeking something external from your organization.

Be kind, do good, don't be a waste of oxygen…
THE END

REFERENCES

Asher Cheses. (2018). *U.S. High-Net-Worth and Ultra-High-Net-Worth Markets 2018: Shifting Demographics of Private Wealth.* Cerulli Associates.

Dieter Holger. (2019, September 10). What Generation Is Leading the Way in ESG Investing? You'll Be Surprised. *Wall Street Journal.*

GIIN. (2020). *2020 Annual Impact Investor Survey.* New York: The Global Impact Investing Network.

IFC. (2019, April). *Impact Principles.* Retrieved from Impact Principles: https://www.impactprinciples.org/9-principles

Impact Management Project. (2022). Retrieved from https://impactmanagementproject.com/impact-management/impact-management-norms/

Johnson, P. D. (n.d.). *Global Philanthropy Report, Perspectives on the Global Foundation Sector.* Boston: Harvard Kennedy School, The Hauser Institute for Civil Society.

United Nations. (2015, December 30). Retrieved from United Nations News Center: https://www.un.org/sustainabledevelopment/blog/2015/12/sustainable-development-goals-kick-off-with-start-of-new-year/

US SIF Foundation. (2020). *Report on US Sustainable and Impact Investing Trends.*

APPENDIX A: GUIDELINES ON PROGRAM-RELATED INVESTMENTS[4]

Program-related investments are those in which:

1. The primary purpose is to accomplish one or more of the foundation's exempt purposes,

2. Production of income or appreciation of property is not a significant purpose, and

3. Influencing legislation or taking part in political campaigns on behalf of candidates is not a purpose.

In determining whether a significant purpose of an investment is the production of income or the appreciation of property, it is relevant whether investors who engage in investments only for profit would be likely to make the investment on the same terms as the private foundation.

If an investment incidentally produces significant income or capital appreciation, this is not, in the absence of other factors, conclusive evidence that a significant purpose is the production of income or the appreciation of property.

To be program-related, the investments must significantly further the foundation's exempt activities. They must be investments that would not have been made except for their relationship to the exempt purposes. The investments include those made in functionally related activities that are carried on within a larger combination of similar activities related to the exempt purposes.

Once an investment is determined to be program-related, it will continue to qualify as a program-related investment if changes in the form or terms of the investment are made primarily for exempt purposes and not for any significant purpose involving the production of income or the appreciation of property. A change made in the form

---

[4] https://www.irs.gov/charities-non-profits/private-foundations/program-related-investments

or terms of a program-related investment for the prudent protection of the foundation's investment will not ordinarily cause the investment to cease to qualify as program-related. Under certain conditions, a program-related investment may cease to be program-related because of a critical change in circumstances, such as serving an illegal purpose or serving the private purpose of the foundation or its managers.

If a foundation changes the form or terms of an investment, and if the investment no longer qualifies as program-related, it then must be determined whether or not the investment jeopardizes carrying out its exempt purposes.

An investment that ceases to be program-related because of a critical change in circumstances does not subject the foundation making the investment to the tax on jeopardizing investments before the 30th day after the date on which the foundation (or any of its managers) has actual knowledge of the critical change in circumstances.

APPENDIX B: SIBISA

One of the innovations that Lumina Impact Ventures sought to improve workforce training for the incarcerated population involved the combination of a social impact bond and an income share agreement. My colleague Elizabeth Garlow, Investment Officer at Lumina Impact Ventures, wrote the proposal in 2018 summarizing the SIBISA concept and how it could potentially serve as a scalable model in partnership with one of its investees, Edovo. While the concept was never launched at Lumina, it provides an example of how innovative financing structures can be developed to drive scalable, sustainable impact.

BACKGROUND

The United States has the largest prison population in the world and the second-highest incarceration rate at 0.91% of the adult resident population. Roughly 2.2 million adults are incarcerated in federal and state prisons and local jails[5]. Incarcerated individuals, on average, have lower levels of educational attainment and often lack vocational skills, making it difficult to successfully re-enter their communities and find employment[6]. This contributes to high rates of recidivism, which are costly to these individuals and society at large.

- There are several positive benefits to providing education for incarcerated individuals, including:
- Significant reductions in the odds of recidivism—studies point to a 43 percent lower chance of returning to prison;
- Higher odds of obtaining employment post-release;

[5]   U.S. Bureau of Justice Statistics 2013

[6]   https://www.bja.gov/Publications/RAND_Correctional-Education-Meta-Analysis.pdf

- High return on investment—on average, educating one inmate ranges between $2,000 and $4,000, while incarceration costs can range from $30,000 to $40,000. [7]

Some newer programs have moved beyond basic education to focus on relevant skills development that will help individuals thrive in an increasingly technological society. For example, a program called Code.7370 provides incarcerated individuals in the San Quentin, CA prison with six months of intensive computer programming classes, and Texas' Prison Entrepreneurship Program teaches individuals how to build a business plan. In these models, participants demonstrate an average twenty-one day turn-around from prison to paycheck.[8]

- However, individuals wanting to pursue education during incarceration to improve their circumstances face significant barriers, including:

- Lack of access to quality educational content and credentialing opportunities;

- Limited access to financing given zero eligibility for Pell grants and downward trends in funding for prison education due to cuts in state corrections budgets[9];

- Difficulty translating education into career opportunities given employer biases against criminal records.

PROPOSAL

While there have been attempts in recent years to expand access to Pell grant funding for the incarcerated population[10], the Congressional ban still remains firmly in place, and no national standards currently exist to ensure consistency in budgeting practices at the state level

---

[7] The Second Chance Act (Public Law 110-199) funded a comprehensive study of correctional education, led by the RAND Corporation in cooperation with the DOJ's Office of Justice Programs.

[8] "Inside the Classroom where San Quentin Inmates Learn Coding." https://www.wired.com/2016/11/san-quentin-inmates-learn-to-code/

[9] In 1994, Congress made state and federal prison inmates ineligible for Pell grants, and in 1998, the Workforce Investment Act seriously limited funding for correctional education.

[10] In 2016, the Obama Administration experimented with expanding access to Pell grant funding for the incarcerated population through the "Second Chance Pell Grant" program.

to fund prison education. A new mechanism to fund and expand education for incarcerated students that focuses on sought-after skills will improve access to credentials, employment opportunities and enhance long-term life outcomes.

The proposed mechanism combines the concept of a social impact bond/pay for performance contract with an income share agreement. Social impact bonds (SIB) incentivize better social outcomes, usually through a contract with the public sector/government agency, which passes on savings realized through better outcomes to private investors. With an income share agreement (ISA) for education, students finance their education by agreeing to make payments after graduation based on a percentage of their income for a set period of time.

In the scenario that follows, the two are combined to facilitate credentialing opportunities for incarcerated individuals that translate into high-demand skills and careers through a unique collaboration between Lumina's partners, including Edovo (an incentive-based education technology platform), private and philanthropic investors, higher education, and technology organizations.

SIB-ISA 5 STEP PROCESS

1. **Deliver Customized Education**

   Edovo contracts with prison and jail facilities to provide inmates with access to proprietary and licensed courses made available through customized tablets.

2. **Partner to Expand Opportunity**

   Through partnerships with higher education institutions, Edovo opens a pathway to credentials for incarcerated students. Edovo partners with a pilot group of technology sector employers to ensure educational opportunities align with in-demand skills, developing a talent pipeline that meets employers' needs.

3. **Finance Education**

   The costs of delivering education are financed upfront by private investors (or by the employers themselves), with a guarantee structure backed by philanthropy to reduce the risk for investors.

4. **Secure Employment**

   Upon release, graduates are placed in tech jobs and engage in an ISA with transparent, pre-defined terms to repay tuition costs to investors.

5. **Measure Impact**

   An independent evaluator tracks metrics on credential completion, job placements, and tuition repayment.

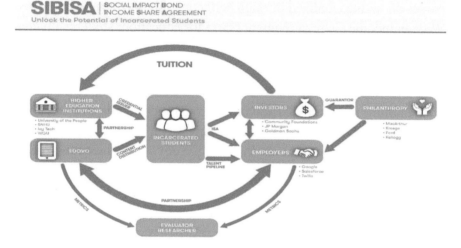

PARTNERSHIPS

This strategy has the potential to catalyze new capital to fund prison education while ensuring quality credentialing that translates into meaningful career pathways. Given Edovo's technology platform, this is a readily scalable intervention. The effort involves a unique configuration of potential partners that Lumina can help assemble to collaborate on this effort.

Education Institutions	Employers	Investors	Philanthropy
Southern New Hampshire University Western Governor's University University of the People Ivy Tech	Google Salesforce Twilio Facebook LinkedIn	Goldman Sachs Community Foundations CRA arms of major banks	MacArthur Ford Kresge Kellogg Lumina

PROPOSED FINANCIAL STRUCTURE

Costs	ISA Terms	Philanthropic Guarantee
Costs of delivering education will vary depending on the institutional partner. A current partnership proposal between Edovo and the University of the People (tuition-free, online) estimates education delivery costs at $2,828 per student per year in the state of MI.	Income threshold Repayment period Repayment caps	To reduce risk for investors and employers, philanthropy guarantees 50 to 70 cents on the dollar.

APPENDIX C: GLOSSARY OF TERMS

Assets Under Management (AUM)

The market value of the total financial assets that an investment company manages on behalf of its clients.

Angel Investor

These investors are typically the earliest stage of investors after a "friends and family's" round of investors. They are typically under $50K in size.

Additionality

The additional impact achieved by the presence of an impact investor, in essence, their catalytic effect.

Asset Class

A category of investment, defined by its main characteristics of risk, liquidity and return. Major asset classes are cash, fixed income, public equity, private equity and real asset.

- **Fixed income** – An asset class, where returns are received at regular intervals and at predictable levels. The most common type of fixed income security is the bond. Some investors include loans and private debt in this category.

- **Public equity** – An asset class where individuals and/or organizations can invest in a publicly listed company by buying ownership in shares or stock of that company.

- **Private equity** – An asset class where money is invested into a private company, or the privatization of a company. Most investors aim to invest into a company, take a majority stake, improve the company and then exit their investment at a large profit.

- **Real Assets/Commodities** – Farmland and forestry are examples of these, typically are held long term and can generate some type of yield/revenue. Oil or other types of hard assets are also considered commodities that have a useable/consumable purpose.

- **Real Estate** – The are essentially buildings, they can be commercial (businesses live in them) or residential (people live in them)

Below Market-Rate of Return / Concessionary Return

An investment made with an agreed-upon rate of return that is less than the current market rate and sacrifices some financial gain to achieve a social benefit. Program-related investments (PRIs) are often referred to as below-market or concessionary investments, given the IRS requirement that no significant purpose of the investment can be the production of income or appreciation of property.

Bridge Financing

Temporary financing to an organization in the form of a grant, loan or other forms of funding to tie the organization's capital needs until it can successfully complete a capital raise in the future. These are usually loans or some form of debt financing.

Capital Stack

A description of the totality of capital invested in a project or entity that combines grants, debt, hybrid debt, and/or equity. The stack is described as containing the most risk at the top, traveling down the stack to the position with the least risk. Typically, higher positions in the stack expect higher returns for their capital because of the higher risk. Lenders and equity stakeholders are highly sensitive to their position in the stack. When a socially-minded funder is involved, they may be willing to take higher risk for lower returns in order to catalyze or (crowd in) other traditional investors, which is counter to the traditional spectrum of risk/reward trade-off.

Cash Deposits

Often foundations invest cash through community-based lenders such as community development financial institutions (CDFIs), credit unions, or regional banks; often FDIC insured, with competitive rates of return. These deposits offer alternative secured financing to communities (sometimes at no interest), increasing access to capital for low-income borrowers and businesses.

Catalytic First Lost Capital

Catalytic first-loss capital refers to socially- and environmentally-driven credit enhancement provided by an investor or grant-maker who agrees to bear first losses in an investment in order to catalyze the participation of co-investors that otherwise would not have entered the deal. Catalytic first-loss capital has gained prominence in impact investing dialogue as more investors look to enter the market.

Collateral

Personal or real property or other assets that the borrower pledges to assure repayment of a loan. If the borrower defaults on the loan, the lender takes possession of the collateral to recover the value of the loan.

Community development financial institution (CDFI)

An umbrella term that encompasses private-sector, community-focused banks, credit unions, and lending institutions that has as its primary mission to provide credit and financial services to underserved markets and economically-disadvantaged populations.

Convertible Preferred Stock

Preferred stock that includes an option for the holder to convert the preferred shares into a fixed number of common shares, usually any time after a predetermined date. Most convertible preferred stock is exchanged at the request of the shareholder, but sometimes there is a provision that allows the company, or issuer, to force conversion. The value of a convertible preferred stock is ultimately based on the performance, or lack thereof, of the common stock.

Convertible Debt

A loan that is convertible into equity on pre-agreed terms.

Convertible Grant

A grant that is converted into equity in the event of the (commercial) success of an enterprise.

Cornerstone Investor (more commonly referred to as "Anchor" investor)

The principal investor in a fund or project whose commitment to invest gives confidence to others to invest.

Corporate Social Responsibility (CSR)

Also called corporate citizenship, social impact, or sustainable business/ responsible business. CSR policy functions as a built-in, self-regulating mechanism whereby a business monitors and ensures its active compliance with the spirit of the law, ethical standards, and international norms. A broad term, CSR, differs vastly based on the industry and firm but can include such issues as increasing volunteer efforts, philanthropy, impact investments, monitoring and evaluating internal practices, and reducing carbon footprints.

Credit Enhancement

Actions that improve the credit profile of a deal, e.g., a foundation provides a guarantee, over-collateralizes, establishes a reserve account, or acts as a subordinated lender. In essence, the structure makes the loan less risky to other investors.

Dilution

Dilution is a result of a reduction in the ownership percentage of a company, or shares of stock, due to the issuance of new equity shares by the company. Dilution can also occur when holders of stock options, such as company employees or holders of other optionable securities, exercise their options. When the number of shares outstanding increases, each existing stockholder owns a smaller, or diluted, percentage of the company, potentially making each share less valuable if the total value of the company did not increase enough to offset the dilution.

Donor-Advised Fund (DAF)

A pool of charitable resources that donors deposit for management in community foundations, corporate-originated charitable funds, or other non-profit institutions, for which the donors receive the full value of their charitable deduction at the time of deposit and out of which they make charitable contributions to eligible non-profit organizations over a period of years. DAF capital is now also able to be invested in for-profit impact investments, with any returns cycling back into the DAF account for further investment or charitable giving.

Environmental, Social and Governance (ESG)

ESG criteria are a set of standards for a company's operations that sustainability-focused investors use to screen potential investments. Environmental criteria look at how a company performs as a steward of nature. Social criteria examine how a company manages relationships with its employees, suppliers, customers and the communities where it operates. Governance deals with a company's leadership, executive pay, audits, internal controls and shareholder rights.

Ethical Investing

Using one's ethical principles as the main filter for securities selection. Ethical investing depends on an investor's views; some may choose to eliminate certain industries entirely (such as gambling, alcohol, or firearms, also known as sin stocks) or to over-allocate to industries that meet the individual's ethical guidelines.

Fiduciary Duty

Refers to a relationship in which one person has a responsibility of care for the assets or rights of another person or entity. Directors, trustees, managers and certain other advisors of nonprofit organizations owe fiduciary duties to the organizations they oversee, similar to the duties of directors at for-profit companies. However, unlike fiduciaries of for-profit companies or pension trusts, fiduciaries of foundations and endowments owe legal duties of obedience to the organization's charitable mission and to the observation of the social purposes required of nonprofits. The fiduciaries of charitable organizations must approach investment and program-related investment decisions with these duties in mind.

Finance First Investors

Investors who prioritize the financial return objective over the social or environmental objectives of an investment. This group tends to include commercial investors seeking investments that offer market-rate returns and also yield social or environmental good. Also included in this group are investors that are required to uphold a fiduciary standard and are therefore unable to make investments that lack the potential to yield market rate returns

First Loss Capital

Socially and environmentally-driven credit enhancement provided by an investor or grant-maker who agrees to bear first losses in an investment in order to catalyze the participation of co-investors that otherwise would not have entered the deal.

Fund Advisor

The person or company responsible for making investments on behalf of, and/or providing advice to, investors. A fund's advisor assigns a manager(s) to make the day-to-day decisions involved in the fund's investments according to stated strategies and investment objectives.

Fund Manager

Responsible for implementing a fund's investing strategy and managing its portfolio trading activities. A fund can be managed by one person, by two people as co-managers, or by a team of three or more people.

General Partner (GP)

In private equity and venture capital funds, GPs raise and manage the funds, set and make investment decisions, and help their portfolio companies exit as they have a fiduciary responsibility to their Limited Partners.

Global Impact Investing Rating System (GIIRS)

Pronounced "Gears," the GIIRS is a rating system applied to both companies and funds that allows impact investors and fund managers to evaluate social and environmental impact (but not the financial performance).

Global Reporting Initiative (GRI)

A multi-stakeholder process and independent institution whose mission is to develop and disseminate globally applicable Sustainability Reporting Guidelines. The guidelines were developed so that companies, government agencies, and non-governmental organizations can report on the economic, environmental, and social dimensions of their activities, products and services.

Green Bonds

A type of tax-exempt bond issued to promote environmental sustainability and the development of brownfield sites (areas of land that are unused and under-developed and may contain low levels of industrial pollution). Green bonds are generally issued by federal, state, or local municipalities. Additionally, Development Finance Institutions have issued green bonds in order to support large-scale projects that address climate change. The proceeds from the purchase of green bonds either fund 'green' projects directly or are earmarked for green projects.

Guarantee

An agreement to perform the obligations of a third party if that party defaults. When a third party guarantees a loan, it promises to pay in the event of default by the borrower.

Hybrid Financial Instruments

Allocation of financial resources to impact-oriented investments combining different types of traditional financial instruments (grants, debt instruments, and equity instruments) in order to achieve the best possible alignment of risk and impact/financial return for particular investments.

Impact-First Investors

Seek to optimize social or environmental returns with a financial floor. These investors use social/ environmental good as a primary objective and may accept a range of returns, from return of principal to market rate. This group of investors is willing to accept a lower than market rate of return in investments that may be perceived as higher risk in order to help reach social/environmental goals that cannot be achieved in combination with market rates of financial return.

Impact Investing

Investments made into companies, organizations, and funds with the intention to generate measurable social and environmental impact alongside a financial return. Impact investments can be made in both emerging and developed markets, and target a range of returns from below market to market rate, depending upon the circumstances. Impact investors actively seek to place capital in businesses and funds that can harness the positive power of enterprise.

Impact Reporting and Investment Standards (IRIS)

IRIS provides a common reporting language to describe the social and environmental performance and ensure uniform measurement and articulation of impact across portfolios. The IRIS initiative defines terms to enable consistent reporting and allows benchmarking of data across companies, funds, investment portfolios and other organizations by serving as a repository for aggregated IRIS-compliant data.

Internal Rate of Return (IRR)

The expected compound annual rate of return that will be earned on a project or investment.

Limited Partner (LP)

LPs are the institutional or individual investors that have invested in the funds of a venture capital firm. LPs could include endowments, pension and sovereign wealth funds, family offices and funds of funds.

Mission Investing

A mission investment can be either a program-related investment (PRI) or a mission-related investment (MRI). Mission investing is the practice of foundations that invest to advance their missions and programmatic goals. Private foundations make PRIs part of their annual distribution strategy. MRIs are risk-adjusted, market-rate investments made from the foundation's assets.

Mission-Related Investing (MRI)

MRIs proactively seek investments based on their potential to advance progress and deliver financial returns that align with a specific mission of an organization without compromising financial returns objectives. They target market-rate returns relevant to similar nonprogrammatic investments, as they are made from the foundation's endowment assets rather than grant budget and seek a financial return similar to its other endowment investment allocations.

Negative Payouts

The base amount repaid from a PRI that has previously been counted toward a private foundation's 5% payout requirement. The amount recovered is added to the foundation's payout requirement during the period received unless renewed or recycled to another investee during the period determined by the IRS.

Negative Screen

Removing from investment consideration companies and industries deemed objectionable for ethical or moral reasons.

Pay-For-Performance (P4P) / Pay-For-Success (PFS) / Payment By Results (PBR)

A term that describes payment systems that offer financial rewards to providers who achieve, improve, or exceed their performance on specified quality and cost measures, as well as other benchmarks.

Payout Requirement

Payout refers to the 5% of endowment assets that private foundations are required by the IRS to expend on program (grants) and program-related administrative expenses. PRIs and related expenses are eligible to be counted in the 5% payout requirement. Foundations do have some ability to pay out more or less than the 5% in a given year as long as the rolling average is 5% of assets.

Patient Capital

Loans or equity investments offered on a long-term basis (typically 5 years or longer) and on soft terms (e.g., capital/interest repayment holidays and at zero or sub-market interest rates).

Program-Related Investments (PRIs)

Investments made by foundations at below-market terms where the primary goal is to advance the programmatic goals (foundation's mission) of the organization and where capital appreciation or income production is "not a significant purpose." PRIs are investments made using the grant budget rather than endowment assets.

Qualified Opportunity Zone (QOZ)

A low-income census tract or a census tract contiguous to a low-income community designated by the US government to be eligible to receive investments from a Qualified Opportunity Fund (O-Fund) via the Investing in Opportunity Act enacted in 2017.

Qualified Opportunity Fund (O-Fund)

A vehicle organized for the purpose of investing in Qualified Opportunity Zones. By reinvesting recently realized capital gains into an O-Fund, investors can receive preferential tax treatment.

Recoverable grant

An agreement under which a grantee commits to repay a grant under certain circumstances, generally, if the project financed by the grant is financially successful. If the conditions that trigger the repayment obligation are not met, the grantee is under no obligation to repay, and no default is triggered.

Responsible Investing

The practice of considering environmental, social, and governance factors when making investment decisions. Approaches include negative screening, shareholder activism, positive screening, and impact investing.

Return on Investment (ROI)

ROI is a performance metric that tries to directly measure the amount of return on a particular investment relative to the investment's cost.

Simple Agreement for Future Equity (SAFE) Note

The renowned venture capital firm/accelerator Y Combinator created these as a simplified form of a convertible note that is much less complicated. Usually issued by early-stage companies to angel investors, these investments allow an investor to purchase shares in the company in the future and usually have a valuation cap.

Seed Investor

Still considered early stage, this is usually the first institutional round of funding during the earlier development stages of a business where there is still less certainty of success.

Sustainability Accounting Standards Board (SASB)

SASB Standards guide the disclosure of financially material sustainability information by companies to their investors. Available for 77 industries, the Standards identify the subset of ESG issues most relevant to financial performance in each industry.

Socially Responsible Investing (SRI)

An investment strategy whereby investors utilize screening and exclusion, divestment, positive reinvestment and shareholder activism to achieve positive social or environmental outcomes. A typical SRI strategy would exclude "sin stocks," such as companies producing tobacco, firearms or alcohol from a portfolio of public equities. SRI is predominantly used with public market securities and is relatively accessible to non-accredited investors.

The 5% And 95% — The Five Percent (5%) And The Ninety-Five Percent (95%)

Refers to the totality of a foundation's assets and the portion that, to avoid excise tax, must be paid out in program expenditures (and administration in support of such)—the 5% payout requirement; and the 95% that is typically referred to as the endowment, and is traditionally invested primarily for financial gain and preservation of the foundation's corpus.

Total Addressable Market (TAM)

The size of the market that a company's products or services serves or can serve. Investors want to know how large the opportunity is and how many competitors are in the space already that the entrepreneur must compete against.

United Nations Principles for Responsible Investment (UNPRI/PRI)

PRI is an UN-supported international network of investors committed to six aspirational principles. The Principles are based on the notion that ESG issues can affect the performance of investment portfolios, and the network supports signatories to facilitate incorporating these issues into their investment decision-making and ownership practices.

United Nations Sustainable Development Goals (UN SDGs/SDGs)

The SDGs are a collection of 17 global goals as "a universal call to action to end poverty, protect the planet and ensure that all people enjoy peace and prosperity." The goals are interconnected and meant to be a guideline for governments, philanthropists, non-profits, and others working towards positive change, such as impact investors. SDGs are recognized across institutions and geographic regions, making them a popular framework for benchmarking impact.

Values-Based Investing

Values-based investing takes a longer-term approach toward investment by marrying one's personal or family values with long-term investment returns.